MW00770198

Super Bomb

A VOLUME IN THE SERIES

Cornell Studies in Security Affairs

Edited by Robert J. Art, Robert Jervis, and Stephen M. Walt

A list of titles in this series is available at cornellpress.cornell.edu.

Super Bomb

Organizational Conflict and the
Development of the Hydrogen Bomb

KEN YOUNG AND
WARNER R. SCHILLING

Cornell University Press

Ithaca and London

First published 2019 by Cornell University Press

Printed in the United States of America

Library of Congress Cataloging-in-Publication Data

Names: Young, Ken (Director), author. | Schilling, Warner R. (Warner Roller), 1925–2013, author.
Title: Super bomb : organizational conflict and the development of the hydrogen bomb / Ken Young and Warner R. Schilling.
Description: Ithaca, [New York] : Cornell University Press, 2019. | Series: Cornell studies in security affairs | Includes bibliographical references and index.
Identifiers: LCCN 2019019716 (print) | LCCN 2019020252 (ebook) | ISBN 9781501745164 (cloth ; alk. paper)
Subjects: LCSH: Hydrogen bomb—United States—History. | Hydrogen bomb—Government policy—United States—History. | Arms race—History—20th century. | United States—Military policy. | United States—Politics and government—1945–1953.
Classification: LCC UG1282.A8 Y68 2019 (print) | LCC UG1282.A8 (ebook) | DDC 355.8/251190973—dc23
LC record available at https://lccn.loc.gov/2019019716
LC ebook record available at https://lccn.loc.gov/2019020252

ISBN 978-1-5017-4518-8 (epub/mobi ebook)
ISBN 978-1-5017-4517-1 (pdf ebook)

Chapter 7 is based in part on Ken Young, "The Hydrogen Bomb, Lewis L. Strauss and the Writing of Nuclear History," *Journal of Strategic Studies* 36, no. 6 (Spring 2013): 815–40. Used by permission of Taylor & Francis.

For Maria Olivia Young (b. 2014)
That she may grow up in a world free from fear

Contents

Preface

This book has had an unusually long gestation period. The idea originated at the Institute of War and Peace Studies (IWPS) at Columbia University in the immediate postwar period and was finally realized at the Department of War Studies, King's College, London, some sixty-two years later.

Columbia's Institute of War and Peace Studies was a pioneering institute established on the initiative of Dwight D. Eisenhower, Columbia's then president, general of the army, and the future US president. Eisenhower confessed to finding it "almost incomprehensible that no American university has undertaken the continuous study of the causes, conduct and consequences of war."[1] As he saw it, the role of such an institute would be to "study war as a tragic social phenomenon—its origins, its conduct, its impact and particularly its disastrous consequences upon man's spiritual, intellectual and material progress."[2] The founding of the institute (now the Arnold A. Saltzman Institute of War and Peace Studies) in 1951 led the international movement toward the academic study of international security, paralleled some years later in the UK by the foundation under Michael (later Sir Michael) Howard of the Department of War Studies at King's College, London, where this project was revived, with its coverage extended beyond President Harry S. Truman's original January 1950 decision to proceed with development of the hydrogen bomb, and was carried to completion.

Columbia's institute was initially headed, and directed for some twenty-five years, by William T. R. Fox, a highly respected scholar of international relations. He was included in the august company of scholars and practitioners brought together by the Rockefeller Foundation in 1954—among them Hans J. Morgenthau, Reinhold D. Niebuhr, Paul Nitze, and Arnold Wolfers—in a historic event to establish the foundations of realism as an academic and practical doctrine in international relations.[3] The follow-up series of discussions that arose from that conference was to take place at the IWPS.

Among Fox's particular interests was the relationship between the military and civilian powers, including the little-researched relationship between scientists and the military. With that in mind he initiated a set of case studies, funded in part by the Carnegie Corporation, the intellectual impetus for which was set out in a memorandum from Fox to the Columbia nuclear physicist Isidor Isaac Rabi:

> My effort is, first, to discover and describe the ways of thinking and acting on national security problems of various kinds of civilians and soldiers when they deal with questions of joint concern. . . .
> A second part of the research is to make fairly intensive studies of actual policy decisions. . . . One of the cases on which we are working is especially designed to clarify the distinctive ways in which scientists talk and act—that is, distinctive in relation to politicians, civil servants, diplomats, professional soldiers, industrial mobilizers, etc. The publication of the transcript of the Oppenheimer hearing of April and May, 1954, seemed to give us the opportunity to make a careful study of the decision to put the research on thermonuclear weapons on a crash basis.[4]

Into that project came Warner R. Schilling, a thirty-one-year-old research associate at the institute. Schilling first came to the IWPS in 1954, shortly after receiving his doctorate in political science from Yale and after briefly serving at the Princeton Center of International Studies. He was appointed assistant professor in Columbia's Department of Public Law and Government, and became an associate professor in 1962 and full professor in 1967. In 1976, Fox retired from the directorship of the IWPS. Schilling, who had succeeded him as the James T. Shotwell Professor of International Relations, then stepped up to the directorship, which he held for the following ten years.[5]

In 1956 that rise to eminence lay in the future. Schilling plunged into the task of exploring the hydrogen bomb decision process through a program of interviews. The list of the interviews he conducted, included in the introduction and bibliography, illustrates the wide reach of the program that he undertook during 1956–58. Using, among other sources, the transcript of the Oppenheimer Personnel Security Board hearing to identify key players, Schilling produced an extensive target list, from President Truman on down. Moreover, he was remarkably successful in obtaining access, a tribute to his discretion and to the standing of the institute.

Yet no research project follows a predetermined path to conclusion. The research process itself is inescapably an iterative one, in the course of which the gathering of insights reshapes the original plan. Interview time was committed to exploring the relationship between scientists and soldiers, and, as

Fox had hoped, Schilling published an important paper on this topic.[6] That subject nevertheless took second place to the need to unravel the politics of the "Super," as the hydrogen bomb project was known.

Part of the charm of reading Schilling's interview notes lies in the personal reactions he recorded, often surprising himself. Some of his interviews—John Manley, William Borden, Joe Volpe, Paul Nitze, Alvin Luedecke, Sidney Souers—stand out for the stream of insight they provided. People to whom contemporary historical writing has been unkind, such as Borden of the Joint Congressional Committee staff and the physicist Edward Teller, Schilling found congenial and helpful. The following characterizations are typical of Schilling's reflective style:

- "My reaction to [Luis] Alvarez was much the same as to Borden and to Pitzer. Point being that contrary to my expectation, these were men who give every impression of emotional maturity and intellectual clarity. . . . Alvarez is a thoroughly likeable guy who demonstrates none of the semi-buffoon like attributes that I had inferred from his testimony."
- "Rather impressed with [Hans] Bethe, especially when he grasped right away some points I stated in far from lucid prose. Also impressed me as a very sincere man in his approach to and recollection of these events."
- "Whether it was just general courtesy and respect for the profession, [Edward] Teller was most generous with his time and seemed quite eager to help. Personally, he like all these participants is both impressive and pleasant. He has [a] tendency to get quite—perhaps this is too strong a term—excited and will walk back and forth while talking, sit and then rise again. Tends to talk rather loud. . . . I would say that I find it plausible that there would be those who would find him difficult to get along with in a joint effort and that there would be those who would find it a joy."
- "I was with [Dean] Acheson from 11:45 to 12:30 PM. I was also charmed off the seat of my pants. This time [unlike his first interview with the former secretary of state] I didn't suffer from stage fright. After the interview was over he said he would walk out with me, and we walked across town to his club where he was meeting someone for lunch. Needless to say, I found this a pleasant experience."
- "[Sidney] Souers was an ideal interviewee; willing to talk at length and with seeming candor. His perspective on Govt service and the people involved appears to be without rancor or ill feeling. Even re people for whom he clearly has little use, e.g. [Louis] Johnson, his words are not barbed."
- "As for general impressions [of J. Robert Oppenheimer], these were anti-climatic, as, perhaps, they were bound to be. I didn't really get much support for any of the common images: JRO the master persuader; the liar; the brilliant analyzer; or what have you. Mostly, he just seemed to be another GAC member, another physicist. He was at times witty and attractive in his discussion; at other times hostile and short tempered."
- "[Kenneth] Nichols himself was about what I had expected. . . . I would say, however, that he doesn't seem to have the subtlety of intellect that I thought

I saw in Loper or in McCormack. There was a little bit of the Groves in him; an element of directness and emotion, a certain harshness of judgment perhaps."

Schilling's fascinating interview notes, spiced with observations such as these, languished in his files as he switched his attention to other projects. He had unwisely taken on three book projects, and, despite the importance he attributed to the subject matter, the "H-case" book, as he referred to it, did not progress far even in draft form. Schilling certainly envisaged completion, and his approach would have been to provide a closely textured analysis of the bureaucratic political environment in which the partisans and opponents of the Super operated.

When in 1961 he published an important (and much-cited) article on the project, he included a footnote revealing that it was based on sixty-six personal interviews with the (unidentified) participants in the events of that time. He added,

> Given the character of the interview data and the particular focus of this article, it is the present writer's conclusion that the best way to meet scholarly obligations to both readers and participants is by omitting citation for the points that follow.[7]

The special value of that article—carried over to this book—lay in its being based on near-contemporaneous interviews with nearly all the key players in that complex game. Their memories were fresher than in later years, when a number of them recollected events in their memoirs or in discussion. That the account given was substantiated throughout by unattributed interviews was tantalizing, but these were people speaking off the record and with a candor that was not to be found elsewhere, a feature that in turn has added value to this book, where anonymity is no longer required and where the detailed description and citation that Schilling promised would "of course, be later available with the publication of the whole study of the H-bomb decision" can be included.[8]

The difficulty of completing that study became more apparent with the passage of time and with the appearance of other publications and archival releases that presented him with a moving target. Schilling also faced various forms of writer's block that only became worse as he got older. Noncompletion of the project remained a matter of great regret to him.

In 2011, Ken Young, a historian of the early Cold War period with a background in public policy, was working through the Lewis L. Strauss papers at the Hoover Presidential Library in West Branch, Iowa, preparing a paper on Strauss and the hydrogen bomb.[9] There he came across a 1957 letter to Strauss from Schilling, seeking an interview for Columbia's H-bomb project. Warner Schilling's later work had been long familiar to Young, and he had benefited from it in particular when writing on the landmark State Department policy study NSC-68.[10] Having confirmed that Schilling was still professor emeritus at Columbia, Young wrote to him in August 2012 to inquire about the Strauss interview. Schilling's reply did not reveal much, but was kindly in its encouragement.[11]

Fifteen months later, Schilling's son Jonathan wrote with the sad news that his father had passed away and that there were indeed notes of interviews with Strauss. Correspondence ensued over a period of months, and eventuated in a meeting at the Schilling house in New Jersey. There, Young and Schilling's sons reviewed together the range and quality of the extensive interview notes and acknowledged that not to have carried that study forward was an opportunity missed. It was accordingly agreed that Young would take over Schilling's interview material and make use of it in writing a full-length account of the Super episode.

The scope of the original Columbia study was restricted to the period up to the key decision of January 1950. Schilling did comb the published transcript of the Oppenheimer Personnel Security Board hearing of 1954, but he did so for the light it cast on the period leading up to the presidential decision on the Super, the period of his particular interest. Young's approach has been different: to take the threads of the debate as it stood at that point, and trace their continuity in the years that followed, as the "H-bomb dissidents" opposed successive manifestations of a reliance on thermonuclear deterrence, raising questions not just about the hydrogen bomb as such, but about the United States' dependence on nuclear weapons and its willingness to strike at civilian populations.

The result is, therefore, a very different book from the one that Schilling planned. The plan is Young's, as is the use of the very many more recent sources unavailable to Schilling. The Schilling interviews provide illumination for what is otherwise an archival study. But Schilling also left many helpful observations, framed during his long teaching career, and these have been drawn on from time to time. The book's origins betray two rather different approaches, then. Yet aside from the difference in temporal focus, this book can be considered the result of a sort of posthumous collaboration between two scholars who, despite differences of academic location and generation, seem to have had a shared sympathy, with much the same perspective on the analysis of public policy.

Acknowledgments

Schilling recorded the acknowledgments that he would have made had his book come to fruition. He listed Nancy Huntington, Renata Minerbi, Lisa Henderson, and Holly Stabler, and to those names may be added individuals with whom he discussed the work as it progressed. These included his wife, Jane P. M. Schilling, as well as the interview participant and family friend J. Kenneth Mansfield, institute director William T. R. Fox, and Schilling's fellow academic experts Richard E. Neustadt, Roger Hilsman, Paul Y. Hammond, and David B. Truman. Young is thereby indirectly indebted to these individuals, and, of course, to all those whom Schilling interviewed.

He is directly indebted to many more. Foremost among them are Warner Schilling's sons, Jonathan and Derick, who agreed to entrust their father's research material to him. As it happened, they did far more than this, acting as a continuing conduit of information, as critical reviewers of draft chapters, and as providers of enthusiastic support and encouragement. Jonathan acted as the principal point of contact with the family and contributed his own considerable scholarly knowledge of the issues addressed in this book, as well as a perspective on his father's teaching and writing over many years—together with a fastidious regard for language. He plumbed his father's lecture notes and other material to offer many useful insights that Young could take up as he judged best. Jonathan Schilling generously accepted Young's decision to take the story in a rather different direction from that his father would have chosen, and supported that endeavor with items from the Schilling archive. Those inputs were invaluable and ensured that the Schilling "voice" would be heard. (And in turn Jonathan and Derick are extremely grateful to Young for his original idea and his subsequent efforts in bringing their father's research and work to full light.) Young of course takes responsibility for the themes, interpretations, and conclusions that run through the account that appears in these pages.

Young also thanks King's College, London, for awarding an undergraduate research fellowship to Jonathan Powley, who helped gather archival material during the summer vacation of 2016. Jonathan's commitment and professionalism were beyond his years and much appreciated. Simon Ertz at Stanford University gave excellent help with the LeBaron papers. Also appreciated is the meticulous help with searching and accessing US archival material provided by Thomas M. Culbert, former US Air Force officer, historian, and friend. As ever, historical research owes much to the professionalism and kindliness of the archivists. Particular mention should be made here of Lynn Gamma at the Air Force Historical Research Agency; Craig Wright at the Hoover Presidential Library; Randy Sowell at the Truman Presidential Library; Kevin Bailey at the Eisenhower Presidential Library; Alicia Kubas, government publications and regional depository librarian at the University of Minnesota; and Ginny Kilander at the American Heritage Center of the University of Wyoming. Joseph Siracusa, a leading analyst of nuclear weapons and international security at the Royal Melbourne Institute of Technology, kindly read the preliminary draft of the manuscript and contributed his characteristically perceptive advice. Cornell University Press provided insightful comments from an anonymous external reader and from one of the press's own series editors, while Roger Malcolm Haydon gave continuous support and encouragement.

In-depth immersion in research can often be a trial to a scholar's friends, who, while not named here, will know who they are and will doubtless be glad that the project has concluded. Finally, among all these debts, the unwavering love and support of Young's wife, Ioanna, proved once again to be beyond price and is, as ever, the most deeply felt.

London, 2018

Unbeknownst to me until very late in the process of working with Ken on this project, he was dealing with cancer during most of this time, and in February 2019 he lost his battle with it. I always knew that this project would involve one author who was no longer alive, but it has been hard for me to fathom that both of them are gone.

Before his health completely failed him, Ken submitted a final manuscript, and that, together with a few clarifications and minor additions to the text, along with the usual amount of copyediting, is what you read here. Ken was forced to prioritize content over citation, so in a number of instances sources have been added by Derick Schilling and myself where the submitted manuscript was lacking them. Some of these sources may be ones that Ken never saw. But in no cases have any changes to the historical interpretations in his manuscript been made.

In this work, special thanks have to go to Derick, whose ability to closely read historical writing is unsurpassed. Many of the same people or institutions that Ken mentioned above, as well as the American Philosophical Society, have provided help with checking archival sources. Finally, thanks go to the editors at Cornell University Press for their patience and assistance.

Jonathan L. Schilling
New Jersey, 2019

Introduction

The announcement by President Harry S. Truman on 31 January 1950 that the United States would seek to develop the hydrogen bomb, or "Super," was dubbed by the former national security adviser McGeorge Bundy "this second great step in the nuclear age," one from which "there was no turning back."[1] It certainly seemed at the time to be one of the most momentous events of Truman's presidency, and perhaps of the postwar world. The president formally made his decision earlier that day after meeting with and receiving the advice of a group of senior officials appointed for that purpose—the secretaries of state and defense, and the chair of the Atomic Energy Commission (AEC). The abruptness of Truman's apparent decision at that meeting—asking first if the Russians could achieve a hydrogen bomb, and then, having been assured that they could, immediately authorizing work to proceed—masked a brief but intense period of confused and sometimes agonized debate within those institutions of government most closely concerned with nuclear energy.

The sequence of events that led up to that decision day is well known and has been exhaustively covered in the literature of nuclear history, not least in the official history of the AEC, the second volume of which provides an archive-based blow-by-blow account.[2] Truman's publicly announced decision to endorse "continuing" theoretical work on the hydrogen bomb has been extensively recounted.[3] His subsequent decision, just weeks later, to authorize going ahead to actual testing and production was not publicly announced.

This book begins with the event that drove this decision forward: the detonation of the Soviet Union's first atomic bomb. There follows an account of the brief but intense period leading up to Truman's decision to proceed. The issue was highly polarizing, with the scientific advisers to the Atomic Energy Commission ranged against the military, and the US Air Force in particular. The events leading up to Truman's decision are well-known, the period that followed less so. It was during the ensuing years that the dissident scientists found ways to continue their opposition, no longer to the

1

Super itself, but to its place in the strategic posture of the United States. The greater part of this book is devoted to that aftermath, which culminated in a concerted attempt by the air force to retain control of policy and carry forward the doctrine of strategic bombing, adopted during World War II but now operating with weapons of formerly unimaginable power.

Much of what went to promote, or avert, these decisions is to be found in the private maneuverings of public people. Truman—with only partial success—demanded secrecy for a project of such profound importance. There was a reticence too. Those involved were aware of just how dreadful a threat to human life the hydrogen bomb would pose were it ever to be used. Sen. Brien McMahon wrote of the "intense personal anguish" with which he advocated the Super's production, and of how he and Truman shared "feelings of horror at the thought of these hideous weapons entering into the arsenals of the world."[4]

The short interval between the surprise Soviet atomic test in late summer 1949 and the presidential decision of January 1950, coupled with the strictly limited cast of individuals who played a part in it, poses the question of why Truman acted as he did. There are few clear answers to be found in the vast body of Truman scholarship or in the president's memoirs, which pass lightly over the decision.[5] Truman, wedded to the idea of US nuclear superiority as a guarantor of peace, paid little regard to the phenomenal increase in the destructive power of the hydrogen bomb, seeing it as no more than a qualitative enhancement of what was already in the armory.[6] One reason for this seemingly casual approach is that Truman had remained remote from consideration of the possibility of a thermonuclear weapon; indeed, he had deliberately isolated himself from scientific advice about nuclear weapons. When, at the eleventh hour, he summed up the issues and made his decision, he was untrammeled by too much information.[7]

Barton Bernstein, a careful analyst of the issues involved in the development of the H-bomb, asks whether the president was "responding to bureaucratic pressures, a technological-scientific imperative, congressional and domestic political pressure, his sense of international needs, . . . a demanding military, and their congressional supporters . . . ?"[8] It seems that all of these factors were present in the clamor of the time and were vigorously articulated within the closed circle of institutions and individuals, who advocated and opposed with equal fervor. But their impact on the president was too readily assumed. Bernstein answered his own question in the only closely reasoned account of why Truman acted to approve development of the Super:

> Truman's decision of January 31 was virtually inevitable. He felt no reason to resist this commitment and many reasons—both domestic and international—to make it. He was not compelled to do so by powerful domestic political and bureaucratic forces, but he would have found those forces hard to resist if he had wished to. He did not.[9]

Resistant to pressure, and acutely aware of his responsibility as president, Truman took note of the bitter contestation of views and reserved his judgment of where lay the national security interests of the United States.

The Closed Circle

The multiagency nature of the US federal government frequently results in conflicts that engage a number of parties as responsibilities collide and overlap. In the case of the immediate decision to be taken on the Super, individual participants in the discussion were limited in number; they were estimated by the physicist Herbert York to be fewer than one hundred.[10] This closed circle reflected the fact that the network of players and agencies involved was predetermined by the organizational structure established in 1946 to deal with atomic affairs. At the center was the Atomic Energy Commission, a five-man body created under the Atomic Energy Act to oversee all atomic programs, and chaired by David Lilienthal. The AEC was served by two key bodies: the General Advisory Committee (GAC) of civilian scientific experts, and the Military Liaison Committee (MLC), the AEC's formal connection to the Pentagon. Beyond this inner circle lay the State Department and the Department of Defense, the Joint Chiefs of Staff, and such technical advisory bodies as the Weapon Systems Evaluation Group.

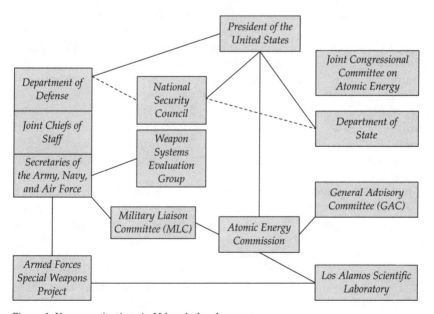

Figure 1. Key organizations in H-bomb development

Keeping a close eye on developments, and by no means reluctant to seize the leadership in the debate, was the congressional Joint Committee on Atomic Energy (JCAE), chaired by the Democratic senator Brien McMahon, who, though a junior senator, had made atomic energy his own issue. McMahon used his position to try to force the pace of US nuclear development. In this, he was supported by the JCAE's ranking Republican member, Bourke B. Hickenlooper, who took the chair for 1947–48 when the Democrats had lost control of Congress. Congress assigned to the JCAE an unusual and formidable arsenal of powers. Its combination of legislative and oversight functions was unprecedented. Its relations with the Pentagon and the armed services were particularly close, while its power of oversight over the AEC was so definite and clearly stated that it was remarked on in a government report written decades later.[11]

Outside the inner circle were a number of scientists, freelancing their influence through Washington's back channels. The attention of all these players focused on the man in the White House. The decision to develop a thermonuclear weapon, or to forgo it, would rest with President Harry S. Truman. How did it come about?

Accounting for the Decision

Most accounts of these events answer Bernstein's question of how the Super came about in terms of the "technological-scientific imperative," begging the question of what lends such pressure an imperative status. They give central place to the politics of atomic science, portraying the debate in terms of the interpersonal drama of contesting scientific figures. For example, Bernstein's own detailed accounts of developments place the scientific community in the foreground, as his work, some written with collaborators, is focused on the scientists themselves and their dilemmas.[12] Richard Rhodes's monumental *Dark Sun: The Making of the Hydrogen Bomb* portrays a scientific race to decision. Gregg Herken's authoritative account presents the Super issue as one of a series of "cardinal choices" in creating a nuclearized world.[13] A mountain of secondary literature adds bulk, but little additional insight.

There are also the histories that did not get written. The physicist Henry D. Smyth, the sole atomic energy commissioner to serve through the entire period of consideration of the Super, from the Soviet explosion up to the first test at Eniwetok in 1952, was regularly pressed by the editor of *Foreign Affairs* to commit his recollections to print. Smyth, the most careful and judicious participant in the affair, drafted and reworked an article but eventually abandoned the attempt at a longer piece as requiring more time, and a greater historical capability, than he felt able to claim.[14]

The most tantalizing absence from the written records is the book planned by the ultimate insider, Robert LeBaron, chair of the Military Liaison Committee and assistant secretary of defense for atomic affairs. Entitled *Decision at H-hour*, LeBaron's unwritten account, he proposed, would aim at "giv[ing] the American public a firsthand view of the actual administrative workings of the military organization" during the period of the development of the hydrogen bomb. Covering the five critical years of the Super project, LeBaron promised to document events "which have been widely misinterpreted and misunderstood in the public mind" and to show how "sound decisions on atomic policy were made."[15]

Whatever LeBaron might or might not have revealed had his book been written, it is clear that the intense politicking that went on scarcely dented the president's calm assessment. Harry S. Truman was his own man and reserved his judgment of the case for developing the hydrogen bomb.[16] In later years, Truman went so far as to deny all sources of influence on his decision, affecting not even to recall the vigorous advocacy of the JCAE. As the president who had overseen the creation of the AEC, the JCAE, and the MLC, and having earlier authorized the use of the atomic bomb against Japanese cities, he was acutely aware of the burden that fell to him.[17] It was not something to share.

Truman's rapid and immediate decision to proceed with the hydrogen bomb when presented with the case by the powerful triumvirate of Secretary of State Dean Acheson, Secretary of Defense Louis Johnson, and AEC chair David Lilienthal—allegedly after just seven minutes of discussion—has been taken by some as a token of his superficiality. For Acheson, his closest adviser, nothing could be further from the truth. The president, Acheson countered, always did his paperwork, and nuclear affairs were no exception. Truman read papers "with the greatest thoughtfulness." When in November 1949 he called Acheson in for a discussion of the hydrogen bomb, the secretary found he was entirely familiar with the issues, including the considerations being advanced at the lower levels of government.[18]

Despite the agonized politics of the time, within a few years the decision had come to be seen by many as perhaps regrettable, but necessary in the light of Soviet advances. By this point some of the original protagonists had become eager to ensure that retrospective credit for the decision went where, in their view, credit was due. It was a time when the temptation to be seen as having been on the right side of history was irresistible. To be labeled as having been opposed to, or even skeptical of, the project in 1949 seemed inglorious, possibly even dangerous, in the inquisitorial atmosphere of the mid-1950s. This J. Robert Oppenheimer found to his cost when he faced a charge that he had opposed, and sought to delay, the development of the hydrogen bomb. Oppenheimer was largely acquitted of these charges, but lost his security clearance on the grounds that he was evasive and untrustworthy.[19] The "trial" of Oppenheimer reverberated through the rest of the decade and beyond, with the release of the redacted passages of the hearing transcript—new material, used extensively in this book—coming only in 2014. Schilling, who was to interview both Oppenheimer and his critics, found it necessary to emphasize in presenting himself that he was not reexamining the case in the aftermath of the hearing.[20]

What were the implications of Truman's January 1950 decision? Schilling's own 1961 article on the subject, explicitly subtitled "How to Decide without Actually Choosing," presented it as no more than a "minimal step" toward the hydrogen bomb: "Of all the courses of action considered and debated during the preceding five months, that chosen by the President represented one which seemed to close off the least number of future alternatives, one that left the most issues still undecided."[21] Thus, cautious approval for further and "continuing" work to be undertaken at Los Alamos could not in itself be reasonably seen as plunging the world into a thermonuclear arms race. To see it as such was to rush the many decision fences that lay ahead. As the physicist Enrico Fermi noted, "One must explore it and do it and that doesn't foreclose the question: should it be made use of?"[22] GAC secretary John Manley disagreed, warning that "a successful test means a commitment to produce and use, if necessary, S-bombs. . . . Once such weapons are proved feasible it will not longer [sic] be possible to choose not to possess them."[23]

While that was evidently so, there was no certainty that nuclear fusion was attainable, still less that it could be weaponized. The military view was accordingly still more pragmatic. Discovering what a thermonuclear weapon could achieve was a necessary preliminary to discussing how it might be employed. Moreover, a decision to make such a weapon did not necessarily presuppose a decision to use it.[24] On the other hand, a limited decision of the type taken on 31 January raised a risk of being "mousetrapped," of ending up with weapon potential, rather than actual weapons, or with no authority to use them once available. The Department of Defense had not considered it urgent to raise production and use issues at the time of the original decision. But after January 1950, according to one air force general, "the passion boiled out," enabling the Pentagon to look for decisions on production and use sooner than it had anticipated, and pending proof of feasibility.[25]

Envisage, then, a chain of decisions in which each one closes off some options for the next while leaving others open. First, the decision to approve further scientific work did not in itself *necessarily* imply the construction and test of a device. It did, however, rule out unilateral renunciation, a position favored by some of the Atomic Energy Commission's scientific advisers. Second, the decision to test a device, if it arose, did not foreclose options on a decision to produce a weaponized version for the US armory.[26] Third, were that decision to be taken, it had no necessary implications for deployment or the authority to use such a weapon. Fourth, were thermonuclear weapons to be developed, tested, and deployed, questions of control over the decision to use—or withhold—them would loom large.

Each of these steps would in the course of time be taken, and were actively sought by some at the outset, and actively opposed by others. But as a sequence, they were not explicitly predicated on Truman's minimalist decision, which seemed indeed to close off the fewest options. As a well-placed air force general pointed out, the president decided the only pertinent point, made the only decision needed at the time. There was no purpose in stirring up opposition to testing or use. Feasibility had first to be determined.[27]

There were few illusions, though, that feasibility, once determined, would be the end of the matter. If feasibility was determined, an impetus for production would follow, and in turn be followed by the preparedness to use such a weapon. To take the first step was to raise the probability of each successive step being taken, albeit with the risk of losing freedom of maneuver. This Oppenheimer's General Advisory Committee had accurately predicted.

The development of the hydrogen bomb was marked by several distinct stages. Initially the prospects of such a weapon depended on the successful development of the fission bomb, which would be required as the starting point in any thermonuclear device. The second stage began after Hiroshima and was characterized by the widespread horror aroused by the use of the atomic bomb, anxiety about a potential arms race, and scientific support for an international agreement to limit that possibility. The third stage began in early 1947 with the failure of the Baruch plan for international control. The detonation of the first Soviet atomic device marked the beginning of a fourth stage, "more intense and bitter than before," as characterized by Peter Galison and Barton Bernstein.[28] A fifth stage—of applied effort—ostensibly began with Truman's endorsement of further work on the H-bomb and gathered pace with the outbreak of the Korean conflict.[29] By this point, the Super was beginning to be seen by the military not as a single panacea, but as one among a "family" of nuclear weapons, including smaller tactical devices. The deep reservations held by the initial critics of the Super proposal had morphed into opposition to the prevailing doctrines of strategic bombardment.

Finally, the breakthrough represented by Stanislaw Ulam's speculations about thermonuclear ignition, taken up by Edward Teller, who saw the potential of using radiation implosion to ignite the device, set the path toward successful development and testing. The opponents called for a moratorium on testing, but their failure marked the last moment at which the iterative progress from research to usable weaponry could have been averted. Thereafter, the expectable process of technological improvement took over to make hydrogen bombs more usable and more flexible—and more ubiquitous.

Executive decisions are contestable and are frequently contested. Rarely simply accepted, they often set up a recursive process of reconsideration, further contestation, and a reluctance to accept what on the face of it has been authoritatively decided. Truman's 31 January 1950 decision—a minimal decision to the analyst, but a maximal decision for the opponents—marked the beginning of a new process of bureaucratic struggle in which dissenters continued to resist those subsequent decisions on testing, production, and use. Many responsible scientists and officials put their best efforts into turning the presidential decision into reality, thereby moving down the chain of possibilities and opening up issues for further subsequent decisions. Those who were skeptical of the wisdom of the original decision, and therefore opposed it, continued to argue, if not against the decision itself—there would have been little point—then against the further choices that became consequential upon it. They worked desperately to promote policies that might mitigate or deflect its consequences.

Table 1 Chronology of "Super" development

Date	Development
1946	
April	Los Alamos hydrogen weapon conference concludes, "It is likely that a super-bomb can be constructed and will work."
1949	
12 May	Study group under Lt. Gen. Hubert R. Harmon reports to the Joint Chiefs of Staff on the limited effects of an atomic air offensive on the Soviet Union.
26 July	Truman appoints Acheson, Johnson, and Lilienthal as Special Committee of the National Security Council (NSC) to study the acceleration of the nuclear weapons program.
16 August	Policy Planning Staff paper on the political implications of a possible Soviet atomic bomb test.
29 August	First Soviet atomic bomb test—Joe 1.
3 September	Monitoring detects the Soviet test.
23 September	Truman announces Soviet atomic test.
5 October	Atomic Energy Commission (AEC) rejects Lewis L. Strauss's call to develop the hydrogen bomb.
6 October	Truman learns of the possibility of a hydrogen bomb.
10 October	Special Committee of the NSC reports on acceleration of the atomic energy program. Truman receives Strauss memorandum urging development of the hydrogen bomb.
14 October	US Air Force chief of staff Gen. Hoyt S. Vandenberg briefs the Joint Committee on Atomic Energy (JCAE) in favor of the hydrogen bomb.
28 October	AEC chair David Lilienthal urges the General Advisory Committee (GAC) to recommend against proceeding with hydrogen bomb.
30 October	The GAC advises against proceeding.

Date	Development
18 November	The *Washington Post* breaks the story of US scientists working on "super-bomb."
19 November	Truman again appoints Acheson, Johnson, and Lilienthal as NSC Special Committee on atomic matters. Working group of representatives from State, Defense, and AEC established to support their work.
25 November	Strauss writes to Truman asking him to direct the AEC to set in motion work on the hydrogen bomb.
	Truman asks Acheson, Johnson, and Lilienthal to jointly study the issue of whether the hydrogen bomb should be developed.
1950	
27 January	JCAE hearing on the H-bomb.
31 January	Following meeting with the Special Committee, Truman announces direction to AEC to "continue its work on all forms of atomic weapons, including the so-called hydrogen or super-bomb."
10 March	Truman accepts recommendation of the Joint Chiefs, through the NSC Special Committee, to instruct the AEC to prepare for H-bomb production.
4 July	Joint Atomic Energy Intelligence Committee reports on Soviet H-bomb program.
1952	
13 June	Joint Chiefs formally define the military requirement for thermonuclear weapons.
September	Truman rejects plea by expert panel headed by Vannevar Bush and J. Robert Oppenheimer to delay thermonuclear test.
31 October	Ivy Mike test—first US test of a staged thermonuclear device.
1953	
12 August	Joe 4—first Soviet thermonuclear test.
1954	
February	First thermonuclear weapon enters US stockpile.

Confronting Complexity

The interview program that Schilling embarked on in 1956 and pursued over the following two years was wide ranging and included almost all of the (then still living) key players, from the president down.

Three points strike the reader of Schilling's interviews and his reflections on them. The first is that the notion that Truman set in motion a crash program to develop the hydrogen bomb, while popularized by the press, members of Congress, and the Oppenheimer security board hearings, and assumed by William T. R. Fox's research mandate at Columbia, continued to be accepted, despite having little foundation in fact.[30] Few of Schilling's interviewees recalled that the term "crash program" actually fitted the events of the time. Most dismissed it.

The second point is that one of the questions on which Schilling's persistent probing concentrated turned out to be something of a blind alley. His interview schedule was designed to focus closely on the opportunity cost of the Super—that is, the diversion of fissionable material from fission bomb production. This issue had been made a major part of the argument among the opponents of the Super. A wide range of estimates were tossed around, on the basis that the effort to produce tritium for the Super would displace much-needed plutonium from the A-bomb production program. It was a consideration that seemed to gain special force following the outbreak of the Korean conflict, when the immediate availability of atomic bombs became an acute concern. As it turned out, as Schilling learned, these future material relationships were unknowable. That failed to deter the claim makers from publicizing what were—according to no less an authority than John von Neumann—"phony" claims, advanced to promote or oppose a position, in this case to block the path to the Super. Briefed on von Neumann's view by the AEC staffer Kenneth Mansfield, Schilling reflected on whether he ought not to

> shift the focus of my question from: how come the ultimate decision ignored this rational point, i.e. economic point, i.e. A-cost, to the question: when you get conflicting scientific advice, whose advice turns out to count. The answer is clearly—those experts who get the most powerful support, politically, are the ones whose advice counts.[31]

This was evidently so, and while Schilling continued to explore his respondents' expectations of the opportunity cost of tritium in terms of plutonium, his wise caveat about power and influence prevailed. In this way he located his study in the mainstream of the intellectual tradition within which he was working, signaling concordance with other Columbia colleagues working at the interface of policy. According to that tradition, simply to describe a series of decision outcomes is to oversimplify the essentially political activity of pressures and counterpressures, bargaining and compromise, alliance and counteralliance that characterizes the politics of policy. In such a struggle, few participants can be truly described as decision makers, but rather as what Schilling's colleague Roger Hilsman calls "inputers, recommenders, vetoers, and approvers," the relative power of whom is at least as important to the final outcome as the cogency of the arguments used in supporting the policies in contention.[32] These near truisms, nonetheless fertile, connect this first author to his predecessor, providing the common ground for a study in which we relinquish all expectation of uncovering a neat and unambiguous record of events. Instead, we presuppose complexity and contradiction, claim and counterclaim.

The third point, then, is that Schilling encountered the full force of complexity and contradiction in his research into the Super decision. He was taken aback by the acrimony that characterized the Super controversy from beginning to end. He was struck, too, by what he termed the "kaleidoscopic" quality of the episode, in which the observed reality shifted dramatically as the perspective moved from point to point, from person to person.[33] Mutual distrust was also apparent, with many respondents attributing suspect motives to their opponents while representing themselves as heroic in their own contributions. Bitterness and denial were widespread.

From what encounters did these conclusions emerge? Schilling cast the net wide for his interview program, from middle-ranking players up to a former president of the United States. Some he interviewed two or three times; with others he was able to follow up interview points in further correspondence. As every oral historian knows only too well, not all the interviews we seek actually materialize. Yet Schilling had very few refusals. Those were on the grounds either that the person sought did not regard himself as a participant in the process or, as in the case of a closely involved air force general, that national security considerations precluded his talking to Schilling about the issues. Schilling accomplished sixty-six interviews, and these, with the subjects' institutional affiliations and positions shown as they were during the September 1949–January 1950 timeframe that the interviews focused on, are listed below. (A separate, alphabetical list that gives interview dates is provided in the bibliography.)

Table 2 Interviews by Warner R. Schilling

Organization	Individual	Position during 1949–50
White House	Harry S. Truman	President of the United States
	Sidney Souers	Executive Secretary, NSC
State Department	Dean Acheson	Secretary of State
	George Kennan	Director, Policy Planning Staff (through 1949)
	R. Gordon Arneson	Special Assistant for Atomic Energy
	Adrian Fisher	General Counsel
	Robert Tufts	Policy Planning Staff
	Paul Nitze	Director, Policy Planning Staff (from 1950)
Department of Defense		
Civilians	Louis Johnson	Secretary of Defense
	Marx Leva	Assistant Secretary, Legal and Legislative Affairs
	John H. Ohly	Special Assistant to Secretary of Defense
	Archibald Alexander	Assistant Secretary of the Army

(*Continued*)

Table 2 (Continued)

Organization	Individual	Position during 1949–50
Military	Maj. Gen. Leslie Groves (retired)	Former Director, Manhattan Project
	Lt. Gen. John E. Hull	Director, Weapon Systems Evaluation Group
	Maj. Gen. James Burns (retired)	Assistant Secretary of Defense
	Rear Adm. Arthur C. Davis	Director, Joint Staff, for Joint Chiefs of Staff
	Vice Adm. Dewey Struble	Deputy Chief of Naval Operations
	Gen. J. Lawton Collins	Army Chief of Staff
	Maj. Gen. James Gavin	Weapon Systems Evaluation Group
Atomic Energy Commission	David Lilienthal	Chair
	Lewis Strauss	Commissioner
	Sumner Pike	Commissioner
	Gordon Dean	Commissioner
	Henry Smyth	Commissioner
	Brig. Gen. James McCormack Jr.	Director of Military Applications
	Kenneth Pitzer	Director of Research
	Carroll Wilson	General Manager
	Joseph Volpe	General Counsel
	Shields Warren	Director, Division of Biology and Medicine
	Norris Bradbury	Director, Los Alamos Scientific Laboratory
	Robert Bacher	Former Commissioner
	Maj. Gen. Richard Coiner	Deputy Director, Military Applications
	Rear Adm. James Russell	Deputy Director, Military Applications
AEC General Advisory Committee	J. Robert Oppenheimer	Chair, Physicist
	Oliver Buckley	Executive, Electrical Engineer
	Hartley Rowe	Executive, Engineer
	Lee DuBridge	Physicist
	Glenn Seaborg	Chemist
	Cyril Smith	Metallurgist
	Isidor Rabi	Physicist
	James Conant	Chemist
	John Manley	Secretary, Physicist

Organization	Individual	Position during 1949–50
AEC Military Liaison Committee	William Webster	Former Chair
	Maj. Gen. Kenneth Nichols	Army member
	Maj. Gen. David Schlatter	Air Force member
	Brig. Gen. Roscoe Wilson	Air Force member
	Robert LeBaron	Chair, Assistant Secretary of Defense
	Brig. Gen. Herbert B. Loper	Army member
	Rear Adm. T. B. Hill	Navy member
	Brig. Gen. Alvin Luedecke	Executive secretary, Air Force member
Other scientists	Edward Teller	Physicist
	Luis Alvarez	Physicist
	Robert Serber	Physicist
	Hans Bethe	Physicist
	Vannevar Bush	Engineer, Administrator
	Jerrold Zacharias	Physicist
	Philip M. Morse	Physicist, Administrator
	Leo Szilard	Physicist
Joint Congressional Committee on Atomic Energy	William L. Borden	Executive Director
	Henry M. Jackson	Representative (WA)
	Chester Holifield	Representative (CA)
	Melvin Price	Representative (IL)
	W. Sterling Cole	Representative (NY)
	John Walker	Counsel (from 1951)
	J. Kenneth Mansfield	Staff
Other actors	Arthur Krock	Columnist
	W. Barton Leach	Legal consultant to US Air Force

Note: The ranks of military and naval officers given here are those they held at the time of the Super controversy. When specifically cited in the endnotes, the ranks given are those held at the time of the interview.

Not all interviews are of equal value. With meticulous candor, Schilling chronicled his encounters, commenting on whether an interview advanced his understanding or contributed little, noting—for example in his unproductive interview with an awkward Truman—that he needed to be more flexible in his questioning rather than follow his schedule:

> Instead of shifting immediately from the prepared questions, once it became clear that these were not going to tap his mind usefully, I instead persisted in following the outline. This meant that the interview consisted of a series of questions from me about particulars which he either did not recall or which he believed to be of almost zero relevance or importance. Given that we parted company from the beginning on the key point of whether there were any issues here, almost no question could have been asked bearing on matters of interest to me that would not have stumbled on this point.[34]

Such are the hazards of "elite interviewing." In this case they were amplified by Truman's characteristic reluctance to disclose his hand on these decisions. Other interviewees responded in a very different fashion and the process was often highly productive.

Schilling was not only persistent in his pursuit of his interviewees; he was also deeply self-critical about the authenticity of what has been called "interview-induced reflection." He applied firmly logical criteria to the interviewer's bête noir issues of misrecall, suggestibility, evasion, and deliberate obfuscation. He noted the extent to which many of his respondents referred to office diaries or consulted their records before or during the course of their interviews. Bearing in mind that these were people speaking off the record and with a candor that would not be found elsewhere, he concluded that, by and large, his material represented a generally valid account of his interviewees' recollections.

Taking the Study Forward

This set of interview notes, correspondence, and reflections is the principal legacy of Schilling's work of some sixty years ago. Oral accounts need to be embedded in a well-documented context, and this Schilling was unable to achieve with the limited archival sources available to him at the time. Although he intended to write a book-length study and prepared a narrative of events to guide his interviewing, the project was sidelined by the flood of subsequent accounts and, indeed, by the need for a young scholar to move on to the next project. The account given in this book obviously benefits from the wealth of memoirs, commentary, academic and journalistic writing, and archival material that has become available in the interim, some of it following declassification—material that was not accessible to Schilling.

Yet material alone does not a story make. It must be interpreted, and we cannot be sure that the two authors—who, it must be remembered, never met—would share the same understanding of the events of 1949–54. But we seem to share a sympathy of approach, a way of interpreting events, even if the passage of the years suggests a more optimistic judgment about great power nuclear rivalry than the sober note on which Schilling signed off his own 1961 article on Truman's decision.

The way in which the story has finally come together places it at odds with other accounts of how the United States moved to produce a thermonuclear weapon. It places a greater emphasis on the politics of the military players, in particular the US Air Force. Soldiers and scientists appear in this book as equal, if generally adversarial, players. The focus adopted here, of continuing contestation through the succession of decision issues, takes the story beyond January 1950 to explore the ways in which the same strains of conflict—and the same cadres of promoters and dissenters—were present in the fraught years that followed.

This is not, however, a story of the politics of technology. Far from offering an account in terms of the familiar technological-scientific imperative, this book highlights the use to which that technology might be put—in a sense, referencing a user rather than a producer account. Thus, centrally placed in the coalition of advocates of the hydrogen bomb, we find the US Air Force and its formidable, agenda-setting Strategic Air Command (SAC), led by Gen. Curtis E. LeMay, who had led the relentless campaign of area bombing of the Japanese cities in 1945. SAC's existence was predicated on a strategic bombing offensive using atomic weapons against the adversary's cities. The coalition of the hydrogen bomb's opponents, centered on the scientist critics around J. Robert Oppenheimer, began by opposing the development of the Super. As events moved on, so did their opposition, to testing, production, and deployment. Opposing SAC's campaigns of massive strategic bombing, the dissenters instead advocated the tactical use of nuclear weapons and secure air defenses as a continuing counterpoint to the emerging development of the "air-atomic age."

The book begins with chapter 1's account of the impact of the first Soviet atomic bomb test on US thinking and policy. It ended the US monopoly of atomic weapons, a development that some had foreseen and others had discounted as a possibility. An atomic Russia triggered fears of a "bolt from the blue" assault on US cities. One reaction was to seek to prioritize US air defenses. Another was to confirm the program agreed to that summer to accelerate the production of fissionable material for atomic bombs. The surge of anxiety also brought hitherto obscure speculations about thermonuclear physics into the public domain. It seemed apparent to some that the Soviet nuclear threat should be countered not by a multiplication of atomic bombs but by an American "superbomb."

In chapter 2, advocates and opponents plunge into the business of campaigning for or against that development. The AEC and its committees were at the epicenter of this debate. The scientific General Advisory Committee, chaired by the former Los Alamos laboratory director J. Robert Oppenheimer, enjoyed a privileged position that it used to block, as it seemed, further activity beyond the theoretical work already accomplished at Los Alamos.

That debate might have remained inconclusive but for shifts in personnel and policy that by the end of January 1950 saw, as chapter 3 recounts, the arrival at a decision. The tide of opinion within the closed circle of participants was beginning to flow against the dissenters, who were skillfully outmaneuvered to provide the authoritative advice that Truman needed to close the debate and authorize not just the expansion of theoretical work, but the path ahead to development and testing.

The fierce debates and personal maneuvering that colored the whole of the Super's history was not confined to practical scientific issues. Chapter 4 examines the controversy's real or assumed moral and political aspects. Moral repugnance inflected the scientific judgments of Oppenheimer's GAC, triggering discussion of the relative moral significance of thermonuclear bombing, the use of the atomic bomb, and the mass urban bombing campaigns of 1942–45. More immediate concerns centered on the impact a decision to develop thermonuclear weapons might have on the pattern of international relations. Given a paucity of intelligence, the effects on the Soviet Union's own weapons program, and thereby on the United States' vulnerability, could only be guessed at: would development of the Super restore the status quo ante-1949 or lead to a thermonuclear arms race and ultimate stalemate—or even Armageddon?

Arguments that had divided US atomic science in the previous months continued, albeit against a changing landscape of decision. In chapter 5, those arguments are examined: arguments about the feasibility of the Super, a matter only decisively settled by the first test, and about its cost, in monetary terms and in terms of precious plutonium foregone. Two other key arguments are reviewed. The first is that even if the Super proved feasible and cost effective, it had little military utility. The second is that even were deployment in war to be considered desirable, so massive a weapon would be undeliverable. On each of these issues the ground shifted under the feet of the participants in the space of just five years.

Chapter 6 shows how the struggle for influence over thermonuclear weapons moved onto new territory, where many of those who had opposed the decision to develop the Super expressed their continuing dissent through the politics of national security policy. The same figures emerged as critics of the air force doctrine of strategic bombardment, and of Strategic Air Command, in which its application was vested. In pointing up the prospects for employing nuclear weapons more effectively in the land battle, the dissenters attracted some support from army officers, while their arguments were anathema to air force generals. As Oppenheimer and another member of his GAC took control of a study of tactical weaponry, the air force began to move against what was seen as dangerous, possibly subversive, amateurism. The offense was compounded by the promotion of an approach to air defense that was seen as another direct challenge to SAC through a disavowal of the deterrent force of strategic bombardment. The first steps were thus taken on a path that would lead to Oppenheimer's "trial" before the AEC's Personnel Security Board, a process that would culminate with his being stripped of his security clearance.

The ousting of Oppenheimer intensified the bitterness that had characterized the politics of the Super from the outset. With the unexpected publication of the transcript of the Personnel Security Board hearing, there now began the process outlined in chapter 7: the search was on for villains, and theories about the slow—and unenthusiastic?—development of the Super abounded. With active encouragement from air force sources, the pillorying of Los Alamos took place in the press, culminating in a widely read journalistic account of where the blame lay. With its dubious claim to extensive research, James Shepley and Clay Blair Jr.'s *The Hydrogen Bomb* owed its paternity and its material to the advocacy coalition that had successfully pushed for the Super. The issues were now public, and the original closed circle of decision widened to include other partisans in the worlds of science and politics. So acrimonious had the progress of the Super been that scores remained to be settled. And they would be.

With the passage of time, many of these animosities—hatreds even—moved downstream. Partisans retired or died. The international politics of the Cold War moved on. The concluding chapter returns to the alignment of forces that worked to sideline those scientists who opposed the then-predominant doctrine of strategic bombing. Schilling's own conclusions from his interview program, included here, stress the confusion and the acrimony of the brief but decisive period in which the Super's potential for US security or global insecurity was contested. With distance, it becomes possible to understand the vigor and passion with which the Super, and the deployment of nuclear weapons for massive retaliation, was resisted, as well as the organizational imperatives of air force leaders to outwit that resistance, the better to protect the deeply embedded air power doctrines that prevailed at that time. The result is that the world was left with the proliferation of nuclear and thermonuclear weaponry. Would that proliferation bring stability or fragility?

The Shock of the "New World"

To the Atomic Energy Commission's official historians, the development of the atomic bomb and its use against Hiroshima and Nagasaki marked the onset of a "New World."[1] Scientifically speaking, that was of course the case. In a deeper sense, though, the new world was a new global order ushered in four years later by the loss of the US atomic monopoly when the Soviet Union emerged as the world's second nuclear power. The Soviet test of August 1949 had an immediate impact on the perceptions and expectations of US policy makers. The shock of a nuclear-armed Soviet Union precipitated both an urgent search for new defenses and a polarization of opinion on the hitherto little-known Super proposal.

What followed—active political consideration of the proposal to develop the hydrogen bomb—occupied a brief and unusually intense moment in US history, from September 1949 to January 1950. The theoretical possibility that a fusion weapon, a "Super" of vastly greater power than the fission bombs used against Hiroshima and Nagasaki, might be feasible had been recognized by Los Alamos scientists before 1945, although the advice from Los Alamos two years later was that such a development was still a long way off without a major investment.[2] So the science had a history, even if political decisions became urgent only with the Soviet atomic test of late August 1949.

Some of the key insiders learned of the test in dramatic fashion. AEC chair David Lilienthal described driving home with his wife from a dinner on Martha's Vineyard one foggy night. As they reached gate of their rented house, a gaunt figure appeared in the headlights, "hooking his thumb in the hitchhiker's gesture . . . on a windswept moor, in the dead of night, on an island, outside a goat field." It was Brig. Gen. James McCormack, the AEC's director of military applications, with a message. They reached the house, Lilienthal lit a kerosene lamp, and they sat down. McCormack referred ruefully to the hard time given to Roman messengers bringing bad news, then went on to explain that on the basis of the detection program, it had been concluded that the US atomic monopoly was over. "By shortly after dawn," Lilienthal later wrote, "we were on our way back to Washington, where other men in government were learning the bitter news."[3]

The Soviet bomb "changed everything," recalled Dean Acheson.[4] Having eliminated the United States' former advantage in atomic diplomacy, the Soviets were now expected to prosecute their intentions with ruthlessness and violence, putting a premium on piecemeal aggression. This expectation would have far-reaching consequences for US policy and was shared by Paul Nitze at the State Department, whose NSC-68 study was set in motion by the president's decision on the Super, initially as a way of drawing in David Lilienthal. Lilienthal's price for accepting the decision was the launch of a general review of US security. Materializing as NSC-68, this review provided the blueprint for the general rearmament that was dictated by the shock of the Chinese revolution, with its amplification of the Communist threat.[5] That blueprint might well have remained a mere aspiration had it not been for the Chinese entry into the Korean conflict, prompting massive rearmament.[6]

The point at issue, now that the gap between the two powers had dramatically narrowed, was whether US policy could be based primarily on atomic superiority. The development of the hydrogen bomb offered hope of maintaining short-term nuclear superiority and providing a protective umbrella beneath which conventional forces could be progressively expanded.[7] Yet in late 1949, the Super project, beguiling to a few scientists and well-informed officials, repellent to others and unknown to most, remained no more than a hypothetical possibility. For it to advance beyond that status would require presidential authority at a time of severe constraint on defense spending.[8]

Officials and observers—and indeed the general public—had long been aware that the United States would be confronted by a nuclear-armed Soviet Union at some point. With greater or lesser degrees of attention and apprehension, they had been waiting for that moment.

Sniffing the Wind

US policy makers were not entirely in the dark, as steps had been taken to get warning of an actual explosion taking place. In April 1947, newly appointed AEC commissioner Lewis L. Strauss urged on his fellow commissioners a new program to monitor the upper atmosphere as a means of discovering whether and when the Soviets detonated an atomic weapon. Strauss thereby gained an honored place in the history of long-range detection, but he did not originate it.[9] During the course of the Manhattan Project, Maj. Gen. Leslie Groves had commissioned Luis Alvarez to devise a means of detecting whether the Germans were operating an atomic reactor. Alvarez produced a filter-based device for atmospheric testing, but it produced no positive indication when flown over Germany in the latter months of the war, leaving uncertainty as to whether the technique was viable.[10]

Proposals for remote monitoring proved highly controversial, partly because there were so many agencies potentially implicated in such a program, and partly because only one of them, the US Army Air Forces (AAF), soon to become a separate US Air Force, subscribed to the belief that a Soviet bomb test might be imminent. The consensus among other agencies was that it was some years away.[11] Vannevar Bush, a key adviser, believed the handicaps of Soviet arbitrary rule would impede scientific progress toward a bomb.[12]

Pressed by Lewis Strauss, and under orders (in the last two days before air force independence) from army chief of staff Dwight D. Eisenhower, AAF chief of staff Hoyt S. Vandenberg—who had recently relinquished his role as head of the Central Intelligence Group—set up an interservice Long Range Detection Committee under his successor at the Central Intelligence Group, Adm. Roscoe Hillenkoetter. The committee adopted the mistaken view that the three basic methods of detection—radiological, sonic, and seismic—were well-developed enough, and that the remaining problem was to identify the agency or agencies that would operate them. While it seemed that the intelligence agencies had an obvious claim, Strauss had worked through his chair, Lilienthal, to press the AAF (as it still was) to take the lead. Having been secretly briefed, Strauss was aware that the AAF operated three squadrons of B-29s modified for weather reconnaissance. They were already designated to monitor the atmosphere on flight paths that would intercept any western-drifting air masses from Soviet territory. In September 1947 the newly independent air force was formed.[13] It inherited the AAF's responsibility to detect the detonation of an atomic bomb anywhere in the world.

A small private company, Tracerlab, won a contract to develop the technology, and during the Sandstone atomic bomb tests of April–May 1948, B-17 drones were flown through the radioactive cloud, in order to develop the system and train personnel in its use. This was not the only means of monitoring the Soviet nuclear program. Sonic and seismic methods were also developed, and a meeting attended by Oppenheimer, Edward Teller, and other scientists wrongly concluded that only seismic methods could offer the evidence the administration needed. Oppenheimer strongly attacked the air force's favored airborne radiological sampling as inadequate, a judgment that would be quoted back at him during his security hearing six years later. The air force paid no regard to this skepticism, and was encouraged by the Sandstone experience. In January 1949, air force officers briefed Strauss on the working of their system of regular "sniffer" flights. He was satisfied that while much remained to be done, "at least the door is no longer left unguarded."[14]

The Joint Chiefs of Staff rejected the various proposals that Vandenberg put forward for a comprehensive long-range detection system to provide detection by complementary seismic or acoustic methods. They backed an interim system of radiological monitoring as the only, albeit a flawed, technique likely to be available in the short run. The Research and Development Board chaired by Vannevar Bush resisted, but the Joint Chiefs made the pragmatic decision to have a flawed system rather than none.[15]

As it happened, the existing technology proved adequate for establishing the fact, if not the precise nature, of the Soviet explosion. The first alert obtained thorough atmospheric monitoring came on 3 September 1949, when an air force WB-29 picked up signs of atmospheric radioactivity.[16] Additional flights were launched over the Pacific, and a week later the British were notified that a mass of air containing activity was passing north of Scotland.[17] British meteorological flights to monitor atmospheric radiation were first discussed with the Americans in September 1948 and were running by April 1949. Alerting the British to the recent Soviet test created a dilemma, with some feeling that such a sharing of information might be in violation of the 1946 Atomic Energy Act.[18] Air force officers pressed hard for immediate sampling as the radioactive air mass drifted eastward. Additional material, collected in the filters carried under the wings of Royal Air Force long-range aircraft, was available for analysis at the Harwell atomic research establishment, and was shared with the US Naval Research Laboratory. By mid-September, analysis of the airborne filter material had exhausted its value and was being superseded by rainwater analysis.[19]

Vandenberg subsequently relocated $50 million of the air force budget to detection improvements.[20] A committee appointed by the AEC under Vannevar Bush to review the evidence meanwhile concluded that the data presented to them were "consistent with the explosion of an atomic bomb."[21] "Joe 1" had arrived. The Joint Chiefs and Secretary of Defense Louis A. Johnson briefed the president, and, mindful of the risk of panic, urged Truman to make a public statement to ensure that Americans would know that he was, as Johnson put it, "keenly aware of the problems involved" and making every reasonable effort to obtain a solution. "If the public is not satisfied," Johnson added, "it may stampede the Government to make hurried decisions that may not be in the best interest of our Country."[22] On 23 September Truman made a low-key announcement of the Soviet test. It was drafted by George Kennan, head of the State Department's Policy Planning Staff, but was the result of many hands; the announcement said that "the eventual development of this new force by other nations was to be expected. This probability has always been taken into account by us."[23]

Generally, official reaction was directed at reassurance. Air force secretary Stuart Symington told Johnson that the air force "subscribed completely to the policy that exploitation of that event might develop a dangerous snowball of fear"; within weeks, however, he became anxious that reassurance might slip into complacency.[24] Gen. Omar Bradley, chair of the Joint Chiefs, did his best to forestall that snowball of fear, telling a journalist that the Soviet A-test was

> no occasion for hysteria. . . . For an industrially backward country, the problem of making an atomic bomb is not so difficult as is the problem of turning it out in quantity and delivering it. As long as America retains (as it can) a tremendous advantage in A-bomb quantity, quality and deliverability, the deterrent effect of the bomb against an aggressor will continue. Sustained research and development can keep us far in the lead with methods for intercepting enemy bomb-carriers. No one can predict what the weapons of the future may be; in the long run our promise of security lies in the combined, unparalleled inventiveness and industrial skill of Western Europe and America.[25]

Despite that timely bromide, reactions were mixed, even within atomic energy circles.

Reactions: "A Good Deal of Fright and Fear"

While the monopoly of atomic weapons gave the United States a seemingly decisive advantage over the Soviet Union, this was a potential, rather than an actual, advantage. War planning did not yet commit to the use of atomic bombs, of which there were in any case only a very small number in the stockpile, and none in the hands of the military. Moreover, few imagined that this advantage would not be nullified at some point by Soviet progress. Eisenhower, army chief of staff from 1945 to 1948, warned of the "transitory" nature of the US monopoly.[26] Foremost among the more far-sighted military planners was Maj. Gen. Curtis E. LeMay, the AAF's deputy chief of staff for research and development, and soon to be the architect of US strategic air power. Speaking in mid-1946, LeMay stressed the compression of time and space achieved by aircraft technology, and the certainty that "other nations" would develop atomic weapons. "When these bombs fall on our industrial heart—that rich and highly developed area that lies between Boston and Baltimore and Chicago and Cairo, Illinois," he warned, "the war may be already over, as well as just begun."[27] Vannevar Bush and Leslie Groves had meanwhile warned the Joint Planning Staff that there was no defense against an atomic attack, once launched.[28]

Predictions of the date by which Soviet progress would materialize in the form of a weapon test had varied widely. While Stalin's low-key response to the Trinity test of the atomic bomb had been intended to convey indifference, within the month he instructed the People's Commissar of Munitions to "provide us with atomic weapons in the shortest possible time. . . .

Provide the bomb—it will remove a great danger from us."[29] In the United States, some thought it unlikely that the "backward" Soviets would ever master the problems of atomic weapon production. The State Department's Paul Nitze was a convinced skeptic—even in the mid-1950s, his personal observations of Russia ("squalor" and "technological backwardness") inclined him to doubt the ability of the Soviet state to achieve major high-technology projects.[30] This view was seemingly commonly held among the State Department's Russian experts, who, like Nitze, were dismissive of Russian technological progress and so discounted the prospect of the early appearance of a nuclear-armed Soviet Union.[31] Another factor was the secrecy surrounding the activities of captured German physicists in the Soviet Union. Others (including Groves) considered the lack of Soviet high-grade uranium a fundamental handicap, although the United States took steps to impede any uranium enrichment program that might be under way. The quality of intelligence was so poor that it was tempting to rely on conservative suppositions. According to Donald Steury, a CIA historian,

> Moscow's lack of high-grade ore, combined with the clampdown on exports of related equipment to the USSR, convinced Western analysts that they had bottled the Soviet nuclear genie. . . . Extrapolating from the US experience, the analysts concluded that a Soviet atomic bomb was at least three years away.[32]

Even those who expected to see Soviet progress on the atomic bomb did not anticipate that it would come so soon. In March 1948, scientific staff from the three US services made their own assessment, which was endorsed by the Joint Intelligence Committee. That assessment, which shaped official thinking, was that the earliest feasible date for a Soviet bomb test would be mid-1950, with the more probable date being mid-1953.[33] Consultation with the British expert Sir Henry Tizard had suggested a date in the late 1950s. The president's Air Policy Commission, seeking what it imagined to be the most pessimistic date, settled on 1952 or 1953. Lower-range predictions were rarely given much credit, and did little to cushion the shock. Most of those involved in the subsequent actions to redress the nuclear balance conceded that the Soviet test had caught them by surprise, and with no contingency planning, responses were necessarily ad hoc.

Even access to the most highly privileged sources of information failed to prepare atomic policy makers. Oppenheimer himself recalled,

> [At] every meeting of the General Advisory Committee nearly we had a briefing on what was called atomic intelligence. It is common knowledge that prior to the Soviet explosion, the earliest possible date was considerably later than the actual explosion and the probable date quite a lot later. The fact is we didn't know what was going on. So this came as an immense

shock, and to everyone involved clearly meant some re-thinking of many aspects of United States policy.[34]

Isidor Rabi later recalled that he "was astonished that it came that soon. If you asked anybody in 1944 or 1945 when would the Russians have it, it would have been five years. But every year that went by you kept on saying five years. . . . It was a stunning shock."[35] Kenneth Pitzer, research director of the AEC, shared with Schilling his recollection that people did indeed seem "stunned," it not being obvious to them what should be done. William Borden recalled the JCAE response as one of "tremendous shock," and Gordon Arneson, special assistant for atomic affairs to the secretary of state, and self-styled "Mr. Atomic," confessed that it would be "presumptuous" to claim that he wasn't surprised.[36]

The State Department had anticipated a need to respond to the Soviet bomb test, whenever it should come. George Kennan was especially sanguine on this issue. He conceded that the test came sooner than expected, but was dismissive of how so many people were "running around in circles" after the announcement.[37] His own view favored diminishing the reliance on nuclear weapons through international control, as the weaponry was more likely to impede than further US policy. His arguments did not convince Acheson, but Kennan was about to leave the State Department in favor of a life of reflection and writing at the Institute of Advanced Study in Princeton. Paul Nitze, hardheaded arch-realist, would take over as director of the Policy Planning Staff.[38]

The remit of State's Policy Planning Staff was oddly limited, and no work was being done to consider appropriate responses, military or otherwise, to evidence that the Soviet Union had acquired a nuclear capability. Nor was it the staff's role to predict a possible test date, or to consider the process by which it might be established. The staff's concern was to discern firm and incontrovertible evidence that such an explosion had occurred. It warned, though, that "only if a high degree of certainty can be placed on systems of detection, would this Government be warranted in basing policy decisions on intelligence derived from them." The principal concern was for those nations that had attached their security to US atomic preponderance and that might be inclined toward greater neutrality in a bipolar atomic world. Reporting just two weeks before the actual explosion, and assuming without question that such knowledge would be made public by the administration, the staff argued that such knowledge could have a steadying effect on the American people by providing a sense of security that—ironically—the US government was not in the dark about Soviet progress and "would be in a position to refute with conviction false claims or rumors."[39]

The Pentagon view tended to be shaped by the misleadingly optimistic intelligence reports, and the near-final war plan Off Tackle was based on the assumption that the Soviets would possess no atomic bombs by 1950. The Joint Chiefs were concerned as much with the demoralizing effect of a threatening Soviet nuclear capability on the morale of the American people as with shifts in the military balance or the impact on US allies.[40] Yet the Military Liaison Committee had been doing some planning for the prospect of an atomic Russia, and from 1947 the US government had initiated training for medical personnel in the event of an atomic attack.[41] The National Security Resources Board established training courses dealing with the effects of atomic attacks, for the benefit of municipal officials.[42] In any event, for the service chiefs, knowledge of the stockpile and the likely rate of production was militarily a more urgent need than firm predictions of the dates of tests. The early, optimistic estimates of Soviet progress were extrapolated to give rather sanguine estimates of the likely size of the Russian stockpile in various years. The confirmation of the Joe 1 test led the Joint Intelligence Committee to hastily revise its projection upward from around 20 bombs in mid-1955 to 120–200 by mid-1954.

Given the urgency of assessing the new situation, a group was drawn together under CIA chairmanship from the AEC, the Joint Intelligence Committee, and the State Department to prepare an estimate of the strategic implications of Soviet possession of atomic weapons. While they were deliberating, the Joint Staff reacted to the confirmation of the Soviet test with a report to the Joint Chiefs warning that the current war plan Off Tackle would need revision when the conclusions of this review became available.[43] That much the Joint Chiefs accepted without quibble, but within the CIA group, the process of registering views of the changed threat produced some sharp differences of opinion. Naval Intelligence put forward the view of Soviet decision makers as essentially cautious, for even were they to assemble a sizeable stockpile of atomic weapons, "it would not follow necessarily that they would attack the United States."[44] The air force view, in contrast, stressed capabilities rather than intentions.

While the Joint Intelligence Committee's assessment, presented on 20 January 1950, considered it improbable that the Soviet regime would deliberately attempt any venture that might lead to war with the United States, it was evident that "the Continental United States will be for the first time vulnerable to serious damage from air and guided missile attack," and that "the loss of the United States monopoly has reduced the effectiveness both militarily and psychologically of the Atlantic Pact." Forward bases, particularly those in the United Kingdom, were now seriously threatened, and it was feared that the UK, conscious of its new vulnerability, could be detached from the alliance. That would have been a major hazard to the US war plan, although ultimately the UK government remained steadfast in its commitment to Western defense. While the Soviet Union would remain far behind the United States in numerical, stockpile terms, its position would improve. The balance of power, the committee argued, could be considered equalized when the Soviets "have sufficient bombs to inflict serious or critical damage on the United States and its Allies."[45]

Tu-4s of the Soviet Air Force, effectively B-29 clones, were capable of reaching targets in the northwestern United States as far south as Portland, Oregon, and as far east as Hanford, Washington, on a two-way mission from air bases in northern Siberia. In-air refueling would greatly extend the arc of threat, as would one-way "suicide" missions.[46] In every bombed area, casualties would be "beyond the capacity of the locality to handle," and estimated to total 1,500,000–1,875,000.[47] For the United States, the requirements for air defense were increased, but no proposals were put forward. Introducing a new note, evidence of a large heavy-water program instituted in the Soviet Union suggested to the Joint Intelligence Committee that work on a hydrogen bomb "may be under consideration."[48]

The Joint Chiefs welcomed the conclusions of this assessment as adding weight to their demands for increases in the military budgets. But while the army and air force both accepted the premise that the Soviets would attack once they had an adequate stockpile, the navy continued to maintain its skeptical position. The State Department and the CIA lined up with the navy, the CIA rejecting the predictions of inescapable conflict in its conclusion that the acquisition of the atomic bomb did not substantially change the nature of the Soviet threat.[49] The several intelligence agencies were at loggerheads; the State Department's Office of Intelligence Research aligned itself with the air force against the CIA, and Maj. Gen. C. P. Cabell, air force director of intelligence, flatly rejected the CIA's views in his briefing to air force commanders at Ramey Air Force Base in April 1950.[50] George Kennan was outraged by this rejection of the CIA argument, which was couched in terms of an assessment of intentions drawn from Marxist-Leninist exegesis by the agency's Sovietologists, a line of analysis favored by Kennan. At root, the conflict between the several agencies and the divisions within them was a disagreement as to what provided the best guide to an uncertain future—Soviet intentions, as understood by the CIA and George Kennan, or concrete Soviet capabilities, as understood by the US Air Force and by Acheson, for whom, in the absence of any evidence as to intent, capabilities provided the surest available guide to defensive planning.[51]

That disagreement ran as a continuing vein through the Cold War years and was scarcely reconcilable. Yet as the argument from military capabilities gained precedence, there followed vigorous reactions aimed at regaining as much as possible the advantages of the former atomic monopoly. This took three forms: making the case for a huge expansion of US air power; launching a program of expanded fission weapon production to amplify the existing numerical advantage; and exploring the possibility that a Super weapon might restore the previous position of US atomic preponderance. Although the case for air force expansion was made in direct response to the Soviet A-test, an expanded fission program and consideration of the

Super equally fed air force ambitions, for, by any reckoning, it would be the principal delivery agency for both fission and (if they materialized) fusion weapons. It would thereby be the beneficiary of any investment in new weapon technologies.

Developing US Air Power

There was no complacency. The air force position, as put forward by Secretary Symington in an urgent memorandum to Defense Secretary Johnson, was that the fact of Soviet atomic capability required immediate action on two fronts: an enhanced ability to carry the attack to the enemy, for which a major expansion would be necessary; and defense against an atomic attack by the Soviet Air Force. Symington warned that the existing plan—itself under threat—"now proves to be inadequate in the light of demonstrated Soviet technical and industrial capabilities."[52]

Expansion was a well-worn argument. Air force leaders, the president's Air Policy Commission, and their supporters in Congress had made a forceful case in 1947 for a seventy-group air force as the minimum peacetime force necessary to ensure the security of the United States. An example of arbitrary force goals being set by an expansionist service, there was scant rationale offered of what such a force could accomplish in time of war in terms of strategic bombing. The bid engendered the fierce opposition of the navy, and a cautionary note from Secretary of Defense James Forrestal in his testimony before the House Armed Services Committee in the spring of 1948:

> I am trying now to avoid getting frozen, particularly in the public mind . . . any figure we put out—we called it in the war the numbers racket. . . . Those concepts are all dangerously erroneous if we give the impression that any one of them gives us complete national security. They do not.[53]

By late 1949 these expansionist ambitions were confronted by incoming defense secretary Louis Johnson's determination to reduce defense expenditure, to which end he browbeat the chiefs of staff into reluctant submission. To that extent he was apparently following the brief given to him by Truman, although the bullying methods of what a Truman biographer considered "possibly the worst appointment Truman ever made" alarmed those around him.[54]

The seventy-group program fell far short of being achieved, and would fall further short as the current budget allocation was estimated to deliver just twenty-nine modern groups by 1955. Annual investment at the level of $2.4 billion—two and a half times the actual allocation—would be required to bring air force strength up to fifty-eight groups by 1955.[55] Johnson was

27

single-mindedly pressing in the other direction, to squeeze down the air force allocation still further. The air force victory in the bitter budget battles secured for it Johnson's support for the massive B-36 intercontinental bomber at the expense of the navy's "super-carrier," the navy suffering defeat in the subsequent "revolt of the admirals."[56] Pursued uncompromisingly by air force leaders for its symbolic expression of an independent service committed to long-range bombing, the B-36 controversy also reflected real doubts—scorn even—about the realism of the navy's atomic strike capability. Moreover, there was more than just a bitter battle over the budget here. The "revolt of the admirals" brought to the surface fundamental differences in navy and air force doctrines regarding how World War III would be fought, with the navy hostile to the bombing of cities and the army sharing the air force's doubts about carrier survivability and navy effectiveness in striking Soviet targets.[57] Yet the B-36 would have been highly liable to interception before reaching a target. This troubled aircraft—underpowered, slow, and unreliable—was an outdated design by the time it entered service.[58] In truth, the weakness of the air force in these initial days was in quality as much as quantity; it was years away from state-of-the-art designs coming into service.

While the argument about air force size and strength had turned on the size (rather than the performance) of the strategic bombing force, the second plank of Symington's argument called for a major investment in air defense. In 1946 the Joint Chiefs had conceded that defenses against the atomic bomb were limited, but still assigned top priority to means of stopping the attacking aircraft.[59] These were prudent, indeed urgent steps, however limited. Long-range bombing with atomic weapons was a new threat, and Vandenberg advocated a substantial reallocation of funds from other priority projects to continental air defense. While this had been noted as a priority in the sequence of emergency war plans, by the fall of 1949 the ability to conduct such a defense was almost completely absent. There had been in the immediate postwar period a degree of recognition of the need for effective air defense of the United States, but from the outset it was seen as secondary to the need to establish a powerful strategic strike force. A reorganization of the army air forces in 1946 established an Air Defense Command as coequal with the Strategic and Tactical Air Command, but the allocation of resources put the Air Defense Command at the end of the queue.[60]

The fact of the United States' monopoly of atomic weapons was taken to mean that the threat of hostile air attack was very small. When it did emerge, it tended to be exaggerated. By the time the Soviet Long-Range Aviation had sufficient Tu-4s for that purpose, the inadequacy of its prototype, the B-29, was becoming apparent in Korea.[61] Yet the US authorities seemed unaware that by 1949 work had already begun to replace the dated Tu-4 design with more modern high-performance jet and turboprop bombers. Deeply impressed by the atomic bombings of Hiroshima and Nagasaki,

Stalin had developed an interest in intercontinental bombing.[62] New design teams were established for this purpose, producing the Tu-95 Bear, which remains in service to this day, and the four-jet Bison.[63]

Prior to the Soviet bomb test, initial US air defense plans were short term and founded on a small number of interceptor aircraft with a view to countering "minor air raids." The Joint Chiefs had been unimpressed by the case made for more substantial defense, while AAF leaders were preoccupied with separating from the army to establish the air force. A long-term plan put forward by Maj. Gen. George E. Stratemeyer, commander of the Air Defense Command, failed to gain support, even as the threat of Soviet strike by massed Tu-4s was officially recognized. A study group appointed by air force chief of staff Carl Spaatz concluded that the United States could not afford to provide adequate air defense for the entire country. To do so would be economically unsustainable and would squeeze out the air offensive, while, the study group noted, "real security lay in offensive capability."[64] The Air Staff, then and later, "believed it had to ensure its views were not misinterpreted as advocating air defense at the expense of the strategic forces."[65]

These two factors—affordability and the unchallengeable primacy of Strategic Air Command (SAC)—dominated discussion throughout the first postwar decade. The stark choices to be made drew in not just senior air force officers, but civilian scientists and commentators, mirroring the polarization of opinion—and of opinion formers—that would characterize the conflict over thermonuclear weapons. A study by the RAND Corporation in 1947 warned against major investment in radar defenses as both ineffective and liable to establish a "Maginot Line" complacency.[66] Rejecting RAND's reservations, the newly independent air force adopted an ambitious plan for a complex radar defense net for early warning and fighter control. It had little chance of early implementation due to cost, and the report of the Finletter Air Policy Commission repeated RAND's warning against a "Maginot Line mentality" and reaffirmed that the best defense lay in the counteroffensive striking force.[67]

Meanwhile, new jet-powered interceptor aircraft had come into service to supplement the wartime piston-engined P-61 Black Widow interceptors. The first major test, in the form of an exercise in which B-29s "attacked" the Pacific Northwest in May 1948, produced discouraging results. The aircraft (redesignated now as F-61s) were too slow to catch the B-29s, and the new jet-powered F-80s lacked both range and bad weather capability. The dismal conclusion was that had the B-29s been Soviet Tu-4s, the attack would have been successful.[68] At the end of that year, a commitment was made to invest in a radar net under the newly formed Continental Air Command, which also began to specify requirements for an effective air-defense fighter aircraft.

US air defense was still in considerable disarray when the news of the Soviet atomic explosion came in September 1949. On 30 September, Gen. Muir

S. Fairchild, air force vice chief of staff, convened a staff conference to confront the implications of this new development. At this meeting, a proposal that air defense should have the same priority as the strategic retaliatory force was decisively rejected. While the need for an air defense was common ground, the priority of SAC as a deterrent would not be questioned.[69] The arrival of Soviet atomic capability would accelerate efforts to provide an effective air defense, but it left overall priorities in place. Few air force officers thought it possible to achieve both offensive and defensive capabilities. An influential article in the *Air University Quarterly Review* argued that an impenetrable air defense system, probably unfeasible, was certainly unaffordable.[70]

On 16 November 1949, Vandenberg expressed his dismay at the current state of aerial defenses to the Joint Chiefs, warning that "almost any number of Soviet bombers could cross our borders and fly to most targets in the United States without a shot being fired at them."[71] He was conscious, though, that even the most complete air defense system would not be sufficient to stop any single determined attack.[72] The following week, Vandenberg pleaded for an aerial defense project to be undertaken at a size comparable to the Manhattan Project, but the other service chiefs were unmoved, thinking such a massive program premature, although they did agree to direct the Joint Strategic Plans Committee to evaluate the soundness of US air defense on the assumption that the Soviet Union was acquiring a stockpile of atomic bombs.[73] The JSPC's conclusion was that US air defense was "inadequate," and specific proposals were made for each service to contribute to a unified strategy.

In December the Joint Chiefs asked Vandenberg to present proposals for investment in air defense. The Joint Chiefs system worked well on this occasion, with chief of naval operations Adm. Forrest P. Sherman taking the lead to write an appraisal of Vandenberg's proposal. He supported the creation of an air defense plan subject to "thorough analytical consideration." Although the operation of air defense was an air force responsibility, the two other services, he said, should be prepared to contribute.[74] On 21 December 1949, the Joint Chiefs informed the Department of Defense's Research and Development Board that air defense should have the highest priority.[75] That month Vandenberg moved to establish the Air Defense Systems Engineering Committee, reporting to him through the Scientific Advisory Board.[76] While the Soviet test heightened awareness of the United States' vulnerability to air attack, the efficacy of the defense against the potential threat, had it eventually materialized, would have been minimal.

In April 1950 a commanders' conference was held at Ramey Air Force Base in Puerto Rico. "One of the reasons we are down here, if not the main reason," SAC commander in chief Curtis E. LeMay warned his fellow commanders, "is to re-evaluate our program in light of the changed situation since Russia has the atomic bomb."[77] The first session at the conference presented a briefing on the extent of the threat posed by a nuclear-armed Soviet Air Force. Looking ahead to 1952, the conference heard that the best intelligence indicated a Soviet stockpile of between forty-five and ninety atomic bombs by that point, with around 400 Tu-4s (rising to 1,200 in 1953), along with the trained aircrew and bases to deliver them.

Maj. Gen. C. P. Cabell presented his appraisal of the impact of various numbers of successful detonations on US territory and concluded that "the total power of the Soviet Union has been and is being increased radically by the possession of atomic bombs, and that the time is fast approaching when the Soviets will possess the capability to attempt a devastating atomic attack on the United States."[78] The probability of war, he concluded, would be reduced if defensive capabilities were such as to guard against a surprise attack, and if offensive capabilities were sufficient to destroy "selected atomic targets in the Soviet Union, and, if need be, to sustain that atomic attack."[79]

Having established the extent of the Soviet nuclear threat, discussion turned to the air defense needed to meet it. The threat would likely materialize as an attack with little or no warning, probably under cover of night or adverse weather, with the Soviet Air Force delivering a large proportion of its stockpile in a single attack so as to maximize the shock effect. This was recognizably a mirror image of SAC's plan under Off Tackle, and indications that the Soviet Union was investing in air defense systems to minimize the effect of a US strike pointed up the need for an adequate US defense. This was still wholly lacking. Maj. Gen. Sam Anderson, director of plans, revealed that twenty-four fighter squadrons and twenty-eight basic radars were stationed in the United States and Alaska, a number drastically below the level needed, whereby a minimum of one interceptor squadron should be available for deployment against any approaching, presumably hostile, formation. A deployment on that basis would require sixty-seven all-weather fighter squadrons.[80] According to present plans, the air force would have a deficit of forty fighter squadrons in 1952. Anderson's plan for expanded air defense, which came to be known as Blue Book, envisaged sixty-seven squadrons of all-weather interceptors, capable of maintaining twenty-four-hour readiness. Importantly, it called for major air defense contributions from the army and navy, reigniting old conflicts about which service took overall control in meeting an attack. By 1954 progress had been made toward achieving the plan, with fifty-five squadrons manned and in place. By this point, planners were looking to air-to-air missiles, some of which would carry nuclear warheads.[81] Thereafter, the expectable threat was likely to be from ballistic missiles. The Soviets were able to build on German technology to develop long-range rockets, and by 1953 US scientists were aware of this development, which would transform the air defense debate—or effectively nullify it.[82]

Expanding Fission Bomb Production

The need for an expansion of fission weapons production was recognized in the summer of 1949 after a period of sluggish and difficult development centered on attempts to refine and improve a version of the Fat Man bomb used at Nagasaki. On 26 May, William Webster, chair of the Military Liaison Committee, notified the AEC that a substantial uplift in production was required if the needs of the National Military Establishment (as it was then known) were to be met. In April the Joint Chiefs had called for an acceleration of the program and for the total weapon requirement to be substantially increased. Lilienthal, the most reluctant weaponeer, instigated a review and replied that the goals set by the Military Liaison Committee "are, of course, considerably beyond those which have been indicated to the President."[83] In July, Truman, urged by the Joint Chiefs, charged a special committee of the National Security Council (NSC) with producing proposals for an acceleration of the atomic weapons program. Johnson had pressed Truman for action, pointing up the different judgments made by the Joint Chiefs and the AEC on the need for expansion, and the special committee—Acheson, Johnson, and Lilienthal—was Truman's device for forcing a decision from warring partners.

The "Big Three" were served by a group of officials under Webster who took the lead in trying to reconcile their different starting points. The exercise was conducted in three separate streams with three groups of officials, an awkward procedure adopted to avoid the risk of the AEC becoming involved in the assessment of military requirements.[84] The outcome was that material was organized in the final version so that, as special assistant to the secretary of defense John Ohly told Johnson, "each agency subscribes only to that portion thereof which relates to its own proper governmental responsibility."[85] The additional funds were substantial at some $300 million, and would have to be acquired through the commission's submission to the White House's Bureau of the Budget, protecting the military budgets from being raided for the atomic weapon expansion.

In its report the special committee took as its starting point the assessment made by the Joint Chiefs. This assessment took a bleak view of the international situation, with Soviet expansionism drawing the United States further into the defense of Western Europe. Recognizing the nature of modern warfare, the Joint Chiefs dismissed the possibility of the United States gearing up for war once hostilities had begun. Instead, the production of the maximum amount of fissionable material would be required to enable the large-scale use of atomic weapons from the outset: "The element of intrinsic scarcity," the committee's report stated, "must be eliminated."[86]

The president's remit stressed the need to consider the adequacy of the then-existing program, as well as the timing of an expansion in relation to the existing budgetary stringency, the possibility of improved deliverability through the development of smaller, lightweight weapons, and the effects on international opinion "of so great an acceleration of visible effort" in this area.[87] By the time the special committee reported in October, the Soviet test had occurred, removing any doubts about the urgency of what was to be proposed. In the first instance, it was considered politic to regard the expansion as "a projection of previous plans" rather than as "a counter-development to the Soviet explosion."[88] As the Soviet explosion came to assume greater priority, Armed Forces Special Weapons Project chief Brig. Gen. Kenneth Nichols encouraged the Joint Chiefs to submit that the test "strongly reinforces and supports the justification and urgency of their previous recommendations."[89]

Johnson's advocacy of the Joint Chiefs' position on expansion was not provoked by the Soviet test, but concentrated on the cost effectiveness of the atomic arsenal and the need for new and smaller weapons for specific targets. Even so, he stressed the need to achieve "overwhelming superiority" in stocks and rate of production "if our atomic weapon posture is to continue to act as a deterrent to war."[90] Acheson was happy to accept these arguments (which he had seen before) and Lilienthal gave his reluctant assent. Truman promptly endorsed their recommendations, and so, as the historian Melvyn Leffler observes, "set the pattern for his [subsequent] support of the hydrogen bomb."[91]

From 1946 on, and under both Democratic and Republican chairs, the JCAE had hounded the AEC and the Joint Chiefs on the question of atomic weapon sufficiency, urging first that the specified military requirement be raised as a driver to increased production of fissionable material.[92] Pressing Johnson and Lilienthal, Sen. Brien McMahon, chair of the JCAE, challenged the doctrine that "we may reach a point when we have 'enough bombs,'" arguing that a considerable increase in the numbers envisaged "would mean the difference between victory and defeat." Hickenlooper pressed the same case, but Truman was cautious about what he saw as "special plead[ing]" by these two congressional heavyweights.[93]

On the day that Truman announced that the Soviets had tested a device, the JCAE formulated a twenty-three-point plan for increased production of the atomic bomb and urged it on the president. Its report to Congress warned that "Russia's ownership of the bomb, years ahead of the anticipated date, is a monumental challenge to American boldness, initiative, and effort."[94] During the run-up to Truman's decision, Hickenlooper criticized the AEC for its lack of "boldness and vigor" in pursuing the Super and went on record as favoring "vigorous research and development" of the potential weapon.[95] Although, unlike McMahon, he did not favor pressing the president on the issue, it was but a small step from there to outright advocacy of the development of the hydrogen bomb. That followed a few weeks later.

Despite the shock that the Soviet test rendered to American confidence, it was the case at the outbreak of the Korean conflict several months later that the United States enjoyed a substantial advantage with respect to deployable air power. The stockpile stood at around three hundred bombs of the Nagasaki-type Mark 3-0 or the improved Mark 4 type, with more than 260 aircraft equipped to carry them. And while both powers dramatically increased their stockpiles and delivery systems over the next three years, the United States' relative advantage held.[96] Truman responded to the rising tide of opinion in favor of strengthening the atomic armory in August 1950 by asking Johnson and Gordon Dean, by then the head of the AEC, to jointly review production as the sense of threat from the Korean conflict mounted. A working group of officials from both agencies addressed the problem and within weeks reported on the need to increase the production of fissionable material by increased investment in ore processing facilities and weapons fabrication plants.[97]

Senator McMahon had used the occasion of the Soviet test to reiterate his demand for an expansion of the existing program of atomic bomb production. While the expansion of fission weapons production had already been set in motion, the further acceleration involved Los Alamos director Norris Bradbury putting the laboratory on a six-day week. McMahon maintained relentless pressure on the administration to expand yet further. Responding in January 1952, the Joint Chiefs insisted that expansion beyond the existing ambitious limits would run into the limits of available fissionable material, and they therefore felt "that the expansion already recommended is the maximum which should be undertaken at this time." The constraint on military effectiveness was less the size of the stockpile than the need to achieve an increased delivery capability.[98] In April, McMahon was worrying away at the Department of Defense, complaining that three months had gone by since the expansion report but no request for the appropriation of funds had been made. "Frankly," he told the secretary of defense, "I feel that this delay implies a lack of the sense of urgency within the Executive Branch which ought to exist and which is stated to exist in the report submitted to the Joint Committee."[99]

Angling for the Super

While there had been discussion of the theoretical possibilities of a superbomb since 1942, work on it had not been granted priority; more was expected of the possibility of a successful "boosted" fission process, which might also provide data on thermonuclear burning.[100] The Soviet atomic test revived work on a thermonuclear weapon. Oppenheimer had chaired an initial conference of scientists in 1942, following which exploratory work was done at Los Alamos during the course of the Manhattan Project. Initially described as "the deuterium bomb or 'Super,'" its prospects were reviewed at a Los Alamos conference in April 1943 following "considerable thought and discussion." The official *Manhattan District History* affirmed that "the proposed weapon, using a fission bomb as a detonator and deuterium as an explosive, could properly be called an atomic superbomb. . . . Its potentialities were so great that research on it could not be neglected completely."[101] Its development, as distinct from theoretical research, remained at a lower priority than achievement of the fission bomb, which was required to ignite a thermonuclear reaction, although systematic theoretical work began in the fall of that year. According to the *District History*, while it was expected that development time would be lengthy—greater than that of the fission bomb—"it was decided that work on so portentous a weapon should be continued in every way possible without interfering with the main program."[102]

Ed Hammel, a member of the wartime team, summarized the state of development in an interview with Martin Sherwin:

> It's of some considerable interest, I think, that at the start of Los Alamos . . . there was an intent, "Let's go right to the Super [bomb]." And for that reason, the very first operational building that was built out here was the low temperature laboratory. . . . It was realized that if Los Alamos was going to put a bomb together and they were going to go the Super route, they needed a low temperature laboratory capable of making large quantities of liquid hydrogen. So therefore, in February, I think, of '44—so that was from April of '43—a building and an air liquefier and a hydrogen liquefier were all constructed. At that time, they were, I think, the biggest ones in the world. By 19 February '44, when that thing was finished, it became apparent that the fission bomb was going to be harder than they thought, and the thing was abandoned. It was turned over and run once and mothballed.[103]

Hans Bethe recalled that the reaction to the Trinity test among the Los Alamos scientists was to look forward to the next challenge. He himself was quite ready to work on thermonuclear development, and so long as the laboratory continued to exist, the Super would be an appropriate next step. This thinking, borne along by Teller's and Fermi's enthusiasm, was predicated on the war continuing for another year or so. Its abrupt end following the bombing of the Japanese cities brought to an end speculation about an immediate Super program. Despite having witnessed the power of the Trinity device, scientists were shocked by the extent of the damage at Hiroshima: within a matter of months, recalled Bethe, they were all talking about international control and no longer talking about weapons development.[104]

The postwar situation had realigned priorities. The atomic bomb no longer posed a theoretical problem, but good scientists would opt to work on the theoretical division's thermonuclear research even at a cost to the fission work, as it posed the more interesting problems (or, as Bethe put it, there was a preference for working on weapons we *didn't* have).[105] Accordingly, more theoretical effort was put into early thermonuclear work than would have been apparent from the public record. Hammel recalled,

> So there was work, there was thinking. I don't believe there was any experimental work here on the Super as such at all. There was no concerted effort until we got the word, "Go ahead." But there sure as hell was a lot of theoretical calculations going on, absolutely. I suspect there may have been physics experiments. By the time we got into it, in the '50s or so, then we had to start looking at some of the low-temperature properties of tritium, of liquid tritium, things like that. But that was all sort of connected with the mainline program.[106]

Groves was emphatic that the Super did not merit serious effort during the wartime years as it could not answer the problem of how to end the war quickly with atomic weapons, his overriding priority. He did, however, approve, in May 1944, the production of experimental quantities of tritium.[107] Later, as a member of the Military Liaison Committee, he favored retaining a small group of scientists to continue theoretical work at Los Alamos in the event of a breakthrough being made.[108] Oppenheimer's Scientific Panel, set up to serve the Interim Committee that bridged the gap between the wartime years and the establishment of a new statutory regime for the control of atomic energy, had acknowledged the possibility of that happening. At the first meeting of the panel with the Interim Committee in May 1945, the chemist James Conant—ironically, in light of his subsequent opposition to the Super—had briefed on the potential of a hydrogen bomb, while Oppenheimer estimated that it would take three years to develop.[109] Following the Japanese surrender, Secretary of State James Byrnes urged that work on the Super should continue. Oppenheimer and his colleagues dissented. Arthur Compton revealed the strength of the opposition of the panel's members: "We should prefer defeat in war to a victory obtained at the expense of the enormous human disaster that would be caused by its determined use."[110]

Meanwhile, having successfully developed the atomic bomb, Los Alamos's first responsibility was to pursue a program of improvement. A further conference in 1946 concluded that the Super was feasible, although that conclusion—or its recording—was heavily influenced by Edward Teller's enthusiasm. The conference had focused on the model proposed by Teller's group, a model that, according to the *District History*, was "chosen for amenability to theoretical treatment rather than for engineering practicability or efficient use of precious material," the aim being "to study the feasibility of thermonuclear bombs in principle, not to propose designs for actual weapons." And there the matter rested. By June 1946, intensive theoretical work was hampered by the loss of personnel from the laboratory.[111] The Defense Research and Development Board of 1948 examined the prospects for such a weapon but deferred further consideration while AEC commissioner

Robert Bacher organized a briefing for military personnel on the potential of a thermonuclear weapon. The Super looked like a long shot and military enthusiasm was understandably muted, although a study by the Air Staff in the summer of 1949 examined the utility of a very large bomb with a yield of one thousand kilotons, concluding that it would enable execution of the current war plan with fewer sorties.[112] By autumn the issue was whether there were new considerations that justified reexamination of the possibility of such a bomb. The Soviet test answered that question decisively.

Whereas the scientific work of the Super had been hitherto shrouded in tight security, Joe 1 unleashed an outpouring of speculations and half truths, to the great discomfort of Los Alamos and the administration. Lewis Strauss, the office holder who argued most vigorously for expansion of the fission program, went one better and now urged the commission at its 5 October meeting to make "a quantum jump" into thermonuclear planning in "an intensive effort to get ahead with the super."[113] The most alarming revelation followed from the secret briefing of the JCAE, when one member, Sen. Edwin C. Johnson, claimed on television on 1 November that Los Alamos scientists were working on a weapon with an explosive power "a thousand times the effect of that terrible bomb that was dropped at Nagasaki." There was no secret now, although comment was surprisingly muted, as had been the case in 1947 when John J. McCloy, former assistant secretary of war, had publicly discussed the possibility of building a hydrogen bomb of immense power and referred to the scale of the effort it would require.[114] The reporter-columnists Joseph and Stewart Alsop ensured that this reticence would end. Joe, the doyen of inside-dopester journalism, picked up the lead, revealing somewhat prematurely that "the theory of how to make [the Super] is already understood and generally accepted. Making it will require immense efforts, yet the job is actually farther along than was the job of making the Hiroshima bomb when the Manhattan District was established."[115]

The uncertain prospect of the Super brought with it a wave of new fears, not least the possibility of severe atmospheric pollution—more generally known as "fallout"—were a thermonuclear explosion to occur. A technical note to the president signed by Sumner T. Pike as acting chair of the AEC revealed that following independent calculations the commission concluded that "this danger is not serious." On the most conservative assumptions, the danger point would not be reached until around five hundred such bombs had been exploded, while more reasonable assumptions suggested a figure of fifty thousand bombs.[116]

Despite the earlier involvement in considering the basis of a thermonuclear reaction, few of the leading researchers reacted to the Soviet test by advocating accelerated work on the Super. In addition to Teller, the exceptions were a group of scientists from the University of California, Berkeley— led by the physicists Ernest Lawrence and Luis Alvarez and the chemist

Wendell Latimer—who campaigned vigorously among their fellow scientists. Lawrence had already been consulting on radiological weapons development, and the shock of the Soviet explosion removed any moral qualms he might still have had regarding an H-bomb.[117]

At the State Department, Paul Nitze took the view that the development of the hydrogen bomb could maintain short-term nuclear superiority and provide a protective umbrella beneath which conventional forces could be progressively expanded. The possibility of snatching back the lead over the Soviets by developing it suddenly became a matter for urgent decision. As Nitze told it, he linked up with Robert LeBaron, chair of the Military Liaison Committee, and took a briefing from a group of colonels who worked on atomic matters for the Joint Chiefs and who had earlier approached him and warned him that the AEC, under the influence of Lilienthal and Oppenheimer, was refusing to pursue the possibility of developing the hydrogen bomb. He also consulted Teller, who convinced him that the Super was possible and that Oppenheimer's technical and scientific objections (that such a weapon was probably unfeasible and certainly uneconomic) did not stand up to interrogation.[118]

The Joint Chiefs remained cautious about the possibilities of the Super until a late stage. A meeting of the Joint Chiefs with the JCAE had been arranged for 14 October 1949, and Alvarez had been actively lobbying for Congress to pursue the Super. Alvarez met Kenneth Nichols, who, accompanied by Maj. Gen. Frank Everest, briefed Vandenberg, who was slated to testify on behalf of the Joint Chiefs at the hearing. Richard Rhodes (who claims it was Lt. Gen. Lauris Norstad, not Everest, who attended) reports that until that day "the USAF Chief of Staff had never heard of the hydrogen bomb."[119] This is hardly likely to have been the case, as speculation about the Super was commonplace in the higher military circles. In any event, it was as head of the Armed Forces Special Weapons Project that Nichols, who was not accountable to the Joint Chiefs, but separately to all three service secretaries, sought out Vandenberg as his sponsor.

Vandenberg in turn sent Nichols over to brief the Joint Chiefs, who, under Gen. Omar Bradley as chair, immediately endorsed the need for the Super, and the next day Vandenberg reported to the JCAE on their behalf in positive terms. While Vandenberg was the active proponent of the Super, Bradley rightly took a more detached view, befitting his role as arbitrator between clashing service interests.[120] Vandenberg's testimony to the JCAE called for reemphasis and even acceleration of development work on the so-called superbomb, confirming it as the military point of view that the superbomb "should be pushed to completion as soon as possible."[121]

Many of the scientists involved took a poor view of the military's readiness to engage with the issues raised by the Super. There was widespread irritation at the reluctance to define the military requirement other than in terms of what the AEC could provide. Scientific leaders, however, for their part, appear to have been blind to the ways in which decision processes in the military establishment operated, with extensive staff work undertaken below chief-of-staff level before a definite position could take shape. By the beginning of 1950, the Joint Chiefs were able to articulate a strong position on the desirability and utility of the Super. Its feasibility remained to be determined.

Advising on the Super

The array of advice and potential pressure on the question of the Super as it existed in late 1949 offered no clear direction to the president. Powerful congressional opinion challenged the advice of the most powerfully placed scientists, but that had not yet been sufficient to swing Truman behind the Super's development. His views began to take shape in mid-January after receiving a report on the military aspects from Secretary of Defense Johnson. In a memorandum to Dean Acheson, Sidney Souers wrote that Truman believed the report "made a lot of sense and he was inclined to think that was what we should do." This report was actually from Bradley on behalf of the Joint Chiefs, but the secretary, eager to seize the moment, had passed it straight on to the president, short-circuiting the normal procedures, somewhat to the irritation of both Souers and Acheson.[1] With the Pentagon and Congress now both pushing in the same direction, only some flexibility on the part of the Atomic Energy Commission (AEC) was needed to provide Truman with the basis for consensual decision. Achieving it would prove an uphill struggle.

The Opening Skirmishes

Among the Washington agencies, the AEC enjoyed an uncomfortable primacy as the body established as guardian of the United States' interest in atomic matters (and, for a considerable period, as the physical guardian of the weapons stockpile). Enjoying almost unprecedented independence, it reported directly to the president. The commission was initially chaired by the urbane David E. Lilienthal, former head of the New Deal's Tennessee Valley Authority. Its other initial members were Robert F. Bacher, a physicist who had held key positions at Los Alamos (and was the commission's only scientist member); Sumner T. Pike, former member of the Securities and Exchange Commission; the banker William W. Waymack; and Lewis L. Strauss, businessman and naval reserve admiral. The commission staff, under a general manager, included a Military Applications Directorate under a brigadier general.

Appointed by the president under the 1946 Atomic Energy Act, the civilian commission took over from the army's Manhattan Engineer District and was itself subject to advice from two other statutory bodies. The first was the Military Liaison Committee (MLC), representing the service interests. It was initially established under air force lieutenant general Lewis H. Brereton, but the chairmanship now rested in the hands of civilian officials. Donald F. Carpenter and William Webster served stints of a year or less during 1948 and 1949 until Robert LeBaron, an assistant secretary at the Department of Defense, took over in 1949 for an extended spell.

The MLC reported to the secretary of defense on all major policy matters and was charged with resolving differences among the departments and agencies involved in the military applications of atomic energy. It was empowered to serve as a committee of the Joint Chiefs of Staff if required, and acted as staff adviser to the secretary of defense and the service secretaries, each of whom appointed two of its members.[2] Commission members held regular joint meetings with the MLC, which for the first years of its life was accommodated within the AEC building.[3] It was regarded by the commission as its channel to the Department of Defense, but was seen by that department as its watchdog over the unpredictable and sometimes obstructive civilian commission.[4]

The second statutory body was the General Advisory Committee (GAC), which provided the scientific, civilian input for the commission's deliberations and was chaired by J. Robert Oppenheimer. Serving with him were James B. Conant, president of Harvard; Lee DuBridge, president of the California Institute of Technology; the physicists Isidor Rabi and Enrico Fermi; Glenn Seaborg, a Berkeley chemist; Cyril Smith, a University of Chicago metallurgist; Hartley Rowe, an industrial engineer who had worked at Los Alamos and was now vice president of the United Fruit Company; and Oliver E. Buckley, an electrical engineer who headed Bell Labs. While both of these committees were powerful players in their own right, the role of the GAC was unambiguous, its statutory remit being to give the commission advice on what would constitute appropriate scientific and technological progress in assuring the common defense and security.

The test of the Soviet atomic bomb had focused minds in Washington. At a 29 September meeting between the AEC and the Joint Committee on Atomic Energy, some of the congressmen wanted to know more about the possibility of developing the Super as a response to the Soviets' unexpected progress. The following day, Strauss prepared a long memorandum to his fellow commissioners calling for intensive effort to develop the hydrogen bomb, with the GAC being asked not to express an opinion on its desirability, but to advise on how best "to proceed with expedition."[5] To his chagrin, the commission would not agree to provide such a steer, leaving the GAC a clear field to provide advice in whatever broad terms it chose.

At a further meeting on 5 October, Strauss found no more support on the commission, even after lobbying individual members in advance. He had intended to present his memorandum, which advocated a "quantum jump" in order "to get ahead with the Super," but Lilienthal had declined to create the opportunity on the agenda for him to do so. Instead, Strauss had to insist on reading his memorandum to the full commission meeting at the end of the formal business. Receiving no encouragement, he then decided to bypass the commission altogether, passing a copy to Sen. Brien McMahon.[6] He also approached the president through Souers, the executive secretary of the National Security Council, who saw Truman daily. When, on 6 October, Strauss explained the issues to him, Souers expressed surprise and revealed that he knew nothing of the H-bomb issue and was sure that the president was equally in the dark. He then checked with Truman (probably on 10 October), who confirmed that he knew nothing of the matter.[7] Souers passed him a copy of the Strauss memorandum, and in Souers's recollection Truman told him to go back to Strauss and ask the commissioner to "go to it and fast." On the twenty-fifth of November, Strauss put the case directly and more formally to the president in a personal letter.[8]

Scientists Meet the Military

Strauss recognized that the president would attend to advice from the Department of State and the Department of Defense, including the Joint Chiefs of Staff, as well as that of the commission. As discussed in the previous chapter, once the Joint Chiefs endorsed the Super, Vandenberg testified on their behalf to the Joint Committee on Atomic Energy. The effect of military figures testifying to Congress on this occasion was not just that the committee members became better informed—military leaders rarely had detailed information at their fingertips—but that the testimony locked the military leadership into the pro-Super position. Service chiefs and senior officeholders were wary about getting out of step with McMahon's committee.

Acknowledging that the policy debate at this level was becoming dangerously polarized, LeBaron took the initiative to bring the military and the scientists together in a bid to achieve a degree of mutual understanding. His own background, both military and scientific (he had a masters of science from Princeton and studied at the Sorbonne under Marie Curie), inclined him to take on this role of bridge builder. He arranged for Bradley to meet the GAC in the hope that face-to-face contact would break down the suspicion and hostility with which the two groups regarded one another.

The Joint Chiefs chair arrived accompanied by Lt. Gen. John E. Hull, chair of the Weapon Systems Evaluation Group; air force chief of plans Lt. Gen. Lauris Norstad; and Rear Adm. William Sterling "Deak" Parsons, joint deputy head, with Maj. Gen. Roscoe Wilson, of the Armed Forces Special

Weapons Project. The terms of the meeting had been set out: at Norstad's particular insistence there should be no inquiry into military plans. LeBaron was sure he had confirmed this with Oppenheimer, who nevertheless went straight to the point, asking Bradley what uses the military intended for nuclear weapons, and how they fitted into the war plans. Bradley, LeBaron later recalled, "clammed up" as it became clear that the agreed terms were being ignored. The meeting made no progress, worsening, if possible, the relations between scientists and soldiers.[9]

If there resulted from this meeting a greater degree of mutual understanding, it was only that the military and the GAC had a clearer sense of the other's opposing views.[10] Some of the scientists, recollected Brig. Gen. Alvin Luedecke, executive secretary of the MLC, were so violent in their views that it was difficult to discuss them.[11] He was not alone among the military men in being surprised and shocked by the vehemence of the scientific opposition.[12] For their part, it had become a common belief among the scientists that the military had simply displayed their ignorance of the issues surrounding the Super, confirming the generally negative view many of them had of the ability of the top brass to understand their own needs. Discussion between the two sides, though, remained confused. Schilling commented that "different participants were talking about different things," adding that the issues "were so interrelated, however, that the participants were not always able to distinguish against what (and even for what) they were arguing."[13]

At the same time, the AEC's recurrent demand that the Pentagon should share more information on the need for atomic weapons (and, implicitly, the plans for using them) was a frequent source of complaint among military men. The constant refusal to do so was interpreted by AEC scientists and some commissioners as a failure of planning for the nature of atomic warfare.[14] AEC commissioners dug their heels in over the continuation of fission weapon expansion through 1952, arguing that while they could agree that the program was feasible, they could not approve the requirement unless they were made privy to the war plans data on which the requirements were based.[15]

General Bradley in particular was derided by the scientists for his seeming reluctance to address the issues. This was parody. The AEC director of military applications, Brig. Gen. James McCormack, who had been present for Bradley's testimony, was surprised by its reception from the GAC members. He recalled the soft-spoken Bradley giving qualified approval to the Super, subject to little being actually known about it, thereby going as far as a professional soldier could go.[16] Among the scientists, there was little appreciation of a military man's sense of obligation, or indeed of the reporting line whereby a service chief must be careful to avoid getting too far ahead of his civilian secretary. For his part, Bradley considered scientists to have no business trying to get into military affairs. He held that as the GAC was not in the chain of authority between himself and the commander in chief, it would have been inappropriate for him to set out the military's position before them.[17] He had reportedly warned the president that to give the AEC a hand in the determination of military requirements would blur his own responsibilities.[18] He now continued as a behind-the-scenes advocate for the Super, discussing its prospects "privately, man-to-man" with the president on three occasions.[19]

The conflict over war plans was sustained in part by the ambiguity of what the term meant. The AEC's demands for specific information could be met, subject to presidential consent. Beyond that, the sharing of overall planning objectives and purposes was unobjectionable to the military. But the details of war planning that specified target designations and weapon allocations were something that could not be shared.[20] Gordon Dean, Lilienthal's successor as AEC chair, expressed the commission's view that the military conveyed its needs simply in terms of the AEC's productive capacity, inflating its demands when, in due course, the expansion process promised more plentiful supply. In his interview with Schilling, Dean related an anecdote about once having received a memorandum from the secretary of defense to the effect that the military required x number of atomic bombs. Dean went to the secretary to discover the basis for this figure, only to be told that the secretary considered it an arbitrary one, advanced for the purpose of discussion. Such vagueness fed the critics' hostility to what they saw as military intransigence.[21]

Nowhere was that intransigence more apparent than in the matter of atomic weapons custody. From the foundation of the AEC and its associated institutions, the military view was opposed to civilian custody. Leslie Groves had the responsibility of negotiating the transfer of property from the army to the new commission, and proposed that the military should retain all weapons and weapon components. It fell to Kenneth Nichols to draft the executive order covering the transfer in uncompromising terms. Strenuously opposed to these key aspects of the transfer, the army, in the persons of Groves and Nichols, "reawakened the old scruples about civilian control," according to Richard Hewlett and Oscar Anderson.[22] The episode left a continuing legacy of mistrust, with echoes of a long-running controversy over civil-military relations. Nor did the threat to the principle of civilian control evaporate, and the next few years saw greater flexibility, with the transfer of nonnuclear components to the US Air Force in the UK upon the outbreak of the Korean conflict in 1950. The following year Truman authorized an initial transfer of a number of nuclear cores to the military, with a more general transfer in 1952.[23] When the decision on the Super came to be made, Lilienthal protested vigorously that the operating assumptions of the military establishment (as he continued to call it) should be subject to review by the AEC; to protect the military from scrutiny at this crucial point, he argued, "definitely removes any notion of civilian participation in a fundamental policy question."[24]

The GAC as Moral Custodian

In addition to the Joint Chiefs, the General Advisory Committee formally consulted a number of other parties, all within the narrow circle of officials and officers who were privy to the discussion of the Super. They included George Kennan, director of the State Department's Policy Planning Staff; Walter F. Colby, the AEC's director of intelligence; LeBaron from the MLC; and Lt. Gen. John Hull, chair of the Department of Defense's Weapon Systems Evaluation Group. Remarkably, though, the GAC chose not to hear from the AEC's own heads of division, provoking a bitter response from Kenneth Pitzer, the director of research, a distinguished scientist in his own right and future chair of the MLC.

When the GAC held a three-day special meeting on 28–30 October, the division directors arrived on the second morning expecting to attend the meeting but found themselves barred. It is on the record that the divisional heads were invited (and, incorrectly, that they attended).[25] Instead it fell to the AEC's general manager, Carroll Wilson, to relay Oppenheimer's decision that they should not be heard, news he delivered in person and with some embarrassment.[26] Pitzer was furious. While he later gave evidence to the Personnel Security Board hearing, none of his vehemence came through in that anodyne account of this occasion.[27] Had he related this story, which he told decades later, to the board at the time, it would have been another damaging point against Oppenheimer.

> This [exclusion] was unprecedented as far as I was concerned. I had always attended any GAC session on a topic to which I could possibly contribute, except for an executive session of the committee alone, or of the committee with the commissioners. Thus, as I say, it was unprecedented that I'd be told I wasn't invited. It was clear to me immediately that Oppenheimer wanted to exclude me. He wanted to prevent me from presenting my views, or explaining and amplifying Lawrence's and Alvarez's views, which I knew, to the other members of the GAC that did not have that background independently. At least, many of them did not.

It was apparent to Pitzer that a major push on the Super would have meant bringing back scientists who had served at Los Alamos during the Manhattan Project, as well as giving a central place to Teller:

> This type of a major change at Los Alamos was what the General Advisory Committee was recommending against. . . . Oppenheimer didn't want me in

on their first sessions while they were formulating their recommendation. He wanted to be able to control the discussion with Conant's backing.[28]

When the GAC met later that day to settle their advice to the AEC, they stated their views on a number of issues relating to raw material and neutron production as well as, almost parenthetically, recommending efforts to develop atomic weapons for tactical purposes. Their report, parts of which were drafted that evening, also included a brief "elementary" account of the nature of a hypothetical fusion bomb and the steps that would need to be taken to bring it into being. The report went on to say that the GAC members were unanimous in hoping "that by one means or another, the development of these weapons can be avoided." The principal reason was that

> the use of this weapon would bring about the destruction of innumerable human lives; it is not a weapon which can be used exclusively for the destruction of material installations of military or semi-military purposes. Its use therefore carries much further than the atomic bomb itself the policy of exterminating civilian populations.[29]

The following day the GAC considered these matters further, commenting specifically on their remit to advise the commission as to whether or not there should be an immediate all-out effort to develop such weapons. In recommending strongly against such action, the committee set out their belief that "the extreme dangers to mankind inherent in the proposal wholly outweigh any military advantage that could come from this development." The United States' stock of atomic bombs was substantial enough to provide an adequate threat of reprisals should the Russians themselves develop the Super. The United States, they concluded, should not proceed with its development, and this act of self-denial would provide "by example some limitations on the totality of war . . . limiting the fear and arousing the hopes of mankind." This further report was signed by all the members, with the exception of Seaborg (who was absent), Fermi, and Rabi.[30] The latter two submitted a minority report asserting that it would be wrong "on fundamental ethical principles" to develop such a weapon and advocating an invitation to the nations of the world to join in "a solemn pledge" not to proceed with the development of thermonuclear weapons. In an important caveat, they conceded that the United States should proceed with the Super if the Soviets ignored this appeal and refused to renounce thermonuclear weapons.[31]

Gordon Dean confided to his diary that

> in the discussions leading to the GAC's conclusion, many things were said, arguments advanced, which do not appear in their written report. They were, I think it is fair to say, visceral reactions. The moral implications were

discussed at great length. It was pointed out that this was something different in kind rather than in degree and that the general tenor of the discussion
was that it was just too big and must not therefore be built.[32]

Leslie Groves blamed the commission for allowing the GAC to pose as a
"moral custodian" of the United States.[33] Dean defended the remit: the
GAC was expected to address the Super question in the broadest possible
terms. Yet he wondered whether their attitude meant that the GAC would
not support sending scientists to Los Alamos to work on the Super.
DuBridge was blunt about that: they would have "roundtrip tickets." Provoked by DuBridge, Dean said he thought that the GAC members were
behaving like a "bunch of college professors."[34]

Equally dismissive was Henry Smyth, physicist and fellow AEC commissioner. Although at that stage opposed to developing the Super, Smyth
bluntly "never understood" the report, found it "no help" to his own thinking, and paid no more attention to it.[35] The reaction to the report among
AEC staffers was one of surprise, even shock. Navy captain James S. Russell, deputy director of military applications, and General McCormack were
reportedly "floored" by it, while Carroll Wilson viewed the report as revealing "troubled souls" wrestling with the problem of the Super.[36] Kenneth
Pitzer had expected no opposition to developing the Super until his invitation to the committee meeting was revoked, alerting him to the likelihood
that the report would be negative.[37] The GAC had isolated itself, and at least
some of its members seemed surprised to find so many key individuals
critical of their report.

McGeorge Bundy, an advocate of alternatives to the H-bomb, remarked
later that the GAC report polarized opinions on the Super:

> Members of the committee were more certain of what they were against—
> what they called a crash program of development—than about what they
> were for, just as their critics were more certain of the dangers of letting the
> Russians win the race than they were of the advantages of an American pro-
> gram of development.[38]

The GAC report was classified top secret, and the details of the argument
did not spread beyond the tight circle of officials most closely concerned
with what the AEC itself would recommend. Lilienthal took the divided
commission report to the president without informing the MLC. Kenneth
Nichols, deputy to Groves on the Manhattan Project and his successor as
chief of the Armed Forces Special Weapons Project, had been abroad in
the UK during this period, and returned to discover that no one would
tell him what the GAC had recommended. "It took considerable effort on
the part of all members of the MLC," he later wrote, "to determine
through our various channels that the GAC had recommended against

developing the H-bomb and that a majority of the Commission was against development."[39] The Joint Chiefs, once briefed by Nichols, produced a lengthy rebuttal of the GAC's arguments. When Lilienthal proposed sharing their response with the GAC members, the request went up the line to Secretary Johnson, who blocked it with the subsequent approval of the president.[40]

A number of other scientists picked up the drift of the GAC report, in part by extrapolating from the known views of Oppenheimer and Conant. But despite Oppenheimer's towering status in the community (and with it, the ability to make the careers of young nuclear physicists), there was dissent, even disbelief. The Berkeley group of scientists in particular, having been at arm's length throughout the process, found it difficult to grasp the GAC argument when it was summarized for them. Luis Alvarez recounted an exceptionally painful episode when DuBridge came to Berkeley in the spring of 1950 to explain it to him and Lawrence. Schilling's own notes of Alvarez's recollection are poignant:

> DuBridge tried to explain why the GAC had done what it had done. Alvarez counts this as one of the most tragic and embarrassing moments of his life. . . . DuBridge found himself unable to make his arguments stand up against the comments and rebuttals of L[awrence] and A[lvarez] and was reduced almost to tears by the experience. He would say but if you had only heard Robert explain it, you would see that it was right.

Schilling reflected on the honesty and regret that shone through Alvarez's memory of this episode, and the regard he expressed for both men, Oppenheimer a personal hero and DuBridge his former mentor at MIT: "He said it was horrible to see a man of DuBridge's stature in such a pitiful state."[41]

There were repercussions not only in California but elsewhere in Washington too. Learning that the Bureau of the Budget might oppose Super development on cost grounds, John Steelman, chair of the National Security Resources Board, sought a meeting with Bradley. Adm. Arthur Davis of the Joint Staff attended instead and was shown a paper signed by a bureau official—"obviously written by some scientist"—setting out the moral grounds for not proceeding. "Son of a bitch" was the verdict of Davis and Steelman both, and no more was heard of it.[42]

Second Thoughts

With the tone set by Conant, Oppenheimer's famed persuasive powers had been deployed to achieve apparent unanimity among the GAC members. "Apparent," as Glenn Seaborg's equivocal dissent was held back, a decision that would in time cost Oppenheimer dearly when it later fell into

Strauss's hands. A purely technical report from the GAC would perhaps have been carefully nuanced. Founding the argument against the Super on moral grounds ensured that the tone of discussion in the committee would be colored by high emotion, despite subsequent recollections that most GAC members did not prioritize the moral issue so highly. Although he signed, Oliver Buckley privately thought the moral aspects of war were not a scientist's business, but, with Rowe, he customarily deferred to the physicists.[43] He later confessed to Sidney Souers, the National Security Council secretary, that he was "embarrassed" by the GAC report.[44] Conant alone had played the key role in persuading the members to hitch themselves to the moral principle.[45]

Oppenheimer was later to claim that had a feasible Super been in sight, the urge to reject it wholesale on moral grounds would have been balanced by the more positive scientific prospects. Similarly, for Lee DuBridge the prospect of a workable device would have transformed the "atmosphere" of the GAC discussion (though not necessarily its decision).[46] As it was, the atmosphere of the committee was distinctly self-congratulatory, although Oppenheimer, who characterized it as a meeting of sensibilities rather than of minds, had some misgivings about its likely reception.[47]

Dissenting opinion was quick to come. The report's content was seen as "visceral." Edward Teller was bewildered, asking how a group with so many good minds could come up with so unoriginal an idea. How could such a group of scientists recommend against research on a scientific problem, as if they were trying to cut off intellectual investigation?[48] Karl Compton, former president of MIT and one-time presidential adviser on the atomic bomb, offered his own influential advice, responding to the GAC report by urging that the United States "should proceed with this phase of atomic weapon development, with increased activity and support, but that we should do so without fanfare or publicity."[49] The military figures who were party to the debate were generally unsurprised, feeling that when scientists got into this realm they were out of their depth and their advice could be discounted.[50] Hans Bethe, when he returned to Los Alamos in 1950, found a great deal of enthusiasm for proceeding with the Super, reporting that with few exceptions the scientists there "hated" the GAC and resented its interference with their plans for development.[51]

To stem the tide of criticism, John Manley, secretary to the GAC, prepared a letter in which he sought to address some of the reservations that were being expressed about the committee's position. By this stage Manley was a vocal opponent of development, despite his earlier involvement with the Super work at Los Alamos and the ambiguity of his continuing role as associate director there.[52] Manley advanced these further points because he feared that the president would not understand that a decision to advance research would lead inescapably to the development of a weapon, so great were the mounting pressures.[53]

His defense of the GAC took a high moral line, proposing that a decision not to proceed provided an "opportunity to apply our standards of life to our actions and to formulation of policy in a more consistent way." Specifically, Manley deprecated the possibility that the Soviets would develop the H-bomb on three grounds. First, there were technical difficulties, as "it involves a big effort." Second, the Soviets had struck a moral posture before the world, and the use of such a weapon would "certainly end Communism at least here." Third, they would fear retaliation by US atomic bombs.[54] These were profoundly weak arguments, even by the standards of the GAC report.

Why then did the GAC embark on so high-minded a course of advice? Some members held that theirs was a *general* advisory committee, and did not see their remit as limited to a narrow range of scientific advice. Hence the impulse to take a "whole problem" approach, reflecting the wide range of engagement that scientists had enjoyed during World War II. This, confessed Rabi, could rightly be seen as arrogance, something for which the GAC members and their supporters in the scientific community would be chastised.[55]

Interviewed a few years later, Cyril Smith was inclined to recant. The GAC had been naive in assuming that international agreement could be reached. It gave insufficient attention to the potential psychological impact of the Soviet Union achieving the Super ahead of the United States. And for a technical committee to formulate a disarmament proposal was to exceed its remit. Smith confessed to Schilling that as scientists, the GAC members should have made due allowance for new ideas, should have had more faith in science. That they did not he attributed to a subconscious desire that the Super would turn out not to be technically feasible. While it seemed so in 1949, they were, he acknowledged, perhaps too unimaginative about the prospects for normal technical improvement.[56]

Nor did the GAC members themselves hold fast to their original report, and at their next meeting in December some at least conceded that they had failed to express themselves clearly.[57] Buckley reflected that the GAC did not do itself justice on the question of further research on fusion. His recollection was that the members wanted to defer a decision on development until the point when clear research results had become available. But they had failed to make this explicit, and on rereading, he felt the report was misleading.[58] Smith agreed that the group had used the doubtful technical prospects of the Super to bolster their concern about its justifiability.[59] For DuBridge, the hurried drafting produced a report that was too short and inadequately worded, and failed to get the main point across; for him, this was that renunciation would not be for all time, but would create a hiatus in which international control could be sought once again, a "damn cheap" means of gaining the moral high ground.[60] Oppenheimer himself conceded the lack of clarity in the report. It might be hard to understand in retrospect, he admitted, but most members had commitments elsewhere and were pressing to get the job done and leave. Hasty drafting produced a document that after eight years remained ambiguous.[61] Several GAC members took the opportunity to send Lilienthal their own further thoughts or elaborations. Buckley's own memorandum was written as a revision of what the GAC had said rather than as the fresh statement that, years later, he wished he had made.[62]

The most startling apostasy, however, was that of James Conant, the moral arbiter of the GAC discussions. It was a long time coming, but in 1970, Conant, jointly with Leslie Groves and Vannevar Bush, was awarded an Atomic Pioneer Award by President Richard Nixon, acknowledging his wartime work and his "pioneering post-war leadership" on atomic energy. The award followed shortly upon the publication of his autobiography, *My Several Lives*. Interviewed about the award and the book, he recanted his opposition to the Super. "My intentions were good," he told a *New York Times* reporter, "but I think history will show I was wrong and that President Truman, who went ahead with the bomb, was right."[63] Lewis Strauss was delighted and, in the silky tones he reserved for triumph over his former adversaries, congratulated Conant for his courage, copying the Oppenheimer Security Board "prosecutor" Roger Robb, now a US Court of Appeals judge, into the correspondence.[64]

A notable exception to the representations following the GAC report was Glenn Seaborg, who had earlier been recorded by Lawrence and Alvarez as a supporter of the H-bomb. Unable to be present at the GAC deliberations on the Super, he had written to Oppenheimer to express his considered view that it would be wrong to hold back from developing the bomb. His dissenting letter had, however, been overlooked, or suppressed, by Oppenheimer.[65] He would pay dearly for this when the letter fell into Strauss's hands. Preferring the United States to go ahead with the Super in advance of any discussions with the Russians, Seaborg did not think the GAC report reflected his views. Alone among the scientists on the GAC, he believed at the time that the committee had exceeded its proper role. He considered writing a protest statement, but decided against it in light of the apparent unanimity that he perceived on the issue at GAC and AEC levels. While Seaborg would eventually advance to become chair of the commission itself and preside over an important reconsideration of the consequences of nuclear war, in 1949 he felt inhibited by his own relatively junior status; he was just thirty-seven years old at the time of the GAC discussion of the Super.[66]

Alvin Luedecke took a mild view of the dispute. In the view of his air force colleagues, the scientists had

created something that they didn't know what to do with, and they wanted to keep the closet door closed just as long as they could. We said to ourselves, we can understand that desire but we think it [is] unrealistic. We think the security interests of the United States dictates that we get busy. We have to do it if we can convince the right people, even though the Oppenheimers and others don't agree and we went on that basis.[67]

The Widening Gulf

While there could be said to have been a "military view" of what some saw as a scientific cabal, views of the Super itself were differently nuanced in each of the three services. These differences did not emerge immediately when the prospect of a thermonuclear weapon first materialized as something requiring decision. Two of those definitely in favor of development were Nichols and his fellow MLC member Maj. Gen. Herbert B. Loper, army men who were in effect rooting for an air force weapon. Although the Super program would in time be competitive with the army's and navy's interest in lower-yield tactical weapons, in 1949–50 appreciation of the possibilities of a wide range of applications was so limited that neither of the other two services would claim proprietorial rights over atomic weapon development.[68] Interservice competition emerged later.

The desirability of the Super was, however, regarded differently by the separate individuals within the services. According to Nichols's self-glorifying claim, only between eight and ten individuals in the military establishment really understood nuclear energy issues. All knew each other well and knew how to influence one another.[69] Roscoe Wilson was one of these and, like Luedecke, could speak for the wider air force constituency:

> From the military standpoint, the danger of losing our dominant deterrent posture was very real; on the other hand, it was difficult to see how our efforts to attain our national objectives could be impaired by our development of the H-Bomb. I do not recall any serious discussion within the military about the moral onus of developing the weapon. It seemed inevitable that it would be developed by someone. The moral aspect was associated with the use to which it would be put. . . . The important thing was to maintain a preponderance of strategic power as the shield behind which . . . our diplomats could work out a modus vivendi with respect to the Soviets.[70]

Robert LeBaron astutely observed that in policy conflicts of this sort it behooves no professional group—scientific or otherwise—to assume a strong position that it cannot back up. The stiff-necked GAC posture simply made it easier for the military to win the argument.[71] The MLC members felt the GAC had made a major misjudgment. There was a keen feeling among those members that the scientists were assuming the role of pundits on military matters, with an unjustified confidence in their own judgment. From the moment of the report, the gulf between the GAC and the MLC widened. The latter committee distanced itself, LeBaron content with keeping the secretary of defense informed.[72]

The dispute left scars. There were few who thought the AEC-MLC-Pentagon relationship worked well. Vannevar Bush was among those who thought the structure of a full-time commission created by the 1946 Atomic Energy Act to be inappropriate and the source of the relationship problems.[73] Throughout this period, under the chairmanships of Lilienthal and Dean, the commission strove to hold the MLC, and thus the Pentagon, at bay. As the production of atomic weapons expanded rapidly in 1951–52, the commission's remit to consult with the MLC "on all atomic energy matters which the Committee deems to relate to military applications, including the development, manufacture . . . of bombs" came under strain. Frustrated by the failure to win the argument about the transfer of weapons custody, the MLC proposed a shift of responsibility for the development of nonnuclear components from the civilian commission to the military services, which would assume overall responsibility for the development and production of these components. The commissioners unanimously opposed this proposal, which would have seen them losing responsibility for the technical problems of hardware, electronics, and marriage to the vehicles of the using service. Attempts to find an agreeable formula failed.[74]

LeBaron, still rather animated about it in his final months as MLC chair and assistant secretary of defense for atomic energy, attempted to redefine the relationships between the key players. Ideally, in his view, the AEC would receive military requirements from the Joint Chiefs, and would submit its programs to a National Security Council special committee for decision by the president. The secretary of defense should coordinate the activities of the commission with the services, and oversight would be provided by the appropriate armed services committees of Congress, for, he said, "the Joint Committee on Atomic Energy does not have any unique rights with respect to the internal affairs of the Department of Defense." The relationship between the MLC and the commission was asymmetrical, and rightly so, providing only a "window for military observation and advice," and despite the wording of the 1946 act, there could be no free flow of information in the opposite direction, from the Department of Defense to the commission:

> Unless the privileged role of the Military Liaison Committee to have working level contact with the Atomic Energy Commission is clearly understood, the superficial use of a two-way exchange of information channel tends to compromise the military posture of the United States by exposing it to the release of internal privileged information which provides security risks which it cannot accept.[75]

LeBaron had little respect for the commission's ability to maintain a tight security net, and he harbored no illusions as to the potential opposition to his proposed streamlining of atomic relationships. To others troubled by the AEC/DoD divide, the problems were attributable less to organizational structure than to LeBaron's own personality and operating style.[76] Gordon Dean, then chair of the commission, was particularly critical; to him, LeBaron was "a pain in the neck" who could not judge the mood of his own committee.[77] If LeBaron was inclined to play prima donna, he was not the first MLC member to do so. With the winding up of the Manhattan Engineer District, Leslie Groves was given a seat on the MLC, a bit-part role in comparison with that he had played in the war years. Unsurprisingly, he proved to be highly active and a thorn in the side of the AEC, using his MLC role to be fiercely critical of the commission, which responded by distancing the organization so far as it possibly could.

A Decision Reached

When Sen. Brien McMahon was briefed by the AEC at the end of October 1949, he learned for the first time of the GAC's advice. Reacting with fury, he was deeply upset and reportedly "almost in tears."[1] The report's position seemed to him "suicidal."[2] He immediately wrote to Truman, warning that his committee was moving toward a unanimous recommendation to develop the Super.[3] He asked for a meeting with the president to press the case for the H-bomb in the event of Truman being disinclined to authorize going ahead. Truman replied that the issue had not yet reached his desk. It did so a week later, with the AEC's unwillingness to push for the Super prompting McMahon to write again, stressing the urgency of a new program. Later that month McMahon wrote once more, imploring Truman,

> The profundity of the atomic crisis which has now overtaken us cannot, in my judgment, be exaggerated. The specific decision that you must make regarding the super bomb is one of the gravest ever to confront an American president. . . . Those who oppose an all-out "crash" effort on the super impress me as being so horrified at the path down which the world is traveling that they have lost contact with common sense and reality.[4]

From then on the press was alert to the gathering debate. The Alsop brothers, Joseph and Stewart, regularly reported on the state of the Super debate, benefiting from the acknowledgment across the defense community that leaking to them was the most effective way of getting a point of view publicly registered. Commissioner Henry Smyth recalled that following one of his first AEC meetings, he was shocked to find an almost complete account of the discussion in the press the next day, by either the controversial columnist Drew Pearson or the Alsops, but he offered no guesses as to the source.[5]

Schilling was impressed by the extent of the press coverage at this sensitive time, and, bearing in mind Souers's advice to him that "there are no leaks in Washington, only plants," he interviewed the Pulitzer Prize–winning commentator and *New York Times* reporter and columnist Arthur Krock. Schilling received little more than generalities, but Krock did intimate that Lilienthal, Oppenheimer, and Strauss were the principal leakers, and that the first two were "liars."[6] The Alsops continued to discuss in their columns the prospect of a superbomb, under the appropriate heading "Pandora's box," to put pressure on the president. The main and perhaps intended outcome of this was to ensure that the JCAE would keep up its own pressure on Truman.[7]

The State Department officials played their cards close to their chests. Acheson weighed the issues, carefully engaging the principal protagonists to clarify their views in his own mind. His decision to advocate the Super was inescapable (as Truman recognized) given that international considerations and domestic concerns—including his own potentially vulnerable position—pointed in the same direction.[8] Gordon Arneson, State's special assistant for atomic affairs, recollected in 1989 that the State Department team, whom he identified as Acheson, Nitze, Fisher, and himself,

> were of a mind that there really wasn't any choice [about developing the Super]. Acheson, I think, showed more flexibility than any of us. He talked to Dr. Conant at length; he talked to Oppenheimer at length; he talked to Lilienthal at length. They were all opposed, and he was not persuaded. He did try. I don't see how we could say we're not going to do this thing, that we will put it in a bushel basket somewhere; because if we didn't do it, certainly the Russians would.[9]

In contrast with their secretary's careful leadership, the State Department's Policy Planning Staff maintained a cool distance from the Super question, avoiding a clear stance and not expecting to be consulted given that the department's prestige was low in matters of military significance.[10] Indeed, George Kennan tended to dismiss the significance of nuclear weapons for international relations, and did not think the Super could be in any way militarily advantageous. He reflected bitterly some years later that "Paul [Nitze] never accepted the premise that I have always started from, and that is that there is no defense against nuclear weapons. . . . These people—and Paul was one of them—would have their way. I didn't expect any good to come of it."[11]

Kennan discussed matters with Oppenheimer, but the scientist-philosopher and the diplomat-philosopher, despite sharing an opposition to the thermonuclear weapon, rated the dangers very differently.[12] Yet Kennan, soon to vacate the directorship of the Policy Planning Staff, was careful to occupy a safe space, looking over his shoulder at Congress. Sen. Bourke Hickenlooper, a fervent critic of Lilienthal and of "moderate" opinion generally, allied with Lewis Strauss in targeting the scholarly Kennan, who told Schilling that Hickenlooper and Strauss had personally given him a warning that if they ever caught him and the department "out of line" on the atomic energy problem, they would "get" him. Recoiling from their "extreme suspicion," he noted ruefully that he had never experienced such strong personal expressions of vindictiveness and hostility.[13]

The commission itself, although split, formally advised Truman against development of the Super.[14] The key date in forming their position was 3 November, when the members came to discuss the GAC report. Lilienthal opposed the demand for an agreed line, urging that the separate views of individual commissioners should be put forward. Against this, Strauss argued in favor of giving the president a comprehensive package of views, incorporating those of the commission and the Departments of State and Defense. While the commission could advise on the feasibility, timescale, economy in terms of fissile material, and probable characteristics of the Super, he maintained that it was not competent to advise on the weapon's military usefulness or on the diplomatic consequences of its possession. As the AEC, State, and Defense were all equally members of the president's "official family," a complete set of opinions, Strauss asserted, should be put before him.[15]

Later that day, Strauss submitted a note elaborating on remarks he had made about questions that he thought the commission ought to be able to answer. These included the cost effectiveness of diverting funds, talent, and material to the development of the Super, and whether it could be justified against the alternative of investing in what he called "ordinaries." He asked whether it could be established that the military actually wanted the Super and wondered whether a decision against proceeding would be considered by European allies as "marking the beginning of a program of our withdrawal from the role of the strong and steady protector."[16]

Before the commissioners, split three to two against the Super, resumed their discussions on 4 November, Truman had been made aware of the differences of views. Meanwhile, Oppenheimer threatened to put the GAC's opposing view directly to the president rather than going through the commission, in the event of the full AEC deciding in favor of the Super. When the commission next returned to the question on 7 November, positions were beginning to harden. Henry Smyth, who had recently joined, made clear his unwillingness to develop a weapon "in the present world circumstances," while Lilienthal was flatly against development at any time. But the tide was already flowing strongly against the AEC majority, and Brigadier General McCormack, the AEC's director of military applications, had once warned that if the commission failed to do its job on grounds of conscience, Truman would "get himself another Commission."[17]

The Breakthrough

McMahon had used his position to persuade Truman to appoint his former law partner Gordon Dean to a vacancy on the commission, and assured Strauss that Dean would support developing the hydrogen bomb, thus changing the balance of AEC opinion. As decision day drew near, Lilienthal was reported to have pressed his opposition in a "secret" meeting with General Bradley, chair of the Joint Chiefs. With a slender grasp of political realities, Lilienthal argued—according to the paraphrase presented by Drew Pearson in his syndicated column, as the meeting was not secret for long—that "we must exhaust every means of reaching an agreement with Russia to outlaw atomic warfare before we make this bomb. We should appeal over the heads of the Kremlin to the Russian people. They will force Stalin to come to terms." Pearson went on to claim that a group of "tormented" scientists were joining Lilienthal to organize church groups in a "crusade" against the hydrogen bomb as soon as the AEC chair stood down.[18]

Following its 7 November meeting, the commission set out its position. It recognized the need to make a public decision, although what that decision should be was a matter on which the commission was divided. To some extent, matters were being driven forward by the Joint Committee, as McMahon announced a special executive meeting to take place in the near future, making it certain that public discussion would ensue, for, as the commission's report acknowledged, knowledge of the Super "is so widespread that a decision not to go ahead could hardly be kept secret." The commission's advice conceded the technical feasibility of such a weapon, pointing out, significantly, that "the Russians are familiar with the ideas and probably can develop a bomb in the period comparable to that which we would need." Nevertheless, Lilienthal, Smyth, and Sumner Pike recommended that the president decide against the development of the Super, citing the support of the scientists of the GAC. Dean strongly argued to the contrary, maintaining that the United States should not forgo the development of a weapon that could be decisive in meeting an aggressive war by the Soviet Union, something he considered a strong possibility.[19]

Days before, Lilienthal had submitted his resignation to the president. Truman, however, prevailed on him to remain in post until a time "when your withdrawal will not upset plans for dealing with problems which may not have been determined by the end of the year."[20] Impatient with this gradualism, Strauss again intervened to urge Truman to act to end the delay, warning that press leaks by the opponents of the H-bomb might crystallize into a campaign against it. Certainly, arguments against the bomb were common currency in the press at this time, with little regard for Truman's requested secrecy.[21]

The Joint Chiefs elaborated their position on 13 January, rebutting the "mass slaughter" objection by maintaining that they did "not intend to destroy large cities per se; rather, only to attack such targets as are necessary in war in order to impose the national objectives of the United States upon an enemy."[22] The paper was drafted by the MLC and sent to the Joint Staff, with the Weapon Systems Evaluation Group probably also commenting at that stage. Johnson insisted that McMahon be briefed on the Joint Chiefs' views, a sure way of making sure the JCAE was onside and fully informed.[23] He also provided Truman with the Joint Chiefs' paper, strongly urging development; the president reportedly commented that it "made a lot of sense and he was inclined to think that was what we should do." Acheson recorded in a memorandum for his files that he himself had "about reached the position that we should advise the President to go ahead." However, there should be no illusions: by recommending such a decision, he wrote, "we are going quite a long way to committing ourselves to continue down that road."[24]

The AEC's report to the president was too equivocal to form the basis of a policy decision. A confidential memorandum that originated with Truman's naval aide set out the issues for a decision on whether the United States should proceed with the construction of a superbomb, deeming it to be "an absolute weapon" that could provide "a most potent and perhaps critical tool to assist in our negotiations for world peace." There was a need to cut through the impasse, and a committee of the Secretaries of State and Defense and the chair of the AEC could address all matters of policy that might arise from the possibility of the construction of the Super.[25] Constituting the group once again as a special committee of the National Security Council, Truman asked Acheson and Johnson to work with Lilienthal to study the alternatives and give him a recommendation.

In this way, Lilienthal's known intransigence was absorbed into the larger triumvirate with the two secretaries. It seems, though, that this device, earlier favored by Truman in relation to the fission expansion program, was designed less as a means of making a decision than as a way to assemble all of the relevant arguments before the president so that the decision would be made by him alone. Johnson, though, believed Truman had already made up his mind to repudiate the scientific advice rendered by the GAC and go ahead with the Super.[26] Robert LeBaron and Stephen Early, deputy secretary of defense and in good standing with both Johnson and Truman, worked out the terms of reference for the group.[27] During the course of the process, Souers ensured that the papers emerging from the staff work would be passed to the secretaries and to the president himself. In this way, Truman was fully up to date with the triumvirate's discussions and able to form his own judgment in advance of their report.[28]

Despite the high level of security, the Alsops were as usual well informed about the appointment of this triumvirate and about the alignments within it, predicting in their column that Truman would override Lilienthal and announce a decision to proceed, unless Acheson chose to advise otherwise.[29] As it turned out, due to their personal and political differences, there was little or no direct contact between the three principals. After their initial meeting on 22 December, the three did not meet again until they finalized their advice to the president on 31 January. Acheson, who loathed Johnson and doubted his mental stability, allowed the defense secretary and Lilienthal to engage in head-to-head confrontation, thereafter blaming the acerbic Johnson for the committee's subsequent failure to meet until decision day.[30] That single December meeting produced no agreement whatsoever: Lilienthal recorded that "we reached no conclusion, which is good."[31]

Each of the three organizations did its own staff work, producing initial position papers. Lilienthal was supported by Henry Smyth in the anomalous position of adviser rather than as a fellow commissioner, and by Joseph Volpe, AEC counsel. Brigadier General Luedecke and LeBaron represented Defense; Paul Nitze, Adrian Fisher, and Gordon Arneson the State Department; and Sidney Souers and James Lay the NSC. The eventual text was crafted so as to minimize Lilienthal's scope for dissent, a process on which a small group—McCormack from the AEC, Kenneth Nichols, and others—"sweated" to produce "fine joint staff work," as McCormack recalled.[32]

Paul Nitze struggled to bridge the gap between the AEC team and the Pentagon, for whom, he later wrote, "an agreed position was impossible." LeBaron favored a crash program, while Lilienthal totally opposed development and proved "hard to persuade." Nitze produced a paper to accommodate Lilienthal's views, the essence of which was that the president should be advised to authorize the AEC to accelerate a program of research and development to test the feasibility of the Super, but that a decision on whether or not to proceed to build weapons should be postponed. The paper said the NSC should review US aims and objectives in light of the likely Soviet fission bomb capability and possible Soviet thermonuclear capability. Acheson initially accepted this position, but Defense Secretary Johnson resisted. Nitze suspected he opposed any review that might point to shortcomings arising from the stringent control of defense expenditure during his stewardship.[33]

Final drafting was left to those State Department staff supporting the process. They did not include outgoing Policy Planning Staff director Kennan, although Acheson invited him, together with Paul Nitze, Kennan's successor, to prepare their own papers. The two, friends and colleagues, reacted to the challenge in radically opposed fashions, bearing out the characterization of the pair as "hawk and dove."[34] Nitze's two-page paper was pithy and to the point. The United States, he said, could not afford not to proceed with the Super, a position that had considerable support in the working group supporting the triumvirate of principals. Kennan's position, on the other hand, cut no ice with Acheson. Kennan had already drafted a memorandum for the president, arguing in favor of forbearance, but this was not what the occasion required.[35]

Given this final opportunity, and aware of his fading influence, Kennan poured all his energies into convincing his colleagues to forsake a strategy based on atomic weapons in favor of a system of international control, however imperfect.[36] He considered his seventy-nine-page paper an impassioned plea against the Super, "one of the most important, if not the most important, of all the documents I ever wrote in government."[37] Why did he judge it so? While Nitze was directing his advice to the immediate policy decision, Kennan was looking far into the future, envisaging an unstable world over which loomed the ultimate threat of thermonuclear weapon use.[38] Therein lay its importance. This paper was surely among the most scholarly of his output, and was centered on a long quotation from Shakespeare's *Troilus and Cressida* in which he adopted an unusual, indeed perverse, reading of the famous passage on "degree" to sustain his argument for moderation.[39] His basic position that strategy should be based on the assessment of intentions, however imprecise, rather than on capabilities, was so out of step with the spirit of the moment that, he later wrote in his memoirs, "one could well understand it if the Secretary of State saw no usefulness, nor even anything worth serious discussion, in the set of views I presented."[40] And that was the case.

Acheson was seen as the swing vote in this three-man group. He was not disconcerted by the inability of the triumvirate to progress through meeting together, remarking to Schilling that it was like a labor arbitration, in that when people are all worked up, it's best to talk to them separately.[41] He proceeded cautiously in his preferred bilateral fashion, insisting on prior interviews with the principal players, holding fourteen meetings between 1 November and 26 January.[42] He disappointed Oppenheimer, with whom he had three meetings, by making it clear that he did not accept his arguments. He also disappointed Lilienthal, who argued that State and Defense had not thought through the strategic implications of the Super. Lilienthal was, in Nitze's observation, "blackballing the H-bomb in order to force a more careful consideration of the meaning to [the] strategy of nuclear weapons."[43] Acheson's reading of this position was already well established: the strategic reservation was a smokescreen for the deeper moral repugnance of which Lilienthal was a leading spokesman.

Acknowledging Acheson's prime position, Oppenheimer reconciled himself to Truman's deciding to push ahead with the Super.[44] Yet he did not abandon his opposition and, in a conversation with Bethe, emphasized the need to keep opposition to the Super alive.[45] Former allies on the GAC and the commission were falling by the wayside, and the expectation was spreading that Truman would approve development. The suspicion that the president had already made up his mind to do so was justified, with Souers reporting that Truman had acknowledged the necessity of proceeding, subject to feasibility and military utility, when first briefed by the NSC secretary.[46]

So much still hung on the advice that the NSC special committee would provide to the president. The day before Acheson, Johnson, and Lilienthal were due to meet again, for what would be the final discussion, *Time* magazine published this appraisal:

> Like a patient sitting in a doctor's anteroom while the specialists discuss his case, the US public . . . sat outside while the President, his military, scientific and diplomatic advisers debated whether to construct the . . . most powerful explosive weapon the world has yet dreamed of. . . . But since the principle of the hydrogen bomb is also known to the Russians, temporizing was risky and might be fatal. The simple fact, unpleasant though it might be, was that if the Russians are likely to build an H-bomb, the US will have to build it, too.[47]

Decision Day: 31 January 1950

By late January the balance of advantage between the two opposing sides was changing. Smyth and Pike were wavering around the Strauss-Dean position, leaving Lilienthal isolated.[48] The GAC's common front was crumbling, while the Joint Chiefs, the MLC, Defense Secretary Johnson, the Pentagon, the JCAE, and prominent congressional leaders and scientists, as well as the team at Los Alamos, were all in favor of proceeding. Acheson generally kept his own counsel but was expected to support the project.

When the special committee met on 31 January, the very different approaches of the three principal interests came to the fore. First, the draft report presented by Acheson included a recommendation that the president defer a decision as to whether thermonuclear weapons should be produced beyond the number required for a test of feasibility. This was excluded on Johnson's insistence. Johnson also supplied an alternative, briefer version of the report to the president. While Acheson argued that the special committee appeared to be in agreement, and that differences between the proposed statements could be resolved, Lilienthal dug in his heels on the key issue of just what direction the president should give.[49] The State Department draft as it now stood read, "Accordingly, the Atomic Energy Commission has been directed to continue the development of all forms of atomic weapons. This work includes a project looking toward a test of the feasibility of the hydrogen bomb." Had it been accepted, this text of the proposed presidential statement would have overleaped the decision to continue research, to the next stage of authorizing a test.

Lilienthal's alternative was simply to direct the AEC to continue its work on all forms of atomic weapons, including the hydrogen bomb. He reluctantly recognized the limited value or effect of advice to the president from him, when it conflicted with a recommendation agreed to by both the secretaries of state and of defense. He insisted that the proposed acceleration of research and development toward a thermonuclear weapon should be preceded by an independent examination of the underlying assumptions, policies, and plans of the military establishment to provide "for our defense . . . if there was to be substance to the principle of civilian control of atomic weapons by the Commission." This investigation should inquire into the best way to further the common defense and security, "to which questions as to our atomic bomb programs and the plans for their use, and the thermonuclear development are subsequent." This, and not "whether we should build the super bomb or not build it," was the central issue. A decision to proceed forthwith "will be to miss an opportunity to re-examine and realign our policy, a better opportunity than may ever appear again to better our security and promote something better than a headlong rush to a war of mass destruction weapons." As to the proposal to proceed with a test in 1952 as a target, "The *act* of directing that this proceed can not be minimized by mere statements such as we recommended to the President. It is too great an act." (Emphasis in the original.)[50]

Acheson was prepared to acknowledge this position but pointed out that "the pressure for an early decision was so great, that the discussion and feeling in Congress had reached the point where deferring the decision to this purpose was an alternative" he could not recommend. Johnson apparently agreed. "We must protect the President," he said. The resulting common ground (if such it was) took the form of a compromise proposal: the AEC would be asked to determine the technical feasibility of a thermonuclear weapon, with the speed and scale of this project to be agreed between the AEC and the Department of Defense; and the Departments of State and Defense would jointly undertake a reexamination of US objectives and strategic plans in light of the "probable fission bomb capability and possible thermonuclear bomb capability of the Soviet Union." Lilienthal continued to press his reservations, arguing that such a presidential directive "would be construed, and inevitably construed, as a very broad and far-reaching decision respecting the hydrogen bomb."[51]

Gordon Arneson recalled Truman musing over his famous "buck stops here" desk plaque as he waited for the three-man committee he had appointed to make recommendations on the Super to arrive at the White House with their report.[52] When the agreed recommendation was put to the president, Lilienthal once again demurred, later recollecting that "it was my unpleasant duty, since the President asked me to express my honest opinion, I said that I thought until we got our whole situation in order [proceeding with the Super] was an unwise course."[53] His dissent was cut off by Truman, who, having inquired, "Can the Russians can do it?" declared, "We have no choice." According to Lilienthal's account the meeting lasted just seven minutes, according to Acheson's less than thirty. Lilienthal was compromised by his apparent agreement to a course of action he considered disastrous.[54]

The president's directive to the AEC "to proceed to determine the technical feasibility of a thermonuclear weapon" followed within hours of the meeting.[55] The announcement was greeted by cheers in the House of Representatives and by a highly supportive public opinion poll, although public support would prove more fickle over the coming months.[56] The following week, Truman explained to some of his staff that, according to his assistant press secretary, Eben Ayers, "there actually was no decision to make on the H-bomb," as the matter had been settled in establishing a sufficient budget for the AEC the previous fall. Ayers added, "He went on to say that we had to do it—make the bomb—though no one wants to use it."[57]

It is interesting to note that by 1957, when interviewed by Schilling, Truman no longer remembered there being any division of opinion on the Super among the AEC, State, and Defense, and that his decision on 31 January was—as he implied to White House staff—essentially a foregone conclusion. All that was needed was for people to be told what to do, he being the one to tell them. It is possible that Truman's recollection of Lilienthal's surface agreement in January 1950 gave him the impression of unanimity. Presidents are often faced with decisions where the differences between agencies or advisers are sharp, obvious, and politically awkward. Truman was disposed to look for advice with all the wrinkles ironed out in advance, hence his use of the triumvirate model. In a case where the issues seem to have been reconciled for him, the question is likely to be remembered by the president as uncontroversial.[58]

Thereafter there was talk of Strauss taking over the AEC to sweep out Lilienthal's influences. But he was deemed too polarizing, and departed the commission.[59] It was the newcomer, Gordon Dean, who replaced Lilienthal as chair. The GAC would change too, and neither Oppenheimer nor James Conant nor Lee DuBridge were reappointed at the end of their terms, it being generally conceded that it would not be fitting for opponents of the president's policy on the hydrogen bomb to serve as the commission's advisers.[60] They had missed the opportunity to appeal directly to the president, as Oppenheimer had proposed. Several members considered resigning in protest, but Lilienthal dissuaded them.[61] It was now too late to influence events.

Lilienthal himself had been sidelined. While his arguments were put to the NSC special committee extemporaneously, he returned to his office and put them on paper in the form of a lengthy dissenting memorandum for the record.[62] Not until September 1952 did Lilienthal commit his memorandum to the files of the AEC, sealing the deposit to restrict its availability.[63] When called before the Oppenheimer Personnel Security Board hearing two years later, Lilienthal came under pressure not to put that memorandum into the public record. He claimed that board chair Gordon Gray—after whom the board would also become known as the Gray Board—and AEC commissioners "intimidated" him to suppress the paper.[64] Yet the passionately written paper was not easily suppressed. Under circumstances that are not quite clear, part of the text was published in an article by James Reston, the *New York Times* journalist.[65]

Humiliated by an aggressive interrogation by the AEC's counsel, Roger Robb, when he appeared before the Gray Board, Lilienthal subsequently found it difficult to substantiate his reservations about the special committee's recommendation to Truman. In an exchange of letters between him and Acheson some years later, Acheson declined to acknowledge Lilienthal's opposition, despite encouragement to do so from Joseph Volpe. He reasonably claimed not to remember such conversations after so great a lapse of time, although he added, "It is, however, my recollection that our recommendation to the President was unanimous and signed by all of us."[66] That of course was true. Lilienthal had found himself formally supporting a decision with which he disagreed.[67] But Acheson's autobiographical version of the issue is rather more nuanced. In *Present at the Creation*, published in 1969, he is more forthright about Lilienthal's objections, recalling that Lilienthal's verbal statement during the meeting was interrupted by Truman.[68]

Aftermath of the Decision

As Schilling's original article observed, the decision of 31 January 1950 was a minimal step toward a thermonuclear capability. However, events moved swiftly thereafter in the direction of developing and testing thermonuclear weapons. Two weeks after Truman announced his decision, Brig. Gen. Herbert B. Loper, a member of the Military Liaison Committee and soon to become head of the Armed Forces Special Weapons Project, submitted a paper to LeBaron titled "A Basis for Estimating Maximum Soviet Capabilities for Atomic Warfare." The paper, to which Kenneth Nichols had contributed, was based on maximum capabilities ("the outside bracket," Loper called it) rather than probabilities. Loper wrote, "While the maximum capabilities at which we may arrive . . . may appear to be of a fantastic order they should not be disregarded." The state of Soviet scientific knowledge of basic nuclear physics was, he said, "at least equivalent to our own." The Soviets' technologies of application might be as advanced, and the Soviets had demonstrated a determination to gain superiority in atomic weapons. There was a greater willingness to take risks, and Soviet advances were underpinned by successful espionage operations:

Russian industrial know-how and technology in the field of metallurgy and chemistry are of a lower order than our own; however, this deficiency is compensated by trial and error procedures, unlimited manpower, disregard of human life, and willingness to accept industrial and material loss, if necessary; and, of great importance, the results of espionage directed at our program, e.g., the benefit of our unprofitable or less promising ventures.[69]

This analysis appears to have been accepted in the Pentagon, with Secretary of Defense Louis Johnson noting at that time that the possibility of the Soviets having a hydrogen bomb development project was being considered.[70] Loper's paper sounded a tocsin, having an electrifying effect on the Pentagon. The possibility that the Soviet Union's stock of atomic bombs might soon exceed that of the United States was alarming enough. More so was the speculation that the Soviets might have tested not just an atomic bomb but a thermonuclear device before the United States' long-range detection system became operational. This was a point that Lewis Strauss would repeatedly make in his powerful advocacy of the Super. What had once been regarded as a crucial limitation on the Soviet atomic bomb program—the scarcity of high-grade uranium in Russia—was now portrayed as an asset, since the dearth of the raw materials needed to make atomic bombs forced the Russians to compensate for that shortage by developing weapons of higher efficiency per available ton of ore. This prompted the conclusion that the Russians could actually have a thermonuclear weapon in production.[71]

Up to this point, there had been no sense of urgency about raising production-and-use issues, but the president's decision encouraged the military to expect that those decisions would come sooner than originally anticipated. The climate was suddenly more favorable, now that, as General Luedecke put it to Schilling, "the passion [had] boiled out" of the debate, following the January decision.[72] LeBaron commended the Loper memorandum to Louis Johnson, who referred it immediately to the Joint Chiefs.[73] The Joint Chiefs received input from the Weapon Systems Evaluation Group, where Rear Adm. Deak Parsons, the senior navy man on the group, was an acknowledged authority on nuclear weapons.[74] Loper and LeBaron authored the first draft of the new submission to the president through Johnson, urging "an all-out program of hydrogen bomb development." Johnson then wrote to Truman to call for such a program. The wily Strauss had shown Johnson copies of four secret documents that had been seen by Klaus Fuchs, the former Los Alamos scientist now revealed to be a Soviet spy, who had been present at the April 1946 Super conference. In this way Strauss ensured that the secretary's plea would be characteristically strong on hyperbole. This indeed happened, with Johnson citing the "extremely serious, in fact almost literally limitless" threats to US security revealed by the new information to which he alluded.[75] Anything short of an "all-out program"

of development, Johnson argued, would leave the United States in "a potentially disastrous position." With the support of the Joint Chiefs, he called
for "immediate implementation of all-out development of hydrogen bombs
and means for their production and delivery."[76]

Truman turned again to the device of a three-man special committee of
the NSC, although in this instance Acheson and Johnson were joined by
Henry Smyth, replacing Lilienthal. The committee, reconstituted with Lilienthal's departure and spurred by the Joint Chiefs paper, reported on the
development program, assuring that "the present research and development program at Los Alamos contemplates maximum effort leading to the
test of a thermonuclear weapon at the earliest possible date." The first steps
of the process would be tested in 1951, followed by a test of a device the
following year. The committee warned that in order to avoid any unnecessary delay between the feasibility stage and the establishment of weapon
production capability, an early decision on tritium production would be
required. The time taken to move from a test device was estimated to be
around three years, although, significantly, the committee advised that "it
is simply not known whether the [thermonuclear] process will work at all
or under what conditions." However, if the program turned out to be futile,
the development work would feed into the fission weapons program.[77]

Thus, having opened the bidding with a seemingly noncommittal decision to continue research on the Super at Los Alamos, six weeks later the
president, acting on advice, called for an acceleration of the program, including a commitment to test and produce a weapon. He had approved
the submission of a supplementary appropriations request to finance the
expansion of production facilities, but sending this to Congress would have
the disadvantage of revealing the nature of the H-bomb program. Secrecy
was a top priority, and the special committee devised a scheme for revealing only "the outer limit of facts" about the program, and only to the top
personnel of the executive branch agencies likely to face the demand for
testimony, or the questions of news correspondents. The guidelines proposed, and approved by the president, stretched the truth by characterizing
the present program as "a continuation and an expansion of the work done
in the past, aiming at a demonstration that it is or is not feasible, and at
preparation for production should that later be necessary."[78] The basic text
of this statement and this particular formulation came from the AEC itself,
in response to a request by Truman.[79]

It was widely assumed that the shock of the Fuchs case propelled the acceleration of the Super program by raising the possibility, however remote,
that Fuchs's treachery would have provided an advantage to any Soviet
H-bomb program. Yet the downgrading of expectations about the effectiveness of SAC's strategic bombardment program from the 1949 report by
the study group under Lt. Gen. Hubert R. Harmon and the first Weapon
Systems Evaluation Group report was probably more significant in making

the need for the Super seem more urgent. Perhaps, though, the key factor was the decision inertia whereby the initial decision to research the Super simply opened the door to the next decision, to test and then produce it. That came sooner than might have been expected, with the disavowal of the GAC's advice.

Through 1951 and 1952, Teller would gather support for the Super project. Impatient and suspicious of Norris Bradbury's Los Alamos laboratory, he pressed for a second laboratory to be established to accelerate research. He took care to stay close to senior air force figures, notably David T. Griggs, the chief scientist. Griggs, Lt. Gen. Jimmy Doolittle, and Lt. Gen. Pete Quesada became strong partisans of Teller. With the support of Air Force Secretary Thomas K. Finletter and his special assistant for R&D, William Burden, Teller's plan for a second laboratory began to advance as an air force project. Whether serious or not, this initiative greatly increased the pressure on the AEC to initiate a second laboratory or risk losing control of the next stage of thermonuclear development.[80] Ernest Lawrence agreed to investigate the options, and asked Herbert York to consult the relevant parties. York later wrote that he "found the whole affair heady and exciting, and . . . was readily persuaded to Teller's point of view." Oppenheimer was known to be an entrenched opponent, but "under the new circumstances he had no other choice," though York did not find him particularly helpful.[81] In September 1952 the new laboratory was established at Livermore, California, as a branch of the existing laboratory at Berkeley.[82] Although the now-complaisant AEC fell in with the plan, it was not an ideal solution, as it set up an ongoing tension with Los Alamos. Relations were, according to York, "strained from the beginning, and rapidly grew worse."[83]

The influential group of scientists who had initially advised against the proposal to pursue the H-bomb shared reservations about the dangers of nuclear testing as well as about the United States' emphasis on the large-scale nuclear bombing of Soviet cities. While logically distinct issues, opposition to the H-bomb development, to its testing, and to its use were inseparable in terms of practical politics. A 1948 report to the National Security Council (NSC 30) had advised that

> in the event of hostilities, the National Military Establishment must be ready to utilize promptly and effectively all appropriate means available, including atomic weapons, in the interest of national security. . . . [And] the decision as to the employment of atomic weapons in the event of war is to be made by the Chief Executive when he considers such decision to be required.

Truman was unequivocal. "I had to make a decision back in July 1945," he said in April 1949 regarding the use of atomic bombs against Japan, adding that if the welfare of the United States and democracies around the world were at stake, "I wouldn't hesitate to make it again." In November 1950 he said—in a confirmation of the Super opponents' fears—that "consideration of the use of any weapon is always implicit in the very possession of that weapon."[84]

Gearing up for possible nuclear war against the unstable situation of the Korean conflict would require a massive investment if the AEC's production capacity was not to be exhausted. This concern only increased following the Chinese entry into the war. From October 1950 the AEC embarked on a large-scale expansion program that over the next three years would cost $3 billion and become one of the largest US government construction projects to take place during peacetime. The facilities built or expanded increased capacity in all aspects of production and included a lithium-6 plant at Oak Ridge, Tennessee, a gaseous-diffusion plant at Paducah, Kentucky, a gaseous-diffusion complex at Portsmouth, Ohio, large reactors and a plutonium-separation plant in Hanford, Washington, and tritium- and plutonium-producing heavy water reactors at the Savannah River site in South Carolina.[85]

Years of Tumult

These were indeed years of tumult for the president. Truman could not have foreseen any of it when the Super issue was first propelled onto the public stage by Joe 1. His basic stance going into the 1948 election had been one of strict economy, and severe restraint on military expenditure. Appointing Johnson as secretary of defense strengthened his hand when he strove for a bipartisan position. But it was not a bipartisan moment. Truman faced an ill-spirited Republican opposition, some of whom had jeered one of his State of the Union addresses. Opinion was coalescing around a virulent anti-Communism as the external threats to the United States seemed to multiply. The announcement of the Truman Doctrine in defense of Greece and Turkey, and by extension all free nations, set a new course for US foreign policy, soon to be demonstrated in the Berlin airlift. The spread of Soviet political control in Eastern Europe prompted new nightmares and fostered fantasies of "roll-back." The "loss" of Chiang Kai-Shek's China to the Communists was readily cited by Truman's critics as a catastrophic failure of foreign policy.

Now the emergence of a nuclear-armed Soviet adversary had forced reconsideration. Truman conceded that disarmament under Johnson had gone too far. It had been welcomed by Congress and the public but now, in light of world events, seemed imprudent.[86] At the same time he stood four-square behind Dean Acheson, the whipping boy for much of the new aggressive spirit in US opinion, airily dismissing his offer to resign. He would need him over the coming years of conflict. Conscious of developing congressional demands, Truman had now set in motion a program of hydrogen bomb development together with a wide-ranging review of the need to reinforce US military strength. He would have known that the financial costs of the Super would be onerous and that it would face fierce opposition on expenditure grounds.

On the other side of the issue, dissident scientists, defeated over the proposal to develop and then test the Super, found subsequent opportunities to put their own weight behind proposals that gave strategic bombardment a diminished place in the panoply of options for pursuing international conflict. Some of those scientists and military officers who advocated a shift of emphasis toward low-yield fission weapons for tactical deployment were convinced that strategic bombardment with high-yield weapons was neither appropriate nor likely to be effective, especially in the most probable scenario—a Soviet ground offensive against Western Europe. According to this analysis, the pattern of resource allocation was distorted by the primacy accorded to Strategic Air Command. Pragmatism, as well as ethics, colored the next stage of the debate.

CHAPTER 4

Moral and Political Consequences

Moral repugnance inflected the scientific judgments of Oppenheimer's GAC, triggering discussion of the relative moral significance of thermonuclear bombing and the use of the atomic bomb. There was little consideration of the area bombing campaigns over Germany and Japan in 1942–45, and atomic attack was seen as sui generis. While there were vigorous debates over what seemed to be irresolvable moral issues, more immediate concerns centered on the impact of a decision to develop thermonuclear weapons on the pattern of international relations, now that the Soviet Union had emerged as a nuclear power. The unipolar nuclear world was drawing to an end. Given the paucity of intelligence, the effects on the Soviet Union's own weapons program, and thereby on the United States' vulnerability, could only be guessed at. Would development of the Super restore the status quo ante-1949 or lead to a thermonuclear arms race and ultimate stalemate—or even Armageddon?

Initial Moral Reactions

Moral considerations had been raised in acute form both before and after the atomic bombing of the Japanese cities. From 1946 five major reports emanated from commissions established by the several churches in the United States and Britain, the first pointedly titled *Atomic Warfare and the Christian Faith*. By and large US churches recognized the necessity of war and accepted the utilitarian justification of the use of the atomic bomb against the Japanese cities. The Church of England, in contrast, made much of just war theory in an argument for proportionality. Just how far the use of a nuclear weapon could be understood as proportionate remained a challenging puzzle.[1] At root, there was no prospect of agreement between the nuclear partisans and their opponents. The idea of a just and proportionate counterforce strike in the event of deterrence failing was acceptable to those who considered nuclear weapons to be different in degree, not in kind, due only to their superior power over conventional weapons. Even this limited use was anathema to the absolutist viewpoint, which held that nuclear weapons *were* different in kind and absolutely evil. In policy, the strength of the absolutist view, coupled with natural prudence, came to sustain a "nuclear taboo" that, it is argued, has served the global order well.[2] Some US officials acknowledged the restraints of the taboo, considering that to use the atomic bomb, for example in Korea, would destroy that frail constraint and open the floodgates.[3] Eisenhower, however, would not rule it out, and a taboo that is not universally observed but subject to pragmatic judgments is no taboo at all.[4]

For many, moral outrage about nuclear weapons stood in the way of the moral reasoning that circumstances demanded.[5] The prospect of the Super simply intensified these concerns for those who already had doubts, and existing debate among scientists became more intense and bitter than before.[6] The Manhattan Project veteran Hartley Rowe admitted that his objections to the Super came from the heart, not the mind, reflecting his "ungodly horror" of both atomic and hydrogen bombs.[7] These feelings found scant reflection in the wider US society, however. The Pulitzer Prize–winning journalist William L. Laurence, who witnessed the Nagasaki bombing, considered Pearl Harbor and the Bataan Death March to have justified the atomic attacks.[8] In that he echoed, and probably shaped, what appeared to be contemporary opinion. A 1945 poll found that 23 percent of the Americans questioned regretted that the Japanese had surrendered before more atomic bombs could be dropped on their cities.[9] Replication of that survey in 1998 showed these extreme and vengeful sentiments to be much diminished.[10] The debate about justifiability remained, but was focused less explicitly on payback for Pearl Harbor, and more on weighing the actual casualties against the American (and Japanese) lives saved by foregoing an invasion.

This argument amounted, in some critics' views, to a moral inversion in which Americans, as Robert Jay Lifton and Greg Mitchell put it, "assigned themselves the task of finding virtue in the first use of the most murderous device ever created." Its legacy, a "Hiroshima syndrome," had developed to act against taking a truly moral stand on nuclear weaponry, "lest our 1945 actions in Hiroshima and Nagasaki become retrospectively unethical and unlawful—in the eyes of the world and, still more troubling, our own eyes as well."[11]

For Oppenheimer, shaper of the debate among the scientists, the moral argument took primacy once it had been established to his satisfaction that the Super probably could not be constructed. Admitting that, in light of the state of knowledge in 1954, the GAC might have written a different report from that presented in 1949, he posited a sharp distinction between the technical and the moral.[12] While arguing in terms of dubious feasibility and lack of strategic necessity, Oppenheimer chose to stand his ground on the moral repugnance of the Super, a vulnerable stance given the lack of certainty about the bomb's feasibility. Speaking on television, he characterized the decision to produce—or not—the hydrogen bomb as involving "complex technical things [that] touch the very basis of our morality." Bernstein prods the logic of his position:

> Was the argument of "no strategic necessity" for the Super sufficient to support [the GAC] conclusion that the bomb should not be sought? Did the strategic argument then liberate them to stress morality? If so, what if new arguments emerged which undermined the position of "no strategic necessity"? Would the moral argument then have to yield? . . . Why did [the Teller-Ulam breakthrough] cancel out the earlier moral or strategic arguments?[13]

This transformation of the moral argument is a puzzle that was addressed in a thoughtful manner by Maj. Gen. James McCormack, the AEC's former director of military applications. For McCormack, a "vast acceleration" of work on the Super directly raised the moral question. For people of a moralizing disposition, a laboratory-based program of pure research was acceptable, but its metamorphosis into a full-scale program for warfare propelled moral considerations to the fore.[14] Oppenheimer's own resolution of the apparent contradiction was to claim a sharp distinction between developing the weapon and using it or, perhaps, being prepared to use it.[15]

In large part, the debate turned on disagreement as to whether the Super should be evaluated in moral terms in comparison with existing atomic weapons, or whether a moral absolute arose in both cases. When the GAC came to report on the Super, the members had united around the moral issue, agreeing that use of the weapon would "bring about the destruction of innumerable human lives. . . [and] carries much further than the atomic bomb itself the policy of exterminating civilian populations."[16] James Conant was at that time, in Lilienthal's recollection, "flatly against it 'on moral grounds.' "[17] He took the lead in drafting the statement by six of the members that a hydrogen bomb would be in a totally different category due to its vast range of destruction; using it would amount to deciding to "slaughter a vast number of civilians. . . . Therefore, a super bomb might become a weapon of genocide." Oppenheimer both at that time and later tended to use the term "genocide" to refer to the effects of the use of the hydrogen bomb on a city. It was a new concept, brought into the public domain at the Nuremberg trials and used rather loosely by Oppenheimer in his later protests. Enrico Fermi and Isidor Rabi in the GAC's minority report also used the term, thereby seeming to foreclose discussion on moral grounds:

> It is clear that the use of such a weapon cannot be justified on any ethical ground which gives a human being a certain individuality and dignity even

if he happens to be a resident of an enemy country. . . . Its use would put the
United States in a bad moral position relative to the peoples of the world.

They designated the Super as "necessarily an evil thing considered in any
light."[18]

The GAC report came under considerable criticism for its vagueness and
ambiguity. Its inadequate argumentation prompted several members to
send Lilienthal their further thoughts on the question. When John Manley,
secretary to the GAC, sought to answer some of the reservations about their
position, he took a high moral line, proposing that a decision not to proceed
would provide an "opportunity to apply our standards of life to our actions
and to formulation of policy in a more consistent way."[19] Lee DuBridge, in
his own further representations, warned that

> [a] moral position in the eyes of our own people and the people of the world
> is not enhanced by the development of a weapon whose sole advantage
> over other weapons is that it will kill more civilians or wipe out larger cit-
> ies. . . . Whatever moral position we have come to occupy by virtue of our
> present program can only be worsened by making a great forward step in
> the production of weapons of mass destruction—weapons of terror. If our
> moral position is already bad why not make it better rather than worse? If it
> is good why not improve it? Taking a bold stand against further advances in
> this art of terror and destruction is certainly a moral rather than an immoral
> act. It may add much or even only a little to our moral stature. It can hardly
> reduce it. But a full-scale attempt to increase our killing power can degrade
> our moral position—possibly only a little, possibly quite a lot.[20]

DuBridge's nuanced argument grounded the debate in relative terms.
The absolutist view, on the other hand, emphasized the values that would
be sacrificed by the use of a hydrogen bomb in war. It took a few years to
develop as scientists reflected on the horrors of Hiroshima and Nagasaki.
During 1944 and the first part of 1945, as Peter Galison and Barton Bernstein
note, "none of the Los Alamos scientists . . . expressed any moral, scientific, or strategic doubts about investigating thermonuclear weapons with
the goal of developing a Super."[21] But while Oppenheimer, Fermi, Ernest
Lawrence, and Arthur Compton advised in its favor in June 1945, after Hiroshima they came to the view that moral considerations should preclude
its development. Compton went so far as to argue that "we should prefer
defeat in war to victory obtained at the expense of the enormous human
disaster that would be caused by [the Super's] determined use."[22] After the
first Soviet test, however, Lawrence changed his view and threw his weight
and that of the Berkeley Laboratory behind the Super project. His hope of
seizing the opportunity to expand the role of his laboratory led Lilienthal to
accuse him of "drooling" over the Super.[23]

Once the decision had been made, discussion of the moral considerations became more widespread. The president's announcement was discussed at the New York meeting of the American Physical Society by a group of prominent scientists, a dozen of whom, including Hans Bethe in a lead role, issued a statement urging the US government to make a pledge never to use the new weapon first:

> We believe that no nation has the right to use such a bomb, no matter how righteous its cause. This bomb is no longer a weapon of war but a means of extermination of whole populations. Its use would be a betrayal of all standards of morality and of Christian civilization itself.[24]

Beyond the United States, the general reaction to the prospect of a thermonuclear weapon was one of revulsion rather than celebration. The Nobel Prize–winning physicist P. M. S. Blackett's 1948 treatise against the atomic bomb, subsequently titled *Fear, War and the Bomb*, had received wide readership in a Britain where the atomic bombings had been received far more negatively than in the United States.[25] The reaction to the prospect of the Super was bound to be more negative still. The Cambridge scientist Sir George Thomson delivered a BBC radio talk in March 1950, and a speech at Chatham House (the Royal Institute of International Affairs) in July. His argument—that a weapon of such power had little real utility, while radioactive contamination put the future of humanity at risk—would have been familiar to an American audience. He supported the pleas of the American scientists that such a weapon should not be used, except in retaliation. He concluded his Chatham House speech with the plea not to "destroy humanity for the sake of a doubtful advantage over our immediate enemies."[26] His talks apparently had a considerable impact on public opinion, though he received a harsh rebuke from Sir John Cockroft, director of the Atomic Energy Research Establishment at Harwell: "The radioactive effects of the Super have thus far, been very grossly exaggerated."[27] On the potential explosive power of such a bomb, another official warned Thomson that "there is . . . no proper scientific foundation for the figure you assume and I feel you should make this clear in stating any conclusion."[28]

Hans Bethe wrote in *Scientific American*, "I believe the most important question is the moral one: Can we, who have always insisted on morality and human decency between nations as well as inside our own country, introduce this weapon of total annihilation into the world? . . . I believe that in a war fought with hydrogen bombs we would lose not only many lives but all our liberties and human values as well."[29] Max Lerner in the *New York Post* lamented that the H-bomb decision "means that one of the great moral battles of our time has been lost."[30] Soviet-inspired sources reflected these arguments. Making a political point in the guise of a moral concern, the labor leader, women's rights advocate, and Communist Party member

Elizabeth Gurley Flynn's column in the *Daily Worker* on 8 March 1950 called for "American women to be gathered in one irresistible voice" against production of the H-bomb. The same issue reported a survey of Seattle church leaders conducted by the *People's World* that showed an overwhelming sentiment against the H-bomb.[31] Harold Stassen, president of the University of Pennsylvania, proposed an interfaith conference to discuss the hydrogen bomb, as it posed an "almost new moral question."[32]

If some of these responses were emotional spasms, a more profound moral critique was advanced by George Kennan. Nuclear weapons, he argued, "negate the principle of life itself. . . . They reach backward beyond the frontiers of western civilization, to the concepts of warfare which were once familiar to the Asiatic hordes. . . . They fail to take account of the ultimate responsibility of men for one another." Acheson, according to his own 1963 account, brutally dismissed this manifestation of Kennan's "Quaker" gospel, urging him to resign from the Foreign Service to preach outside the State Department.[33]

Acheson recollected to Schilling that Kennan and others (by implication, Lilienthal and Oppenheimer) were "wild" on the issue, "at sixes and sevens" and wrestling with their consciences while subjecting themselves to "overpowering emotional pulls." He recalled that "these people" would come to his house at night and pace up and down, agonizing over whether the H-bomb should be turned loose on the world. Acheson assured them that *it was the president's decision, and not theirs to worry about* (emphasis in Acheson's voice). They needed to find "common sense" and be shown they were not in a "terrible moral fix." There were, he noted perceptively, political dangers in being later unmasked as trying to take a decision that was the president's to make. That said, Acheson the ultrapragmatist hoped the Super would prove infeasible, as development by both sides would constitute a long-run net gain for the Soviets.[34]

Broadening the Moral Argument

The popular image of scientists united against thermonuclear weapons was misleading. There was a range of opinion, from moral absolutism to realism, even among the physicists. Frederick Seitz, a professor at the University of Illinois, argued that his fellow physicists should not be concerned with the moral argument, but should concentrate on the preservation of the state in which the "most important ideals" of civilization "represent the principle goal."[35] For their part, the Joint Chiefs unsurprisingly dismissed the GAC's objection, countering that "it is difficult to escape the conviction that in war it is folly to argue whether one weapon is more immoral than another. For, in the larger sense, it is war itself which is immoral, and the stigma of such immorality must rest upon the nation which initiates hostilities."[36]

Likewise, and in contrast with the moralists, Lewis Strauss and Brien McMahon, the principal advocates, were both of the view that the greater power of the Super raised no particular ethical considerations. Contesting the GAC recommendations, Strauss rejected the fundamentalist argument that "as armament, the super is qualitatively rather than merely quantitatively different from the A-bomb." He fastened on the lack of logic in the GAC recommendation to push development of boosted fission weapons in preference to fusion: "The booster is designed to 'improve' the 'ordinaries' by a factor of, say _____. Would the GAC have disapproved the booster if the factor had been [redacted]?" Renouncing the means of killing millions in favor of killing hundreds of thousands "leaves something to be desired from the standpoint of consistency. The booster is certainly not a pinpoint weapon."[37] McMahon pleaded to the president in similar terms:

> There is no moral dividing line that I can see between a big explosion which causes heavy damage and many small explosions causing equal or still greater damage. Where is the valid ethical distinction between the several Hamburg raids that produced 135,000 fatalities [*sic*], the single Tokyo "fire" raid that produced 85,000 fatalities, and the Hiroshima bomb that produced 65,000 fatalities? . . . Is a given weapon to be adjudged moral or immoral depending upon whether it requires hours, days or weeks to take its toll?[38]

Whereas the absolutists attributed an almost mystical quality to nuclear weapons, McMahon, in relating nuclear attack to the bombing of Germany and the Japanese cities, established a more obvious metric of casualty numbers.[39] His argument touched on but did not address the firebombing of the Japanese cities—sixty-six of them were burned, including the destruction of much of Tokyo—raising the moral issue in a challenging, and to American opinion deeply uncomfortable, fashion. Moral reservations about population targeting were well established in the US Army Air Forces and its high command. Whereas the daytime bombing raids of the German cities by the B-17s and B-24s sought "pinpoint" targets (with no great success), the British nighttime bombing, directed by Air Chief Marshal Sir Arthur "Bomber" Harris, sought to deliberately "dehouse" industrial workers.[40]

The moral argument turned on the shock of the sudden and decisive destruction of a city and much of its civilian population in the course of a few hours. The initial intentions of the XXI Bomber Command under Brig. Gen. Haywood Hansell were to hit industrial and military targets located in Japanese cities, in line with the strategic bombing doctrines Hansell had developed and refined as an air power planner.[41] The B-29 force faced major problems in accurately bombing targets from altitude, and Hansell faced criticism for the ineffectiveness of the effort. Army Air Forces leadership enforced a change to incendiary attacks, which Hansell, a convinced advocate of precision bombing, resisted but reluctantly implemented. Without a defined strategic system of targets, he protested, the impact of incendiary bombing on the Japanese war economy was indirect, and fell largely on civilian morale.[42]

Brig. Gen. Lauris Norstad, chief of staff of the Twentieth Air Force, arranged for Hansell to be abruptly relieved of the command, replacing him with Maj. Gen. Curtis E. LeMay.[43] Hansell was deeply shocked, and continued to maintain, well into his retirement, that to have continued precision bombing would have shortened the war without recourse to the atomic bomb. LeMay had no greater initial success until he shifted attacks to low altitudes—just five to nine thousand feet—with the stripped-out B-29s carrying the maximum possible loads of incendiaries.[44] The shift to low-level incendiary bombing peaked with the firebombing of Tokyo on the night of 9–10 March, which killed an estimated eighty-five thousand people. From then on, dozens of cities experienced the fate of Tokyo as LeMay's B-29s systematically burned them. Brig. Gen. Thomas S. Power, future commander in chief of SAC and widely regarded as a coldhearted man, gave eloquent testimony:

> I watched block after block go up in flames until the holocaust had spread into a seething, swirling ocean of fire, engulfing the city below for miles in every direction. True, there is no room for emotions in war. But the destruction I witnessed that night over Tokyo was so overwhelming that it left a tremendous and lasting impression with me.[45]

The firebombings established a new norm, and paved the way to Hiroshima. Vannevar Bush, advising Gen. Henry "Hap" Arnold, chief of the Army Air Forces, on the potential of incendiary bombs, did not pause in his support of an all-out air assault on Japan, nor did he resist the use of the atomic bomb.[46] Thus, it can be argued that Strategic Air Command's concept of massive retaliation originated from both kinds of raids on Japan.[47]

The shock effect of the atomic bombings, their concentration and speed of effect, was new. The suffering caused was not. They were, notes Beatrice Heuser, "not unique in the number of casualties" and, "if at all, then barely, in the quality of their suffering."[48] In terms of broad effect, the firebombings could be distinguished from atomic destruction mainly in the effort deployed.[49] The US Strategic Bombing Survey concluded that

> the damage and casualties caused at Hiroshima by the one atomic bomb dropped from a single plane would have required 220 B-29s carrying 1,200 tons of incendiary bombs, 400 tons of high explosives and 500 tons of antipersonnel fragmentation bombs, if conventional weapons, rather than an atomic bomb, had been used.[50]

"What," asked the political theorist Ernest Lefever in the *Los Angeles Times* in 2000, "is the moral distinction between killing people by an atomic blast or by a rain of fire bombs?"[51] It was not a commonly heard question in the previous half century. American opinion was steadfastly and, initially, overwhelmingly in favor of the atomic bombings. A poll ten days after Hiroshima showed that around 85 percent of those questioned approved of the use of the atomic bombs or saw it as inevitable.[52] There were dissenting reactions, including from former president Herbert Hoover, for whom the indiscriminate killing "revolts my soul."[53] There was, however, no inclination to weigh the atomic bombings against the strategic bombing of the German and Japanese cities earlier in the war. A naval officer attached to LeMay's operation was appalled by the scale of the Tokyo fire-raid casualties, but noted in his memoirs that American reactions to the firebombing were muted in comparison with those to the atomic bombings; strangely, military historians have themselves reproduced that comparative neglect.[54] Oppenheimer himself recalled learning of Secretary of War Henry Stimson's surprise that there had been no protest over the firebombings of the Japanese cities, and of Tokyo in particular: "He didn't say that the air strikes shouldn't be carried on, but he did think there was something wrong with a country where no-one questioned that."[55]

If ordinary Americans were silent about the morality of strategic bombing, so too, initially, were the atomic scientists. The most serious criticism came from elsewhere in the defense establishment, from the navy. As the navy gained a share of the nuclear stockpile, initially for the carrier-borne AJ-1, it developed targeting doctrine that gave first priority for conventional and atomic bombs to those targets that could threaten carrier operations—submarine pens, naval bases, shipyards, ports, and air bases that could support anticarrier strikes. Then later, once the defense of Western Europe became a factor, it added targets that could slow down the advance of the Red Army, such as petroleum-oil-lubrication facilities, railroads, and other air bases. The navy did not plan to hit Soviet cities for population or industrial destruction.[56]

In October 1949, Rear Adm. Ralph A. Ofstie, an MLC member who had served on the Strategic Bombing Survey for Japan, testified before Congress that "we consider that strategic air warfare, as practiced in the past and as proposed in the future, is militarily unsound and of limited effect, is morally wrong, and is decidedly harmful to the stability of a postwar world." He denounced the bombing of cities as "ruthless and barbaric policy" and stated that the air force's plans would lead to the "random mass slaughter of men, women, and children in the enemy country." This, he said, is "contrary to our fundamental ideals. It is time that strategic bombing be squarely faced in this light; that it be examined in relation to the decent opinions of mankind."[57] Oppenheimer applauded these sentiments, and made a number of comments to Schilling about his fear that the Super would be required for area bombing.[58]

The navy argument failed to convince, in part because the army allied itself with the air force instead of the navy. Joint Chiefs of Staff chair Gen. Omar Bradley stated before Congress that it was war itself that was immoral and (implausibly) that the strategic bombing of the Soviet Union would be carried out "with minimum harm to the nonparticipating civilian populace."[59] There was no congressional or public outcry about the morality of dropping nuclear weapons on Soviet cities, and the moral arguments of the navy were dismissed by the air force as hypocritical and self-serving. Interviewed by Schilling, the air force's Maj. Gen. David Schlatter quipped that "an immoral weapon is one too big for your service to deliver."[60]

We see, then, that the moral line drawn by the Super's opponents was highly tenuous. They condemned the prospect of using a thermonuclear weapon, equivocated about the atomic bombings, and averted their gaze from the area bombings of World War II. To make a judgment about the distinctiveness of nuclear war required deeper consideration of what became, for several of them, a catch-all aversion to strategic bombing. Leaving aside for the moment the meaning of that term, none of them essayed a serious attempt to take moral stock of policies that had targeted civilian populations during 1942–45. It would take the philosopher A. C. Grayling to analyze the issue in depth some half a century later, when he would judge those policies to be moral crimes.[61]

The Impact on the International Order

Expectations of the effect that a decision to pursue the Super would have on international relations were sharply divided. Some expected success in that endeavor to simply reestablish the status quo ante-1949, with a return to the atomic primacy the United States had enjoyed since the war. Others feared that merely to announce such an intention would be to initiate a thermonuclear arms race, hence their proposal to make development of the Super a bargaining chip in a new phase of negotiations with the Soviets. Acheson was dismissive. The Russians, he argued, did not operate in that kind of "deliberate way." There were times when the United States could negotiate with them and times when it could not; the period 1949–52 was one when it could not. As to Conant's idea that if the United States did not proceed to advance knowledge of the Super and undertake its development, neither would the Soviet Union, such a proposal was too risky: "This is ostrich policy, not foreign policy."[62] The idea of mutual renunciation, with both sides remaining in ignorance, was wholly unrealistic. So too was the prospect of a negotiated moratorium—which Acheson called a "stupid" idea.[63] Strauss similarly dismissed the idea that the Soviets ("a government of atheists") would be dissuaded from producing the Super in response to the moral example of the United States.[64]

Lee DuBridge, elaborating his contribution to the GAC report, contested the idea that US diplomacy must be backed by the strength of overwhelming nuclear power. To consider renunciation would provide an opportunity for the diplomatic possibilities to be explored.[65] Rejecting this view, Lewis Strauss asked,

> What will be the effect on the free countries of Western Europe of unilateral renunciation of the Super? We do not know the answer to this question, and while in any case it is of course only a matter of opinion that the State Department should be the source of the best informed guess. For instance, it might very well be taken in friendly European quarters that this marked the beginning of a program of US withdrawal from the role of strong and ready protector.

He continued,

> Let us suppose that an advisory group studying our military situation should recommend the maintenance of an army, navy and air force, but specifically not to maintain an army, navy and air force as strong as the supposed enemy country. . . . Obviously [this course] would [not] be likely to be acceptable to the people, and yet . . . from the purely defense point of view [it is] similar in kind if not in degree, to the situation before us.[66]

Strauss followed this rebuttal with his November letter to Truman, urging him to direct the AEC to proceed with the development of the thermonuclear bomb as the highest priority, subject only to the judgment of the Department of Defense as to its value as a weapon, and the advice of the Department of State as to the diplomatic consequences of its unilateral renunciation or its possession. A substantial memorandum set out in detail his reasons for urging this course of action. He concluded that

> until . . . some means is found of eliminating war, I cannot agree with those of my colleagues who feel that an announcement should be made by the President to the effect that the development of the thermonuclear weapon will not be undertaken by the United States at this time. This is because: (a) I do not think the statement will be credited in the Kremlin; (b) that when and if it should be decided subsequent to such a statement to proceed with the production of the thermonuclear bomb, it might in a delicate situation, be regarded as an affirmative statement of hostile intent; and (c) because primarily until disarmament is universal, our arsenal must be not less well equipped than with the most potent weapons that our technology can devise.[67]

In March 1950 Harold C. Urey wrote, "Judging from our past decisions, we have apparently decided to lose the armaments race. Suppose instead of deciding this, we decide we will build the hydrogen bomb. . . . Suppose that two countries have the hydrogen bomb. Is it not believable that sooner or later an incident may occur which would precipitate the use of bombs? . . . An exact balance of power is very difficult to attain. This is what we know in physical science as a situation of unstable equilibrium."[68] Frederick Seitz warned that if the Soviet Union attained a thermonuclear weapon, the United States would lose its European allies. If Soviet troops could occupy Western Europe with impunity, the Soviet bloc could double its industrial output and military strength.[69]

State Department officials were less emphatic than this, but subscribed to the view that Soviet foreign policy had a penchant for risk taking. Now nuclear armed, the Russians were, according to Melvyn Leffler's portrayal of departmental thought, "more rash, more willing to take chances, more supportive of revolutionary movements around the world. . . . If the Soviets should also develop the hydrogen bomb, they would be further emboldened."[70] US superiority had underpinned a confident strategy of containment, and officials balked at the thought of losing the competitive advantage that encouraged them to take risks. With a (notionally) level playing field, Soviet policy could become more aggressive, banking on greater US caution. The existing configuration of power had served US foreign policy. In this new world, the reacquisition of former nuclear preponderance via the development of thermonuclear weapons would serve to contain Soviet recklessness.

It took the archrealist Hans Morgenthau to focus this argument. Writing in the immediate aftermath of Truman's decision, Morgenthau declared that the first priority of the United States was to avoid conflict. Morgenthau had no moral scruples about the acquisition of the most powerful weaponry; rather, he considered the achievement of parity to be a moral imperative. His bottom line was negotiation as the only road to peace. His arguments about the H-bomb centered on four areas. The first was feasibility, judgments about which could not be left to the layperson. The second was moral justification, which from his perspective entailed the modern state acquiring the latest weapons. Third was politico-military neutralization by means of disarmament, which in the present world was not feasible. Finally, a decision not to develop thermonuclear weapons would not preclude the development of other weapons of mass destruction.[71] Beyond these speculations lay a practical calculation. Would the US decision to proceed with the development of thermonuclear weaponry provoke the Soviets into following suit? Or might a Soviet program already be under way, leaving it to the United States to play catch-up? Given the nature of international conflict and the awesome power of nuclear weapons, the only hope for peace lay in US-Soviet negotiations, achieving security through political channels.[72]

Impact on the Soviet Program

Late in October 1949, when the GAC met to consider Lilienthal's request for advice, he set the scene for them with a powerful statement against embarking on a new arms race. Strauss, meanwhile, was privy to information from FBI director J. Edgar Hoover that had yet to reach his fellow commissioners—namely, that Klaus Fuchs, a physicist on the Manhattan Project, had probably been a Soviet spy. Fuchs, who had returned to Britain to take up a key position in atomic energy research at Harwell, had been involved in the theoretical discussions on the possibility of a fusion device and might have passed this information to Moscow through his Soviet handlers. He had also taken out a patent jointly with John von Neumann to provide a thermonuclear ignition device. Strauss was therefore concerned that there could already be a Soviet hydrogen bomb program, and this possibility made the opposition of the GAC, and of Oppenheimer in particular, all the more frustrating. Subsequent news of Fuchs's confession cemented this concern.

Among the scientists, Hans Bethe, while opposing development of the Super, nevertheless acknowledged the realities of Soviet capabilities:

> The prime requirements [for developing a nuclear weapon] still are a group of highly capable scientists, a country determined to make the weapon and a great industrial effort. We know now, if we ever doubted it, that the USSR has all of these. For the Soviet scientists the information [from Fuchs] must simply have resolved many doubts as to which steps to take next and saved a number of costly and futile parallel developments.[73]

Karl Compton tendered similar advice to the president, arguing now that "we should proceed with this phase of atomic weapon development with increased activity and support." In his view,

> it is clear that Russia could proceed with the development of this type of weapon quite irrespective of any high-minded decisions and announcements on our part. There is no basic scientific secret standing in the way and there are some brilliant atomic scientists among the Russians and collaborating Germans. . . . We are more likely to underestimate than to overestimate their capacity.[74]

Soviet scientists had indeed begun speculating on the possibilities of building a hydrogen bomb as early as 1946 and at that time were at least as far advanced theoretically as the United States.[75] Robert Bacher recalled his period as a UN adviser, when Soviet scientists impressed him with their awareness of the key scientific issues in developing nuclear weapons. In

1946 he had been asked directly what the United States intended to do about the Super.[76] And Loper's MLC paper had posited a maximum Soviet capability already in action.

Others, though, deprecated the possibility that the Soviets would develop the H-bomb. Writing on behalf of the GAC, John Manley cited three grounds. First, the technical difficulties, as the effort involved would be very large. Second, the Soviets had struck a moral posture before the world, and the use of such a weapon would spell the end of support for Communism in the United States. Third, they would fear retaliation with US atomic bombs.[77] These were weak arguments, but Manley elsewhere identified the heart of the matter: "Our policy in international affairs neither is nor should be independent of moral considerations. . . . Development or use of terror weapons does not contribute to increase of moral stature." With a rhetorical flourish characteristic of these arguments, Manley asserted that "other nations can hardly turn to Russia for leadership on moral precepts. Shall the U.S. also take steps to abandon its role of leadership toward building a better world?"[78]

The declaration of the dozen scientists of the American Physical Society introduced a key issue: the likelihood that a US program to develop the Super would incite the Soviets to follow. "Perhaps," they wrote, "the development of the hydrogen bomb has already been under way in Russia for some time. But if it was not, our decision to develop it must have started the Russians on the same program. If they had already a going program, they will redouble their efforts."[79] Later, Oppenheimer would admit to the Personnel Security Board that "what was not clear to us [in 1949] and what is clearer to me now is that it probably lay wholly beyond our power to prevent the Russians somehow from getting ahead with it."[80] Paul Nitze accepted part of Oppenheimer's 1950 analysis, but his response was more nuanced. A short-run view of security policy—say, three years or so—might incline toward holding back from development to avoid incentivizing a Soviet project. But a longer-term view acknowledged that the Soviets would eventually succeed in developing their own Super, and the US could not tolerate a Soviet thermonuclear monopoly.[81]

A detailed appraisal of this crucial issue was made subsequently by Herbert York, a physicist who became a critic of the 1950 H-bomb decision. York compared, in graphical form, two hypothetical outcomes of a US decision not to proceed to develop the Super, paired with a Soviet decision to go ahead anyway: "the most probable alternative world" and the "worst plausible alternative world." York made the argument that in the first world, Soviet development would have progressed but more slowly, which might have led to delayed development on both sides to the point where a new era of arms control could begin; while in the second world, there were political imperatives and technological advantages such that the United States would have reacted quickly enough to any Soviet developments to ensure that the nuclear balance would not be altered between the two countries. Instead the US decision to proceed with the Super catalyzed the Soviet decision.[82]

Timing is crucial in estimating this effect. In July 1950 the Joint Atomic Energy Intelligence Committee, an interagency body with CIA participation, reported on the Soviet program, claiming that the decision to start a thermonuclear production program was made in late 1949 "on the condition that there be no serious interference with the production of fission weapons."[83] In his definitive *Stalin and the Bomb*, David Holloway shows that theoretical work began in earnest in 1946, with a report on "utilization of the nuclear energy of light elements" using deuterium as the explosive material; this report may have been prompted by knowledge of the April 1946 Los Alamos Super conference, attended by Klaus Fuchs. In December 1946, the Soviet atomic scientist Igor Kurchatov acknowledged the importance of information about "American work on the superbomb," calling it "probably true and of great interest for our work in this country."[84]

Although neither Fuchs's treachery nor information provided from other espionage sources pointed Soviet scientists in the right direction toward a feasible device, it encouraged their work, albeit, initially at least, down profitless routes. It has been argued that Soviet research was aided, not by Fuchs, but by the analysis of radioactive debris from the first two US thermonuclear tests, and it was with this risk in mind that Bush and Oppenheimer opposed the Mike test.[85] There is only limited support for this supposition, as it seems likely that Soviet detection technology had yet to advance to that usable stage.[86]

Soviet nuclear scientists were drawn together by the challenge posed by a project of such scope and significance, and were willing to work on such a project to equalize the balance of power with the United States. Holloway notes that by late 1948, in advance of their first fission device test, Soviet scientists had established the basic design concept for a workable thermonuclear weapon, with "none of the soul-searching that took place in the United States." The development of the hydrogen bomb was now a top priority for the Soviets, and their positions on the issues involved were more akin to those of Teller than Oppenheimer.[87] The Soviet nuclear program scientist Andrei Sakharov reflected,

> I cannot help but feel deeply for and empathize with Oppenheimer, whose personal tragedy has become a universal one. Some striking parallels between his fate and mine arose in the 1960s, and later I was to go even further than Oppenheimer had. But in the 1940s and 1950s my position was much closer to Teller's, practically a mirror image.

But, recalling that time, he scoffed,

> Any U.S. move toward abandoning or suspending work on a thermonu-
> clear weapon would have been perceived either as a cunning, deceitful
> maneuver or as evidence of stupidity or weakness. In any case, the Soviet
> reaction would have been the same: to avoid a possible trap, and to exploit
> the adversary's folly at the earliest opportunity.[88]

American abstention would have been pointless.

CHAPTER 5

Dissent and Development

The wide divergence of views on the morality of nuclear weapons and on
the likely consequences of the United States proceeding with the Super did
not evaporate with Truman's decision. The Soviet test had brought into the
public domain the hitherto scarcely known speculation that a "superbomb"
or "hydrogen bomb" could be created. As that speculation moved into the
political arena, it came to be regarded by some as a practical project, shame-
fully neglected and urgently needed; by others as too improbable to be
worth pursuing; and by still others as a uniquely sinister, immoral, and
destabilizing prospect.

The many reservations of the GAC and its sympathizers were readily
satirized by Rep. Henry "Scoop" Jackson, a member of the JCAE:

> In late 1949, when there was the controversy on the question of whether or
> not we should really try to build the hydrogen weapon, a very influential
> group of experts argued against this step. First they said it would be
> immoral. Then they said, even if making it in self-defense were moral, it
> could not be built. Then they said, even if it could be built, it could not be
> delivered. Then they said, even if it could be delivered, it would cost too
> much. Then they said, even if it would not cost too much, it could do noth-
> ing that A-bombs couldn't do.[1]

Parody indeed, but the attack captured the key issues that would continue
to be contested as the United States moved beyond Truman's initial decision toward the acquisition of a thermonuclear arsenal. During this postde-
cision period, many of the issues first raised during the preceding months
reemerged to be replayed—and with undiminished vigor.

Was the Super feasible? If the scientific uncertainty that predominated
during those few months and those that followed centered on the possibility of engineering a fusion reaction in a usable weapon, a secondary, but
no less severe, concern was the supposed opportunity cost of such a project. Would development of the Super divert resources—especially nuclear

material and scientific talent—away from the production and stockpiling of much-needed fission weapons? Would a Super program culminate in a test or lead to expensive stockpiling? If built, could it be delivered? If deliverable, did it have any obvious utility?

The arguments between advocates and opponents turned largely on these issues, creating an impression of intense debate on evidential premises. In reality, the positions people adopted reflected their institutional and personal affiliations, from which consensual conclusions were unlikely to follow. John Walker, who was hired as counsel to the JCAE in 1951 and who constructed a chronology of the events in question, observed, in Schilling's paraphrasing,

> People's opinions on the Super question in 1949 were fixed before the facts came in. This [was] true of both sides. The real issue was whether or not to build this horrible new weapon. People divided on this, but the form of their division was in the character of wrestling over various technical considerations about which very little was really known on either side.[2]

And, as it happened, progress in the design of both weapons and carriers confounded the early objections of the dissidents.

Feasibility: "If Wishes Were Horses"

This catchphrase, from a traditional nursery rhyme ("If wishes were horses, beggars would ride"), was Acheson's, reflecting the hope, shared even by some of the Super's advocates, that it would not, in the end, prove feasible to develop such a fearsome weapon. Either way it was not something on which he would place a bet. With several years of scientific speculation behind the laboratory, by 1947 Los Alamos was prepared to address the question of whether a thermonuclear bomb might be feasible. A key report endorsed by the AEC and the MLC concluded that it was probably so, and essayed an estimate of the amount of fission required to ignite deuterium.[3] Yet the road from scientific reasoning to practical application would be long and uncertain. Doubts would persist, and for many their personal hopes and fears shaped the judgments they made.

The 1949 GAC report on the Super set out, with admirable brevity, the process required to create thermonuclear fusion. The basic principal of the design, explained the report, was the ignition of deuterium by a fission bomb, with the accompanying high pressures, temperatures, and neutron densities it would bring to bear. Tritium would be required as an intermediary in "overwhelming probability." To make the superbomb a reality would therefore require not just the provision of tritium but also further theoretical studies "aimed at reducing the very great uncertainties still inherent in the behavior of this weapon under extreme conditions of temperature, pressure and flow," followed by the engineering of designs suggested as hopeful by the theoretical work and carefully instrumented test programs to determine the ignitability of the deuterium-tritium mixture. There was no experimental work short of an actual test that could establish the feasibility of any given model, and "because of the unsymmetric and extremely unfamiliar conditions obtaining, some considerable doubt will surely remain as to the soundness of theoretical anticipation."[4]

The doubts expressed by the GAC in October 1949 had ample precedent. Indeed, unlike the Manhattan Engineering District's atomic bomb project, the history of the Super is a history of widespread doubts about its feasibility, and widespread recognition of the opportunity costs that would be incurred in pursuing it. Norris Bradbury, in a talk given in October 1945, warned that

the word "feasible" is a weasel word—it covers everything from laboratory experiments up to the possibility of actual building—for only by building something do you actually finally determine *feasibility*. This does not mean we will build a super. It couldn't happen in our time in any event. But someday, someone must know the answer: Is it feasible?[5]

At this time, the problems of igniting a mass of deuterium seemed formidable. The challenge for Los Alamos scientists was an order of magnitude greater than that faced during the Manhattan Project.

The April 1946 Los Alamos conference had concluded optimistically that "it is likely that a super-bomb can be constructed and will work. Definite proof of this can hardly ever be expected and a final decision can be made only by a test of the completely assembled super-bomb."[6] While the conference report claimed feasibility for the Super, a number of the participants dissented, attributing the tone and conclusions of the report to Teller's enthusiasm. Carson Mark, a mathematician who subsequently headed the Theoretical Division at Los Alamos, later reflected that

the very proof of feasibility required the fully detailed calculation of its behavior during an explosion. Without this, no conclusive experiment was possible short of a successful stab in the dark, since a failure would not necessarily establish unfeasibility, but possibly only that the system chosen was unsuitable, or that the required ignition conditions had not been met.[7]

With the victory over Japan, the initial effort made on the Super came to an end as wartime personnel returned to their civilian occupations, leaving Los Alamos seriously short of scientific manpower.[8] The case of Luis Alvarez illustrates the sudden evacuation of talent from the laboratory. Credited with having devised the postbomb release escape maneuver for the B-29, his last assignment had taken him overseas to fly in the observation aircraft during the Hiroshima drop. "As soon as I got back from Tinian," he recalled, "I packed up my household goods as quickly as possible and moved my family back to Berkeley; yes. There was nothing essentially for me to do at Los Alamos. Both of my jobs were complete."[9]

AEC research director Kenneth Pitzer estimated that of the 7,100 scientific staff at Los Alamos at the end of the war, some 5,500 left to return to their civilian lives in universities and other laboratories. He reflected that

> during the war you could get absolutely top people to stop what they were doing and go do something that appeared to be terribly important to the war effort. You simply don't have that level of drawing power for recruitment in peacetime, even in a relatively exciting new technological area like atomic energy.[10]

Bradbury briefed the newly appointed AEC commissioners that the program for a superbomb would involve a laboratory effort every bit as extensive as Los Alamos at the peak of its wartime activity. Meanwhile, the laboratory had restricted itself to research and theoretical calculations that might bear on the Super's feasibility. It remained the case, however, that this work had led to "no decrease in our expectations that such a weapon could be constructed were the necessary effort to be expended thereupon."[11] The effort needed would be considerable. In late 1947 the Super was defined at Los Alamos as no more than a possible long-range weapon development, on which an estimated 2 percent of the laboratory's man hours were spent investigating its feasibility and general design.[12] However, cautioned Bradbury, this apparent neglect "has been not entirely a matter of choice, but has been dictated in part by the caliber of personnel obtainable in the interim period and the extremely high degree of scientific competence required to attack the complicated problems of thermonuclear weapons."[13] Theoreticians, rather than engineers, were required for such a development.

At this time, then, the Super looked like a distant prospect. Oppenheimer's General Advisory Committee commended the program of basic studies at Los Alamos as "a healthy and useful part of the work of the . . . laboratory," but noted that even with the most optimistic assessment, "the realization of thermonuclear weapons is many years in the future, and that in many cases our knowledge of the subject is fragmentary and inadequate."[14] In 1948 the Department of Defense established a panel on long-range military objectives in the field of nuclear weapons, with Oppenheimer as chair. The panel saw no immediate prospect of progress on the Super, which would in any event be very expensive in terms of tritium. More immediately feasible and attractive was the boosted fission design as an alternative to the possibility of very high-yield thermonuclear weapons.

When Bradbury reviewed the Los Alamos program again in 1949, he warned again that an effort comparable to that mounted by the Manhattan Project would be required for probably twice as long just to demonstrate whether or not such a weapon could be made. He considered that "such devices are certainly not in the near future and may possibly never exist except on paper. . . . The actual amount of research and development effort to be expended must, however, be related to the foreseeable national need, if any, for a weapon of these characteristics."[15]

The Soviet explosion redefined the urgency of that national need. It galvanized Edward Teller to urge definitive work on the feasibility of the Super, warning of the possibility that the Soviets would achieve a super-bomb within a short period of time. Los Alamos also reacted, recommending further theoretical work to the General Advisory Committee. Under pressure from the JCAE, Bradbury cautioned that in order to advance the Super project he would require thirty additional scientists and an expansion of several hundred personnel over the laboratory's present complement.[16]

Truman's January decision did no more than authorize further scientific work, the end of which could not be foreseen. Explaining to the readers of *Scientific American*, the physicist and dissident former AEC commissioner Robert F. Bacher set out the technical requirement to

> figure out how a sizable fraction of the energy of the heavy hydrogen can be released before the material is cooled too much by emitted radiation or dispersed by the explosion. . . . Whether this can be done will of course not be certain until it has been done. There are many opinions as to how difficult it may be. Since the President has directed the Atomic Energy Commission to continue with the development, we can assume that it is regarded as both possible and feasible.[17]

At that point, many scientists believed—and some, even among the advocates, hoped—that the technical problems of building a fusion weapon would prove unsolvable. The lack of computer capacity and the sheer absence of data about the behavior of materials at the high temperatures envisaged to ignite light elements meant that a high degree of faith was required to pursue the Super in any of its forms.[18] Teller had that faith and did his utmost to ensure that it was shared. In that, he networked energetically and effectively outside the AEC's purview. He enlisted McMahon and Borden of the JCAE, Strauss, and the Department of Defense, where, reports the official history of the secretary of defense's office, air force officials and Robert LeBaron lent powerful support.[19]

Teller struggled to convince colleagues with calculations of a model—now generally known as the "classical Super." He later floated another concept, to be known as the "Alarm Clock," a label chosen to dramatize the urgency of the need for a weapon of vastly greater yield than the fission bombs then in the stockpile. His breakthrough came in a collaboration with Stanislav Ulam that redefined the problem from igniting the light elements with the heat from nuclear fission to compressing them with the radiation from a fission explosion. This, the Teller-Ulam version, was to prove successful.[20] In June 1951 Oppenheimer appeared to have swung his support behind the project, acknowledging it as a "technically sweet" solution. With his backing, the GAC judged it an "interesting, possibly encouraging line of attack" and foresaw the possibility of a test within a year.[21]

However appealing the model seemed, the prospect of a successful thermonuclear explosion was conjectural. "About the so-called hydrogen bomb," a government panel wrote at the time, "there has always been this one great question: 'Is this possible?' This question will be answered if the projected test succeeds."[22] There was no dissent from that proposition; all accepted that only a test could provide the proof.[23] But doubts and fears began to emerge. In April 1952 Acheson appointed Oppenheimer to chair the State Department's disarmament committee, from which position, with the support of fellow scientists (in the person of the always-influential Vannevar Bush), State Department officials, the intelligence community (CIA deputy director Allen Dulles), and prominent individuals from law and education, convened as a State Department Panel of Consultants. At their second meeting in May, the panel, fearing that a first test would doom any chance of controlling this new class of weapon, proposed that the forthcoming test of the Super at Eniwetok be postponed.[24] In resisting the now-established course of development, the panel advocated exploring an agreement with the Soviet Union not to test the weapon, noting that tests could be detected by unilateral means. They argued that the test would aid Soviet development by providing detailed atmospheric evidence of the process, and worsen relations between the great powers. For Bush in particular, it was a significant turnaround from his earlier support for unrestricted atomic warfare.

In summary, the panel's argument for a ban on H-bomb tests took this form. A test would spur the Soviet H-bomb program and would make the United States look like the leader in preparation for nuclear war. Going ahead with H-bomb development would result in a net military loss for the United States if it led to a Soviet H-bomb, as there were more targets in the West suitable for being hit by H-bombs, while the Soviets could use their smaller amount of fissionable material more effectively in H-bombs than in A-bombs. Importantly, this point might be the last stage in the nuclear arms race that offered an opportunity to stop and take stock of where the world was going. The United States was far enough ahead in A-bombs that it could afford to take a chance.[25]

The advice to reject their case was put to Acheson by Paul Nitze. If a ban was to the United States' advantage, he argued, the Soviets would not accept it. If the Soviets were behind, they would use the ban to catch up and then test themselves. Means for detection of tests that then worked might not work in the case of later test procedures. Agreement might make sense if the Soviets would be willing to accept major verification and inspection measures—but they would not. Therefore, a test ban could not bring to a halt the arms race of thermonuclear research. The United States might have a lead in thermonuclear weapon development and could use this advantage, plus its A-bomb superiority, to coerce the Soviet Union into a disarmament agreement.[26]

The NSC special committee, in action again at this point, urged that the test should proceed. Truman approved it, but worried about the test taking place in the final days of his presidency. He encouraged postponement, if valid technical grounds could be advanced. They were not, and the Mike test of the Ivy series went ahead, with spectacular results, on 1 November 1952 (early morning local Pacific time; 31 October in the United States).[27] It had been the last attempt by the dissenters to arrest the road to a thermonuclear arms race, but was doomed due to its members' lacking political allies. US thermonuclear development had now, in Bernstein's telling phrase, "crossed the Rubicon."[28]

Costs—and Opportunity Costs

Still unproven as a deliverable weapon, the superbomb, as distinct from a vast experimental device, was looking more feasible. Yet the question remained of whether it would be worthwhile in cost terms. Truman's January 1950 decision was virtually uncosted. No attempt had been made, prior to the report of the triumvirate of Acheson, Johnson, and Lilienthal, to estimate the financial cost of the commitment the president had made. Continuing as the special committee of the NSC, but with Lilienthal now replaced by Smyth, the reformed committee reported that the research and development program at Los Alamos aimed at a test of a thermonuclear weapon "at the earliest possible date." The first steps of the process would be tested in 1951, followed by a test of the process as a whole the following year. Dollar costs for the expanded weapons program were estimated at $50 million, with the production of tritium for the tests adding a further $5 million. Thereafter, the construction of ten weapons a year was envisaged at a cost of $200 million.[29]

By September 1950, therefore, it had become possible to estimate the likely costs of the AEC's future program in relation to both the expansion of fission weapon production and the new requirements imposed by the Super. A figure of $5.4 billion, tentatively put forward, had the support of the AEC itself, the Department of Defense, and the National Security Council. This proposed expenditure predictably drew opposition, with the Senate Appropriations Committee warning that it could undermine the government's fiscal policy. Congressional opposition could pose a major threat to the program, and so Gordon Dean revised the figure down to $4.6 billion and took the precaution of seeking the president's intervention in support.[30]

Truman, until this point adamant about the need to limit federal expenditure, courageously threw his weight behind the AEC, recognizing that there were other voices that urged pushing the expansion program still further. Acknowledging concerns about the magnitude of federal expenditures, he appealed to Sen. Burnet R. Maybank, chair of the Subcommittee on Independent Offices, insisting that "we must nevertheless continue our efforts to buttress the security of this country and of the free world. Not to do so invites disaster. I am convinced, therefore, that we must and that we can accomplish the proposed expansion in our atomic energy program." He had asked the special committee of the NSC, which had been set up to keep the Super project under review, to confirm that the expansion program was integral to the necessary strengthening of US military capabilities and that international conditions required that strengthening. Truman insisted that the resources needed for the program were within the capabilities of the commission and the expected availability of raw materials. Moreover, he said,

> the manpower, power and construction materials required for the new facilities can be made available without unduly adverse effects on the rest of the defense program or on our economy generally. . . . The program has been carefully reviewed in order to bring its total cost down to a practicable minimum. Every effort has been made to exclude facilities not essential to achieving the expanded production goals.

The current cost estimate, Truman pointed out, was substantially below that initially made. He concluded by urging the importance of undertaking the expansion program without delay, taking care to also enlist support from Sen. Brien McMahon of the JCAE.[31] Expenditure on atomic weaponry fell partly on the AEC (for research and development) and partly on the Department of Defense.[32] The sums mentioned above were opaque, however, as no satisfactory expenditure data existed for the atomic weapons program through the 1950s.[33]

Real costs aside, there remained the question of whether the Super provided economic advantages over the use of fission weapons. Given the small number of atomic bombs available to Strategic Air Command, would development of the Super divert resources and so weaken, rather than strengthen, the US capability to strike? During the period of extreme shortage of fissionable material, air force leaders were unwilling to compromise the effectiveness of SAC's deterrent force by diverting effort to smaller fission weapons.[34] While the theoretical feasibility of a thermonuclear bomb was first discussed in a colloquium at Los Alamos in 1946, when it was assessed that such a weapon could be built in one or two years, in December 1947 the laboratory reported that progress had been limited and that it would be "many years before we develop the thermonuclear reaction for weapons purposes." If the government wanted the Super, "we had better get more brains to work."[35] Oppenheimer, as chair of the long-range military objectives panel on atomic energy, submitted his draft report in August 1948, arguing against making the Super "in view of the magnitude and complexity of the problem, the special personnel requirements, and the uncertainties." Considering also the "extraordinarily difficult problems" of delivery, cryogenics, and tritium production, he recommended that preference should be given in the short term to developing a boosted fission weapon.[36]

AEC acting chair Sumner Pike declared that the commission would strive "to maintain the position of the United States in the field of fission weapons in both numbers and effectiveness" but warned that "specific phases of this effort" might be delayed by H-bomb work.[37] The NSC special committee appointed to report on the progress of the thermonuclear program warned that weapon-grade U-235 would be required in sizeable quantities for the research and test program at Los Alamos. In addition, tritium would be needed, which could be produced only at the expense of plutonium. Producing it would divert some of the capacity at Hanford, with the result that "the total estimated cost in weapons, spread over a period of two to three years, will be on the order of 30 or 40 fission bombs."[38] A major uncertainty here was the amount of tritium needed and available. When Gordon Dean testified before the JCAE in November 1950, he suggested that the opportunity cost of one hydrogen bomb might be between 100 and 150 atomic bombs, a figure that appeared to have no support elsewhere.[39] Lee DuBridge took a more nuanced position, weighing all the factors before advising in a memorandum that the advantages of the Super would equate to two or three fission bombs.[40]

While quenching enthusiasm, such estimates soon became dated, as technological progress produced greater efficiency in weapon design. Although the costs of tritium production figured largely in the scientists' argument against development of the Super, the military personnel involved tended to accept that this was indeterminate, or even, at that time, undeterminable. Estimates kept changing, and for the scientists a clear picture could not be seen.[41] At the AEC, Carroll Wilson took the view that so much emotion had become attached to the issue that it prevented clear alternative costs from being established.[42] Schilling's interview program focused closely on the opportunity cost issue in terms of fissionable material, as this had been made a major part of the argument among the protagonists. He found that a wide variety of estimates had been tossed around, on the basis that the effort to develop the Super would draw material from the A-bomb production program, a consideration that seemed to gain special force following the outbreak of the Korean conflict, when immediate availability became an issue should there be a decision to use the weapon there.

Uncertainties about the availability of scarce fissionable material were compounded by doubts that Los Alamos in peacetime could succeed in attracting the necessary scientific manpower. In February 1950 the AEC's full Military Liaison Committee paid a visit to Los Alamos and spent two days reviewing the program and its priorities in order to advise the secretary of defense. Robert LeBaron wrote that the factor limiting the AEC from moving ahead with the H-bomb activity would be the recruitment of a sizeable number of scientists to return to Los Alamos.[43] The wartime sense of urgency was no longer a factor, while reservations about nuclear weapon development had spread more widely among the scientific community. LeBaron was worried. In a separate memorandum he elaborated his concern about "some of the forces acting outside the physical program of H-bomb development which are intimately related to the progress of the work and which may in final analysis be decisive." Those forces included the attitude of leading nuclear physicists and scientific counselors in universities and other public centers, and "the attitude of the country as a whole, particularly as it may apply to contractors and others." He added that he was "convinced that there are subversive elements" actively working to confuse the issue by disorganizing scientific thinking and fermenting dissension among citizens in general.[44]

This was not, however, Los Alamos's initial problem. So great was the postwar loss of scientific staff from the laboratory that the initial efforts of the AEC were devoted to managing the takeover from the Manhattan Engineer District and keeping the laboratory going. Robert Bacher judged that the laboratory did not begin to feel its strength again until the Sandstone test series in 1948. Many of the wartime staff had been given commitments that they would be released back to their universities or companies at the end of the war. It was well understood that they had been given leave for a specific task, not engaged indefinitely on weapons work. It was difficult to build up the strength again, and the universities, intent on training the next generation of scientists, objected volubly.[45]

Los Alamos director Norris Bradbury agonized over the problem of attracting top theoreticians back to the laboratory. He urged the GAC and AEC to help, and saw the stance taken by GAC members, in particular Oppenheimer and Conant, as a major barrier.[46] Momentum did build, but gradually. Under attack in 1954 for Los Alamos scientists allegedly dragging their feet on thermonuclear development, Bradbury responded vigorously. In October 1954, *U.S. News and World Report* published his detailed rejoinder to Los Alamos's critics. Bradbury pointed out that the laboratory grew from 1,200 employees in 1946 to 3,000 in 1954, bringing back many of the wartime staff as consultants. He maintained that much of the effort went to the improvement of fission weapons, but the laboratory was not "idle in the thermonuclear field," a subject on which work "never stopped." In response to the president's directive, in March 1950 the laboratory had gone to a six-day week for the next three years in order to accelerate progress.[47] This spirited defense notwithstanding, it remained the case that the Super's opponents on the GAC both excluded themselves from the new developments and continued to cast doubt on the feasibility, utility, and morality of the new weapon.

From his seat on the commission, Lewis Strauss kept up the pressure against them. He continued to contest the GAC's assessments, confident that the "economics" of having the Super were justifiable by comparison with "ordinaries."[48] Alone among the commissioners, Strauss disputed the amounts of tritium and U-235 required, as well as the estimated yield for the Super. This was put at a median figure of one thousand kilotons, or, in later parlance, one megaton, which Strauss thought "actually on the low side by a sizeable factor." He also rebutted the GAC's position on the number of Supers required, insisting that that was a matter for military determination.[49]

For SAC, the crux of the matter was whether initially scarce nuclear resources should be diverted in part to smaller-yield weapons. Curtis LeMay was fiercely hostile to any such diversion. SAC would be the undisputed sole customer for the first, massive versions of the Super at a time when resources were scarce and no other service could deliver them. When the development and large-quantity production of smaller, lighter nuclear weapons came onstream, the air force still earmarked such weapons for *strategic* use, particularly as warheads for future ballistic missiles.[50] And when LeMay had under his command a force of F-84F fighter bombers equipped to carry a lightweight fission weapon underwing, he insisted that he would not contemplate arming them until such time as his entire fleet of heavy and medium bombers had a high-yield weapon to carry.[51]

Serving and former GAC members and their supporters continued their opposition. William A. Fowler, a nuclear physicist at Caltech, made public speeches opposing the H-bomb. In May 1950, Lee DuBridge, speaking before a Pacific University audience in Portland, doubted the value of the hydrogen bomb, even were it "possible to make one." DuBridge argued that several hundred fission bombs in the stockpile sufficed to provide enough retaliatory power to destroy the entire industrial areas of any possible enemy.[52] Robert Bacher elaborated the point that same month, going to the heart of the "few large versus many small" debate and attracting widespread attention:

We can easily see that a hydrogen bomb is capable of destroying any major city, with the exception perhaps of some of the outlying districts. How does this compare with what could be done with atomic bombs? We have been comparing the hydrogen bomb with the fission bomb used at Hiroshima, but it has been stated that since the war there have been significant improvements in fission bombs. These improvements have resulted in more powerful bombs and in a more efficient use of the valuable fissionable material.

Most large metropolitan areas include many sections that are covered by water or otherwise unsettled. Thus a hydrogen bomb would blast many square miles whose destruction would contribute in no way to the effectiveness of the bomb. Atomic bombs, on the other hand, could presumably be dropped so as to avoid overbombing uninhabited areas. . . . It seems likely that there is no metropolitan area which could not be thoroughly destroyed with 25 atomic bombs at most, and perhaps as few as 10. It also appears that two atomic bombs would completely paralyze a city, even a large one. . . . In view of this, one begins to wonder just how useful a military weapon the hydrogen bomb would be. . . . It looks very much as if everyone is simply fascinated by the idea of "the bigger the better."[53]

These arguments were very much in accord with the position Lee Du-Bridge set out as a follow-up to the GAC report. Arguing that as "30 properly placed fission bombs is all that could be used against any conceivable target," he maintained that "the stockpile of fission bombs now on hand is already equivalent in damage power to many super bombs." Moreover, developing the Super "must employ fissionable material equal to that of about four A-bombs—plus an amount of tritium. . . . A super only provides about 2 to 3 times the damage power per unit cost of present A-bombs."[54]

Military Utility

While the GAC had been dismissive of any possible military value to be achieved from the Super, the Joint Chiefs made a different assessment in their rebuttal of the GAC's arguments.[55] The United States, they (and soon the Defense Department as a whole) argued, might be unable to overcome the psychological effects if the Soviet Union were to acquire the bomb first: "We shall be unable to counter possible enemy exploitation of the frightening and paralyzing fiction which has become associated . . . with thermonuclear explosions." This would have a "demoralizing effect on the American people," might lead to a destabilization of the international order, and "would provide the Soviet leaders . . . with a psychological boost which in peacetime could lead to increased truculence in international affairs." Sole possession by the Soviets would also present a "blackmail" opportunity for the Soviet Union. Soviet possession would lead to a scenario where they had both the nuclear and the conventional forces to "risk hostilities for the rapid achievement of their objectives."

With sole possession by the United States, the Super could, in addition to its deterrent value, be used offensively. The military argued that the Super would help "against those important tactical and strategic objectives which are particularly adapted to a thermonuclear weapon." Large concentrations of enemy troops and supplies could be destroyed with only one Super rather than many fission bombs.[56] The Joint Chiefs' view on this was derived from the study undertaken by the Weapon Systems Evaluation Group. Lt. Gen. John E. Hull, the group's chair, thought the battlefield use of a thermonuclear weapon would neutralize the Red Army's traditional doctrine and practice of amassing vast concentrations of armor and troops prior to an attack.[57]

These speculations notwithstanding, the principal argument for US possession of the Super was, then, not its use in war, but its anticipated political and psychological effects. It was in deterrence, rather than war fighting, that the weapon's significance was to be found. If deterrence failed, then the atomic strike plan would be triggered, but this was predicated on massive multiple attacks using the fission bomb, the number of which that were stockpiled, in the Mark 4 version, was increasing, albeit slowly. There was no consideration of what changes in the plan would be advisable in the event of a weapon of such hugely enhanced power becoming available. Indeed, as SAC's strength grew and the modernization of the strike force continued, it seemed that for strategic purposes, "high-yield" (generally thermonuclear) weapons would simply replace fission bombs within an existing strike plan.

Turning for the first time to tactical utility in the European theater—a prospect that had been entirely discounted by the GAC—the Joint Chiefs' study pointed out that it would take only one Super, rather than many fission bombs, to destroy a target. A hydrogen bomb could destroy an airfield and its associated facilities and render it useless for a considerable period of time. Once destroyed, targets would be unsalvageable, obviating the need to revisit them. "Effective destruction of the above target types may well lead to decisive results since such concentrations normally occur in connection with critical operations in war." The Super might force the enemy "to avoid concentrations of troops and material," and as a result, "we shall have forced them to abandon the source of their greatest strength, employment of mass."[58] These considerations, aside from operational factors, established a military requirement for superbombs.[59] Although this variety of deployment was not the first concern of the air force, the possible proliferation of target types resulting from the Joint Chiefs' case for the Super had the ironic consequence of undermining the "all eggs in one basket" aspect of SAC's strategic bombing posture by raising the possibility of a diversion of resources to nonstrategic targets.

In December 1949 John Manley set out an extended argument as to the military worth of the "S-bomb." His starting point was that "there are problems of use sufficiently different from those relating to A-bombs that serious questions of significant increase of [the] military worth of S-bombs over [the] equivalent numbers of A-bombs arises [sic]." His paper distinguished carefully between "those considerations which involve matters relating to the weapon itself—its characteristics, how it can be kept in suitable readiness and how it can be used" and "those considerations relating to the value of military power as deterrent to the outbreak of war or as affecting the power of a people to either resist or wage war once an outbreak has occurred."[60] Manley's arguments were directed at rebutting the views of the Joint Chiefs (or the NME—the National Military Establishment—as it had been known) and paid particular attention to the psychological and political aspects that were recognizably the weakest areas of the Joint Chiefs' position.

As to the military utility more narrowly conceived, strategic targets appropriate for attack by an S-bomb would be those of either great area (major cities) or exceptional physical strength.[61] Manley argued that the damage effects of the Super were exaggerated, and that an attempt to maximize the radius of damage would limit the pressure at ground zero to no more than that attainable by a fission bomb, a weapon that also enjoyed flexibility advantages. Moreover, he said, "existing target-vulnerability studies show negligible gain in worth of a weapon as its yield is increased beyond 100 kilotons."[62] Regarding the need for a successful test, "here, again, . . . the NME view appears to lose sight of the objective of comparison between A- and S-bombs."[63]

Deliverability

The utility of any new weapon depends on the ability of the user to apply or deliver it. In the case of the Super, this seemed to have been effectively ruled out by the GAC. While the scientist opponents of the Super framed their case mainly in terms of moral revulsion and military futility, they also expressed a deep skepticism that such a weapon could be delivered to an enemy target. Oppenheimer complained to Conant about the vigorous promotion of the Super mounted by Lawrence and Teller. "I am not sure the miserable thing will work," he complained, "nor that it can be gotten to a target except by ox cart." Oppenheimer's jibe, while perverse, captured the spirit of the GAC's denial of the Super's practicability. The consensus was that even were it feasible to build a thermonuclear bomb, it would be of such size and weight that it would be quite difficult to deliver by air.[64] The physicist Norman F. Ramsey, who as seconded to the Manhattan Project had played a major role in planning the aerial attacks on Japan, and who was still a consultant on atomic matters, recalled feeling that the delivery problem was "a pretty dismal proposition." There was little prospect of such an aircraft being built in the foreseeable future, for, as Ramsey recalled thinking, "it takes a much longer time to develop an airplane than it does at our present rates to develop new bombs. . . . Not only a new airplane but a rather fantastic airplane had to be developed."[65] Those military officers familiar with the research and development continuum were not discouraged. Maj. Gen. David Schlatter, when head of the air force's

Research and Development Command, acknowledged that at one time things appear impossible, other things look certain, and still others fall in between. He was betting on the future with his faith in scientists and aircraft designers to solve the deliverability problem. On taking up his post in 1948 he initiated work to marry the potential weapon and the delivery system.[66]

That the availability of an atomic weapon preceded the availability of a suitable aircraft to carry it was a persistent problem during the early years of the air atomic age. The problem was framed in chicken-and-egg terms: the air force wanted to be able to see the weapon before it would commit to being able to carry it, while the AEC and GAC wanted to get that commitment before proceeding with weapon development. The mismatch of weapon characteristics and carrier capability had bedeviled the B-29 used in the attacks on Hiroshima and Nagasaki. It proved necessary to carry out extensive modifications on these aircraft and on those that followed into service as the air force's strength built up. Code-named Silverplate, the special B-29s were subjected to substantial upgrading, with specific modifications to ensure that the Fat Man atomic bomb and its production versions, the Mark 3-0 and the Mark 4, could be fitted into the very limited space of the bomb bay. This work amounted to some six thousand man hours on each aircraft.[67] In view of these difficulties, the Army Air Forces decided that all new aircraft capable of carrying bombs as heavy as the atomic bomb should be configured so as to be able to carry it.[68]

An improved version of the B-29, later designated the B-50 (possibly because an apparent new aircraft type would strengthen the air force's bargaining position in the budgetary process), was intended to come off the production line ready to carry the bomb. This proved to be an unrealistic expectation. Despite being in many respects a better-developed aircraft, the B-50 experienced major delays in introduction due to the need for remedial work and in many cases the conversion in service to the standard required for carrying the atomic bomb. The reported cost of these postproduction modifications was six thousand man hours, the same figure as required to produce a Silverplate version from the standard B-29.[69] Nevertheless, sufficient progress was made to permit a mass deployment of B-50s, carrying their inert Mark 4 fission weapons, to the United Kingdom at the time of the Korea crisis.

Fat Man, in its original and later improved versions, weighed over ten thousand pounds and was some five feet in diameter and more than ten feet long. Loading it into the aircraft initially required an elaborate provision of a loading pit containing a hydraulic lift, until a more convenient method of loading was devised.[70] The B-29 and B-50 were the only air force aircraft capable of lifting this weapon, and that with some difficulty on anything but the longest runways. Much to the chagrin of air force generals, the navy, eager to stake a claim on this new mode of warfare, established a presence at Kirtland Air Force Base in New Mexico to try out its own AJ-1 aircraft, designed from the outset as an A-bomb carrier.

The prospect of the Super raised the deliverability problem in much more acute form, although the military remained relatively sanguine about the prospects: feasibility needed first to be established to set the parameters for a deliverable weapon.[71] A report of the Long-Range Objectives Panel that Oppenheimer chaired concluded in August 1948 that "since the Superbomb proper will certainly involve extraordinarily difficult problems of delivery, as well as of cryogeny, the panel believes that as a long-term objective design studies for a vehicle capable of delivering such a bomb should be carried out in parallel with the bomb itself."[72] The air force's advice on the development of carriers pointed out that delivery vehicles for the 1954 period, by which date an operational Super was expected, "are essentially limited to equipments already under development. . . . A new weapons system will require a minimum of five years from initiation to beginning of production."[73]

Did this mean that a "fantastic airplane" would have to be developed to carry it? That would depend on the size and weight of the weapon. In that regard, the unknowns were formidable. Whatever trade-off between weight and yield was chosen, it would lead to a heavy and cumbersome weapon. In March 1950, a probable forty-megaton hydrogen bomb was expected to weigh up to forty thousand pounds, with the estimated diameter varying between three and eight feet, and the length between fifteen and thirty feet. Los Alamos assistant technical associate director Harold M. Agnew pointed out that the larger the bomb, the better in efficiency terms.[74]

The problem of constructing a testable device was successfully addressed when Richard Garwin came to Los Alamos in the summer of 1951. His contribution, realized in the Mike test, was to devise a huge sausage-like steel container some twenty feet long and seven feet in diameter within which the entire thermonuclear device was contained, including a vacuum flask–like innermost container with the liquid deuterium, the thermonuclear fuel, maintained at around -249 degrees Celsius by cryogenic plumbing. A fission bomb "detonator" was located at one end of this shape, which, with telemetry and ancillaries, was estimated to weigh around eighty-two tons.[75]

The success of the Mike test, which produced a yield of around ten megatons against the estimated seven, effectively set the parameters for the design of a droppable hydrogen bomb. Size and weight remained a problem, but so too did the orientation of the device, which was a vertical structure. Garwin set out to design what he later called "a deliverable, cryogenic version of Mike that would lie down rather than stand up."[76] In May 1952 guidelines were proposed for the design of a thermonuclear weapon designed on the Teller-Ulam principles. A "recumbent Mike" would have to be within the lifting limits of the B-36, and capable of sustaining forces up to 8 g to cope with turbulence and hard landings. The most severe limit was cryogeny. The deuterium would have to remain frigid once in the air, when separated from the ground-based refrigeration equipment. The device would be known as the TX-16, and an emergency capability committee was established to put it into the national nuclear weapons stockpile as quickly as possible. Three weeks later, on 13 June, the Joint Chiefs formally established the military requirement for thermonuclear weapons. The TX-16 went into development engineering at Los Alamos in June 1952, and the first few "emergency capability" TX-16s were produced in January 1954. Cumbersome and dangerous, only five were built before they were removed from the national stockpile three months later, to be superseded by Mark 17 weapons.[77]

The Mark 17 design, released by Sandia Laboratory in December 1954, was an improved design within similar parameters of size and weight: it was under twenty-five feet long and five feet in diameter and weighed a little under forty-two thousand pounds. Among the design improvements was provision for arming by in-flight insertion. The yield was over thirteen megatons, and the Mark 17 was one of the most powerful nuclear weapons ever built by the United States. It entered the stockpile in March 1955 and was withdrawn in November 1957.[78] This massive weapon, and its predecessor, came close to realizing the doubts of the Super opponents. Yet despite those doubts, it could be carried, if only by the massive B-36, one of which released a Mark 17 accidentally, taking the aircraft's bomb doors with it. And as huge as it was, the B-36 was not the "fantastic airplane" that had been envisaged, the design process having been set in motion as far back as 1941.

Senior air force officers were designated with key roles in the development process. In December 1949, Maj. Gen. Donald L. Putt, former head of the Experimental Bombardment Aircraft Branch during the development of the B-36 and now the director of research and development, set out the considerations that would need to be addressed in finding a more suitable carrier vehicle for a thermonuclear weapon. The first stage visualized the modification of existing aircraft, followed by a "progressively planned deliverability program."[79] The estimates of future nuclear bomb sizes were extremely generous, due to the denial of classified bomb weights and shapes to aircraft designers. As a result, they worked in the dark to design around the largest expectable bombs, while at the same time the bomb designers were working to force size and weight downward. Due to the stringent classification of bomb dimensions in contract proposals, aircraft designers, according to George Lemmer, could never be sure "for more than a few days at a time what the new bomber had to carry." It was painfully clear that the dimensions and weight of what was jocularly described as "the unmentionable device" were as variable as anything else.[80]

In the interim, the air force had to make do with the only possible match of weapon and carrier. B-36 drops of TX-14 ballistic shapes weighing up to fifty thousand pounds had begun at Kirtland in advance of TX-14 procurement, and the first trial model TX-14 began testing there in May 1953. Loading and drop tests started soon afterward. The modifications envisaged by Major General Putt were not extensive. B-36 bomb bay racks and fittings were adapted from equipment once used for the air force's postwar experimental forty-four-thousand-pound high-explosive blockbuster bomb. In June 1948 a B-36 dropped seventy-two-thousand-pound bombs on flight test to demonstrate the aircraft's vast lifting capacity, of which the maximum bomb load was eighty-six thousand pounds.[81]

The much smaller B-47 medium bomber could carry a maximum bomb load of twenty-five thousand pounds, the weight that had been determined as the practical maximum without compromising range and speed. The B-47 was originally designed to fly weapons over twenty-five feet long, but this requirement was overgenerous. In due course the bomb bay would be redesigned, shortened to about fifteen feet, and the saving used to increase fuel capacity—and hence improve the aircraft's range.[82] The new weapon that permitted this reduction in the requirement was the Mark 15 bomb, which became the mainstay of US thermonuclear power in the early years. The difficult problems of cryogeny had been bypassed by the development of "dry" thermonuclear technology, enabling massive reductions in size and weight. The breakthrough had been realized by the Castle test series in March–May 1954, in which the cumbersome cryogenic apparatus was made redundant by the replacement of liquid deuterium by lithium deuteride.[83]

Table 3 Examples of nuclear weapons' weight and yield

Weapon	Year	Weight in lbs	Yield in kilotons	Lbs/kiloton
Atomic bombs				
"Little Boy"	1945	9,700	15	647.0
"Fat Man"	1945	10,300	21	490.5
Mark 4	1949	10,800	31	348.0
Mark 5	1952	3,175	120	26.5
Mark 6	1951	8,500	160	53.0
Mark 12	1954	1,200	12	100.0
Thermonuclear bombs				
TX-14	1954	29,000	6,900	4.2
Mark 17	1954	42,000	13,500	3.1
Mark 15	1955	7,600	3,400	2.2

Source: Polmar and Norris, U.S. Nuclear Arsenal, 36–41, 43–45.

Note: Weight and yield figures are approximate.

The way was now clear for the development of a usable armory of thermonuclear weapons. Just eleven feet and seven inches long, and a mere two feet ten inches in diameter, the Mark 15 weighed a relatively modest 7,600 pounds and was carried by SAC's B-47 and B-52 aircraft and the navy's AJ-1 and AJ-2 carrier-borne strike aircraft. Far from the massive, terrorizing prospect of forty megatons, the Mark 15 delivered a low-megaton yield.[84] Progress continued in the same direction. Bomb diameters in the late 1950s could be as small as eighteen inches, lengths as little as nine and a half feet, and weights as low as one ton. Bombs of this size were available with yields of a little over one megaton. These weapons were readily carried externally on a range of fighter-bombers, raising the prospect of the employment of thermonuclear weapons on the battlefield.

The success of Operation Castle in March 1954, Lemmer notes, "foreshadowed a complete revamping of the national nuclear stockpile."[85] The tests convinced skeptics that thermonuclear weapons were practical, and by early 1956 thermonuclear weapons smaller than anything conceived two years earlier were being produced.[86] These dramatic shifts in size and weight were not foreseen in 1948–50, when work to resolve the carrier problem started on the basis that, as Brig. Gen. Roscoe Wilson argued in 1950, "the development of the H-bomb and the carrier must proceed hand in hand."[87] The B-47 was confirmed as the most appropriate carrier, to be operational by the time the feasibility tests of the weapon had been completed. By 1954, aircraft then in the early stages of development, such as the B-52, could be equipped for the carrier mission. A radically new aircraft, no longer needed, might have cost $50 million.

Air force officers recognized that the deliverability problem was not restricted to lift capability. The critics of the Super project held that it was not deliverable by air, as even if it proved possible to lift it, the carrier vehicle would be annihilated in the blast from a multimegaton bomb. It was beyond argument that the aircraft, in addition to having sufficient range and altitude to reach the target, should ideally be capable of delivering the weapon while escaping its own destruction in the blast. The B-29s used at Hiroshima and Nagasaki had employed a steep turn of 155 degrees after release and, though buffeted, survived. The blast from a megaton weapon, while limited to the cube root of the increase in yield, would still be many times that of the early fission weapons and could not be avoided as readily.

The initial position of the air force was to insist that all methods of delivery should be assessed. Maj. Gen. Sam Anderson, director of plans and operations, pointed out that the likely lethal radius of the bomb appeared to rule out final delivery to a target by means of a conventional bomber and crew. One alternative would be an unmanned drone aircraft guided by a mother aircraft that would stay outside the lethal range of the bomb. Another would be some form of missile, although major missile developments were still some ways in the future and no missile in the surface-to-surface guided missile program was judged to be sufficiently advanced to be given consideration as a possible carrier of the first-phase thermonuclear weapon.[88]

Adaptation for air launch of some soon-to-be-available missiles might be a possibility for standoff operation. But given the importance of weight considerations, which would be critical for missiles, "the pilotless aircraft seems the most feasible means of delivery . . . of the 'Super,'" Anderson wrote.[89] Lt. Gen. Kenneth B. Wolfe, air force deputy chief of staff for materiel, did not agree, believing that a piloted aircraft should be able to drop an H-bomb and turn away in comparative safety. As far as the B-47 was concerned, General Wolfe maintained that thrust could be added to increase its turning speed and that there should be some way to reduce the speed of the H-bomb's descent in order to increase the carrier's margin of safety.[90]

Two special studies were then set in motion. Caucasian was a project to equip the TX-14 with a parachute, enabling weapons up to forty megatons in yield to be delivered by an aircraft—the B-36 was the only option—that would escape to a safe distance as the slowed bomb made its way to the target. Another study was set up to determine the effectiveness of an unmanned drone attacker, a technique that had been developed, with scant success, using B-17s against German targets during World War II. Brass Ring was a study of the feasibility of drone B-47s as high-yield H-bomb carriers.[91] Given the uncertainties and the other obvious disadvantages of the unmanned drone, attention was paid to the option of an air-launched missile. None existed at that stage, although the air force was in due course to carry a formidable range of air-to-ground missiles, including the Hound Dog with a one-megaton warhead. By mid-1952, Brass Ring reached a dead end as initial testing had shown the B-36 could deliver a parachute-equipped H-bomb about as accurately as a conventional bomb. Moreover, if a B-47 were to carry out the operation, as General Wolfe anticipated, the degree of safety would be more than adequate due to the aircraft's superior speed.[92]

Discussion of these options could not be kept out of the press, as the security net thrown over the Super controversy continued to prove remarkably porous. In early January 1950 the Alsops returned to their theme of explaining the Super to their readers, revealing on this occasion that so far as deliverability was concerned, "the most talked-about design is a stripped-down, pilotless jet bomber capable of several thousand miles of flight, at just subsonic speeds and at very high altitudes."[93]

The failure to stop the Mike test was a turning point in the campaign against the Super. Its feasibility as a weapon remained in doubt for a while, then it proved that even the first gigantic weapons could be married to an existing aircraft with surprisingly little difficulty. Within the space of a very few years, the objection that a thermonuclear weapon would be so large as to be undeliverable had been conclusively dismissed. The ground had decisively shifted under the feet of the initial dissidents. The argument now moved to new territory, on which not the weapon itself, but the use to which it might be put was contested. The rationale of the US defense posture in a thermonuclear age now came to the fore as the ground on which disputes would center.

Tactical Diversions

By mid-1950 the Super controversy was already moving on from in-principle opposition to thermonuclear weapons to the question of how and where they might be deployed. Up to that point, much of the principled opposition had been expressed in a smokescreen argument about feasibility and opportunity cost, notably the tritium cost of plutonium foregone. Now the center of gravity of the argument moved from scientific speculation to strategic doctrine.

Such a move raised the political stakes considerably, as the US strategic posture was by that time firmly embedded in the doctrine of strategic bombardment, made manifest in the form of Strategic Air Command, the dominant force within the US Air Force. For Oppenheimer and the Super dissidents to enter the argument about strategic nuclear bombardment was to implicitly challenge the role and existence of SAC, air force policy, and the formerly settled issue of the allocation of nuclear primacy to the air force at the expense of the army and navy. In particular, the specious claim that SAC would concentrate on counterforce targets (military) rather than countervalue targets (centers of industry and governance) cut little ice with critics who recognized that nuclear, and especially thermonuclear, bombs were inherently indiscriminate. But these were dangerous waters. No longer a matter of scientific controversy, where being on the losing side of an argument would have few consequences, opposition to the Super would now become a high-risk game of bureaucratic politics.

The Doctrine of Strategic Bombardment

Debates about strategic aerial bombardment accompanied the emergence of the airplane as a weapon of war. During World War I, the US Army Air Service regarded strategic bombing as a way of bypassing trench warfare. Col. Edgar S. Gorrell, head of the strategic aviation section of the American Expeditionary Forces, argued that instead of bloody ground attacks, the way to defeat the German Army was to destroy the factories that made its weapons: after such a bombardment, the "manufacturing works would be wrecked and the morale of the workmen would be shattered."[1] Even at that stage, then, there was ambiguity about the proposed target: was it the industrial structure itself, or the people who manned it?

Other thinkers bypassed this awkwardness to advocate the unrestricted bombing of civilian populations, a proposal indelibly associated with the Italian theorist Giulio Douhet and, in the United States, with the air power advocate Billy Mitchell. In seeking to establish a doctrine for this new mode of conflict, they advocated "total war," with high-explosive bombing followed by incendiaries and rounded off with poison gas to hamper the rescuers.[2] This approach did not become embedded in US doctrine as taught at the Army Air Corps Tactical School, where Douhet's writings were ignored and Mitchell was a prophet without honor. The accepted approach was instead one of precision bombing of those industrial assets that would have a "multiplier" effect: ball bearing factories and oil plants.[3] This came to be known as "industrial web theory."[4] Mitchell continued to dissent, arguing that the necessary precision could not be attained, and that cities should be the targets.[5] Admittedly, the necessary precision would be hard to attain, and the doctrine of precision bombing was little more than aspirational. According to Lynn Eden,

> To be effective, this doctrine required the ability to understand which target systems were indeed vital, to locate crucial enemy structures within that target system, and to deliver the proper weapons accurately to small targets. Yet all of these capabilities were weak before and during World War II.[6]

In January 1943, the US and British war leaders meeting at Casablanca resolved that strategic bombing would be a war-winning weapon, using long-range bombers to achieve the destruction and dislocation of the German military, industrial, and economic system, and undermine the morale of the German people "to a point where their capacity for armed resistance is fatally weakened."[7] Defeating Germany was given priority over dealing with Japan, and by August 1941, war planners defined the US Army Air Forces strategy against Germany in terms of 154 key targets in four economic areas. Area bombing was not ruled out, but was considered useful only after war-supporting industry was destroyed and the enemy realized the war was lost. There was an important caveat: if people in the targeted cities were already demoralized by a belief that the war was lost, then the bombing of cities could crush civilian morale. But if this condition did not exist, bombing would stiffen resistance.[8]

After World War II, the air force manual *Strategic Air Operations* continued that approach, emphasizing the interdependence of modern urban-industrial societies, where the "interweaving" of the urban fabric would, under sustained aerial attack on "vital centers," lead to the progressive collapse of economy and society. This was the presumed "strategic" effect of long-range bombing campaigns.[9] But the findings of the post–VE Day Strategic Bombing Survey concluded that, to the contrary, the decisive blow had been the bombing of Germany's transportation network. Careful assessment demonstrated just how limited had been the effects of the area bombing campaign relative to precision attacks.[10] That lesson was not extended to the final assault on Japan when, over Brig. Gen. Haywood Hansell's protests, precision bombing was hurriedly abandoned in favor of overwhelming area bombing with incendiaries. While precision bombing would regain favor in the limited regional conflicts of the post–Cold War era, as technology made precision weapons possible, the high level of civilian suffering occasioned by the firebombings and the atomic bombings left a lasting stigma on the doctrine of strategic bombardment.

The coming of what has been termed the "air-atomic age" called into question the established approach to strategic bombardment. Sustained bombing over a period of time was unlikely to be needed. For George Kennan, the prospect of even quite limited attacks using atomic bombs would be more than sufficient to deter Soviet leaders. Even without expansion of the atomic bomb program and the inclusion of thermonuclear weapons, he said, "there is a possibility that what we already had would have been enough. . . . I have felt that the Soviet Union was fairly vulnerable to this type of bombing due to the high degree of concentration of its industrial strength in the individual plants."[11] Before the prospect of the thermonuclear bomb arose, Bernard Brodie had criticized the air force planners' stubborn adherence to historical experience: the atomic bomb did not permit a simple extrapolation from the past. Now, with the Super, the logic of strategic targeting was crumbling. "Ties with the past, tenuous enough at best," Brodie wrote, "were immediately threatened by the appearance of the modern type of thermonuclear bomb."[12]

Even with the limited stockpile of 1949–50, the air force was confident of its ability to inflict crucial damage on the Soviet Union through its air offensive, although this confidence was not shared by all the service chiefs or by the first secretary of defense, James Forrestal. When Louis Johnson replaced him in early 1949, the balance tilted decisively in favor of the air force, although there was no real consensus as to the effectiveness of strategic atomic bombing as it was then conceived.[13] While strategic versus tactical attack was a key distinction for war planners, strategic bombardment was not an undifferentiated concept. Especially as more—and more types—of nuclear weapons entered the stockpile, the distinction between countervalue and counterforce became a hotly contested issue.[14]

While official announcements might emphasize counterforce targeting, the details of SAC's Emergency War Plans were settled in Omaha, Nebraska—where SAC was headquartered, near the geographic center of the United States—not the Pentagon. This arose from the unique status SAC enjoyed as a "specified command," reporting directly to the Joint Chiefs of Staff and enjoying the widest control over functions and strategic assets.[15] Although counterforce targeting gained favor as an official doctrine as the 1950s wore on, in actuality SAC continued to select for their aiming points industrial and governmental centers. The goal was not only to incapacitate the Soviet Union's military machine in one swift blow, but at the same time, in keeping with time-honored doctrine, to destroy the enemy's will and ability to continue or resume hostilities.[16] Once nuclear weapons became more plentiful, the SAC plan was to use them, with crushing force, from the outset. A driving consideration at the time was how to make the most effective use of the limited stock of atomic weapons. Due to the great cost and scarcity of fissionable material, atomic weapons were expected to remain relatively few in number and were reserved to achieve the maximum damage.[17] Supply constraints dictated a countervalue strategy in which, according to Stephen McFarland, "cities were the only useful targets."[18] In mid-1950, SAC was prepared for immediate strikes on 60 of 123 listed industrial centers. Strikes against the remainder awaited better target reconnaissance. The initial attack plan was for the Soviet borders to be penetrated simultaneously by two major forces attacking from the northwest and southwest, using two hundred UK-based B-29 and B-50 medium bombers and ten B-36s flying from the Zone of the Interior—the US mainland. Of the medium bombers, only one in a formation would carry an atomic weapon.[19]

The effectiveness of this strategy was not unquestioned, even within air force circles. In February 1949 the Joint Chiefs appointed a board of senior officers to examine that question, choosing US Air Force Lt. Gen. Hubert R. Harmon as chair. Harmon and his team visited SAC headquarters in Omaha, and sought briefings on targeting plans, aircraft availability, crew training, and performance. Curtis LeMay objected to Harmon's questions, but air force chief of staff Hoyt Vandenberg warned him that "we cannot afford to be hypersensitive when we are questioned about our capabilities."[20]

The Harmon report, *Evaluation of Effect on Soviet War Effort Resulting from the Strategic Air Offensive*, presented in May 1949, cast doubts on the effectiveness of the prevailing doctrine of strategic bombardment, even given the generous assumption that SAC could fly all its missions and deliver atomic weapons on the designated targets with the claimed accuracy. The Harmon board also had to assume a sufficiency of atomic weapons, an untestable assumption given the tight security surrounding the stockpile.[21] The board concluded that the atomic offensive "would probably affect the war effort, and produce psychological effects upon the Soviet will to wage war." Between 30 and 40 percent of Soviet industrial production would be neutralized for a period, depending on Soviet recuperative powers, although certain key industries, including petroleum, would be particularly hard hit. Harmon judged that notwithstanding the assumed success of the air offensive, the attack would not result in the collapse of Communism or the power of the Soviet leadership, and Soviet forces would still overrun most of Europe, the Middle East, and the Far East.[22] When the report was presented, Vandenberg submitted the air force's dissenting opinion to the secretary of defense, claiming far greater impact for the offensive.[23]

The issues got a second run with the launch of a further study of the bombing plans by the Weapon Systems Evaluation Group (WSEG), in a report that became known as WSEG-1 or the Hull report, named after the WSEG director, Lt. Gen. John E. Hull of the army. While the purpose of the Harmon report was to assess the results of the Emergency War Plan, assuming the plan worked as expected, the Hull report's purpose was to judge whether SAC was actually capable of executing the plan. The WSEG was established in December 1948 to provide multiservice analytical support for the Joint Chiefs and the secretary of defense. Its principal task was to apply scientific and technical expertise to the evaluation of discrete weapons systems, and the group's initial program reflected a set of urgent needs for guidance, several of them dealing with the future potential of guided weapons. However, air force director of plans and operations Maj. Gen. Sam Anderson seized the opportunity to insist that the WSEG should reevaluate the projected success of the strategic bombing offensive, pushing it to the top of the agenda, despite the topic seeming far broader than the initial remit of the group.[24]

Truman, the cabinet, the Joint Chiefs, and the service secretaries were briefed on the report on 23 January 1950. It estimated that between 70 and 85 percent of the bombers would reach their targets, but of these, only 50–70 percent would return, a very high loss rate compared with that written into SAC's first Emergency War Plan. Moreover, due to poor bombing accuracy, only 50–67 percent of the industrial targets hit would be damaged beyond repair.[25]

The Hull report also noted additional deficiencies in SAC's capabilities: aerial refueling was not fully operational and the overseas bases were not yet developed. This was certainly true of the vital SAC-deployed bases in Britain, which fell under the control, not of SAC, but of the Third Air Division of US Air Force Europe. In repeated inspections they were frequently deemed to be far from combat ready. The WSEG concluded that as plans for conventional attack were of such limited likely impact, they should be shelved in favor of dependence on atomic weapons.[26] The effect of the Harmon and Hull reports in combination cast doubt on whether the proposed strategic bombing plan could be considered likely to be decisive. By one subsequent calculation, these atomic attacks would cause less industrial damage to the Soviets than the Germans did when they invaded the Soviet Union during World War II.[27]

During this period, SAC's stance, as expressed in the annually revised Emergency War Plan, would follow technological change in a move from traditional high-explosive precision bombing of industrial assets to population targeting with atomic weapons. Initial Air Staff targeting plans in fall 1946 had assumed only conventional bombs, as planners had no information on stockpile numbers or the production rate. Those plans had stressed avoiding population attacks and targeting war-making capacity. But by early 1947, the Air War Plans Division emphasized atomic attacks against "large industrial centers." Subsequent targeting studies for the first Emergency War Plan noted the co-location of a number of industrial targets in the seventy largest urban areas, to be targeted by 133 atomic bombs. Air force planners now began to consider hitting cities in a way that would not only destroy industry but have the "bonus" of killing the area's population. But by the time of Emergency War Plan 1–49 in late 1948, the bonus had become the main goal; aim points were selected with the "primary objective of the annihilation of [the urban-industrial] population, with industrial targets incidental."[28]

With the Super in prospect, war planning had come to follow, rather than lead, technological possibilities. Using large-yield weapons to attack countervalue strategic targets, cities, and industrial complexes played to SAC's capabilities. Equally, thermonuclear weapons, with their greater destructive power, compensated for SAC's principal weakness, the inability to hit specific targets with an acceptable degree of accuracy. The effective weapon radius for the most developed version of the Fat Man bomb (the Mark 4) was five thousand feet, and the best B-50 performance rendered a CEP (circular error probable—a measure of bombing accuracy relating to the likelihood of 50 percent of the bombs falling within a defined radius) of three thousand feet. LeMay assured his fellow commanders shortly before the outbreak of the Korean conflict, "We are confident that targets can be accurately bombed."[29] LeMay was eager to acquire the Super. Once available, it would enable his command to ensure the destruction of targets that he could not be certain of destroying with the prevailing standards of bombing accuracy.

These issues came up again with a later WSEG report in 1954, known as WSEG-10. This report provided some endorsement of SAC's targeting plan, observing that the alternative, attacks against military targets such as troop concentrations, while of some immediate value, would not be lasting or conclusive. On the other hand, without destruction of the Soviet urban industrial sector, the WSEG-10 report said, "Russia could support *immense* armed forces for at least two years of intensive warfare." As to targets, and despite the counterforce orientation of SAC's war plans, the WSEG concluded that the best chance of success was to concentrate its bombardment "against the civic-political structure of the interior of Russia," acknowledging that the suffering inflicted on civilians would be substantial.[30] A rejoinder drafted for air force chief of staff Gen. Nathan A. Twining argued that the group had failed to fully understand the intentions of the SAC targeting plan. They not taken into account the higher-yield fission bombs now in stock, or the number that would soon become available. Nor did the report consider the impact of thermonuclear weapons soon to enter the stockpile.[31]

Others were less confident of SAC's claims. Bombing accuracy was one such area of obscurity. After an unsatisfactory discussion of the subject with LeMay, the air force scientific staff—assistant for development planning Ivan Getting and chief scientist Louis N. Ridenour—resolved in June 1951 to establish an independent review. Ridenour was apparently in a strong position to take this questioning further.[32] In 1944 Hap Arnold had set up under the physicist Theodore von Kármán a scientific advisory group, a body whose status was formalized as the Scientific Advisory Board in 1946. When in 1949 Vandenberg asked for a review of air force research and development, Ridenour, a young physicist and radar specialist, was assigned to lead the process. The Ridenour report, delivered in September of that year, recommended the establishment of a separate Air Research and Development Command and a new Air Staff deputy chief of staff for research and development. In accordance with Ridenour's advice, Vandenberg established the Air Research and Development Command under Maj. Gen. David M. Schlatter early in 1950, and appointed Ridenour as the first chief scientist of the air force.[33]

Acting on their own initiative, Getting and Ridenour agreed to approach Oppenheimer as the only man with the "integrity, reputation, and stature" to undertake a "comprehensive study for SAC . . . with an understanding of national objectives, major strategic concepts, et cetera." Offered the role by Ridenour, Oppenheimer readily agreed to lead a review of SAC's strategic bombing capabilities. It was not a wise move, as Getting recalled:

> Ridenour came back to my office looking pale as a ghost. He reported that when he had given the good news to General Vandenberg, the general had immediately ushered him into the office of [Air Force] Secretary [Thomas] Finletter, saying "Tell him what you told me!" According to Louis, somewhat amazed by the fast turn of events, Louis again reported his success in enlisting Oppie to help the air force on a strategic study. After a moment of silence, the secretary was reported as saying that under no circumstances was Oppenheimer to have access to air force classified information and certainly none having to do with AF strategic targeting policies and plans.[34]

Abstruse issues of strategy were no longer the property of planners at the Pentagon and SAC headquarters. Military proponents and scientific opponents of the Super were locked together in this "socialization" of nuclear strategy, in which the unthinkable consequences of general war electrified scholars, journalists, and concerned citizens alike. Paul Nitze had led the fundamental review of US strategy that accompanied the decision to proceed with the Super. The result, in NSC-68, was a powerful case for diminishing US dependence on nuclear weapons by building up conventional forces at considerable cost. Against the background of the Korean conflict that report proved a turning point.

Later, for the attention of the incoming Eisenhower administration, the soon-to-depart Nitze would express his doubt that SAC's approach would be appropriate for anything other than a response to an attack on the United States itself.[35] However, the post-NSC-68 balance of conventional and nuclear forces was overturned with the adoption of Eisenhower's New Look strategy. As the United States was faced with the evidently increasing capabilities of a nuclear Soviet Union and pressures on the US budget, a stronger emphasis was placed on SAC and the massive nuclear attack, which, according to Elliott Converse, "solidified the Air Force's position, already apparent during the Truman administration, as the nation's first line of defense."[36] Henceforth, aggression would be met by massive response with nuclear weapons "at times and places of our choosing." Addressing the NSC in March 1953, Eisenhower maintained that "somehow or other the taboo which surrounds the use of atomic weapons would have to be destroyed," and in May 1953, when discussing the use of them in Korea, he said, "We have got to consider the atomic bomb as simply another weapon in the arsenal." In October 1953, NSC 162/2 removed an uncertainty that the Joint Chiefs had faced during the Truman years by stating, "In the event of hostilities, the United States will consider nuclear weapons to be as available for use as other munitions." The New Look was an "all eggs in one basket" strategy of massive retaliation.[37]

There still remained the hope, burning bright in some quarters, that conflict with the Soviet Union need not lead to a general war, with its mutually punishing exchange of nuclear weapons. With Europe the expected site of a conventional attack from the East, the tactical, or battlefield, use of nuclear weapons might buy time and serve to avert Armageddon.

Tactical Possibilities for the Super?

Using the first atomic bombs tactically against Japanese troop concentrations had been briefly contemplated in 1945, when Gen. George C. Marshall feared that the bombing of the cities had failed to produce the desired surrender, and invasion would still be necessary.[38] Thereafter, little consideration was given to the deployment of weapons specifically for tactical purposes until 1949. That year, the GAC had proposed that more resources be given to smaller, lighter weapons. In October 1949 the NSC special committee reported on the acceleration of the AEC program as recommended by the Joint Chiefs in July of that year. Consideration by the Joint Chiefs had extended awareness of the range of possible uses of atomic weapons, including their use against relatively small targets. Gathering concern about the defense of Western Europe turned attention to what the Joint

Chiefs called the "swift and tremendous striking power" of atomic weapons, including the development of smaller, lighter bombs.[39] Recognizing that this would increase demand for fissionable material, the Joint Chiefs placed their faith in the greater efficiency that was now promised in weapon development. The AEC, for its part, considered it feasible to meet these increased military requirements, while the State Department deemed the proposed expansion "not untimely" in light of Soviet developments. The additional capital costs were estimated at $267 million.[40]

In terms of battlefield use, the obstacle was discovering safe, accurate means of delivery. The WSEG certainly considered the battlefield uses of a thermonuclear weapon, and in 1950 it produced a study on the use of the atomic bomb on tactical targets—troop concentrations, air bases, naval bases, naval task forces, and heavily fortified positions. A key figure was US Army Maj. Gen. James "Jumpin' Jim" Gavin, who, on being posted to the WSEG, was assigned to review the possible use of nuclear weapons in the tactical setting.

The iconoclastic Gavin wrote an extensive report and convinced himself that the case was made for tactical deployment of small-yield atomic bombs, although he was informally warned off pursuing a line that at that time was contrary to air force policy.[41] The other services did have their general positions. The army awoke slowly to the questionable value of atomic artillery on the battlefield, while naval officers tended to regard the bombing of civilian targets as anathema and contrary to their professional ethos, forged as it was in an era of ship-on-ship warfare. Gavin discovered that the idea of tactical nuclear weapons was not widely accepted in the army either, and he had difficulty getting clearance to publish his ideas. He remarked to Schilling that talking about tactical atomic use in those days was like talking about interplanetary travel—difficult for anyone to take seriously.[42]

Schilling was surprised to find that Gavin, who enjoyed enormous respect as a combat leader, nevertheless had a reflective style of discussion (unlike the orderly verbal tracking that other generals he interviewed showed), with "a slight tendency to sort of take off on stream of consciousness conversation."[43] When the Super controversy arose, Gavin recalled arguing that the issue was not whether SAC was right or wrong in its commitment to all-out strategic bombardment, but that the United States might, by proceeding down that path, get caught in the wrong (regional) war and be unable to produce enough tactical atomic weapons quickly. He doubted that the Soviets would mount their aggression in a way that presented the United States with many suitable strategic targets. He was thus one of the key progenitors of tactical nuclear use, and on a favorable view his work represented what Maj. Edward P. Gavin calls "a significant step towards improving the nation's ability to win limited wars."[44] In that respect he was unwittingly in accord with the view expressed by the General Advisory Committee that efforts should be intensified to make atomic weapons available for tactical purposes, with priority given to integrating bomb and carrier design.[45]

Reviewing the possible uses of the Super, Sam Anderson made the delicate observation that SAC's plan "permits very little cushion for diverting part of its forces to other than strategic targets such as retarding the advance of Soviet ground armies"—something that Curtis LeMay regarded as a fatal misuse of his forces. For tactical deployment, the Super had advantages and disadvantages. Deployed against enemy troops massed for an attack or breakthrough, it could destroy an entire army or force the adversary to change his tactical dispositions. The corresponding disadvantage of the Super was that use in such a setting would involve the destruction of a large proportion of a friendly civilian population.[46]

In 1950, as scientific effort to develop the Super began to gather pace, the outbreak of the Korean conflict had the effect of shifting short-term attention from strategic bombardment to tactical air warfare, sidelining the potential of the Super in the minds of some. Planners considered the possibility that Korea was but a feint that could presage an opportunistic Soviet attack in Europe, and thirty atomic bombs, less their fissionable cores, were transferred to the air force bases in the United Kingdom for use if required in SAC's strategic bombardment campaign.[47]

Lunching with Brien McMahon and other officials in July 1951, Secretary of Defense George C. Marshall was treated to enthusiastic advocacy of lightweight nuclear weapons being used tactically in any future conflict in the European theater.[48] Korea focused minds on what the atomic bomb might achieve there. Speaking in the Senate, Henry Cabot Lodge advocated a defensive line of atomic bomb craters across the peninsula, after warnings had been given to civilians.[49] Meanwhile, Gavin led a visit to Korea to study the problems of air support to ground operations and became convinced that the use of the atomic bomb in Korea should not be ruled out. That he made little headway was attributable in part to the army's unwillingness to consider the potential of atomic weapons. Army leaders had been effectively shut out of the debate after a Forrestal-led conference of the Joint Chiefs in Key West in 1948, intended to clarify the roles and missions of the services. At that conference, primacy in nuclear attack was conceded to the air force (although the navy was not to be denied the use of the A-bomb against specific targets associated with its mission).[50] When, in 1953, President Eisenhower seriously considered the use of the atomic bomb to break the deadlock in Korea, army chief of staff Gen. J. Lawton Collins resisted on the grounds of its ineffectiveness against troops well dug in.[51]

Gavin ploughed a lonely furrow, publishing as extensively as he was permitted. Writing in the *Combat Forces Journal* in November 1950, he reflected on his work on the WSEG and on his visit to Korea, arguing pragmatically that the tactical use of the atomic bomb could make a major contribution if employed "whenever it is possible to deliver it profitably."[52] In a later article Gavin represented the army as able to use atomic weapons to defeat an enemy force without "destroying the foundations upon which a firm and lasting peace can be built at the cessation of hostilities," a clear dig at SAC's reported aim of leaving the Soviet cities "a smoking, radiating ruin at the end of two hours."[53] Gavin was personally opposed to strategic bombing of the cities and believed that the availability of thermonuclear weapons would make "massive retaliation" even more destructive.[54] It was a mark of Gavin's unique standing among nuclear scientists that the *Bulletin of the Atomic Scientists* reprinted his paper of November 1950, citing him as the only prominent military expert looking at uses of the atomic bomb other than strategic ones.[55] Following his resignation from the army, Gavin elaborated his arguments in a book, *War and Peace in the Space Age*, a project he was working on when Schilling interviewed him. In this book he recalled that

> the feeling was beginning to grow that the more dangerous problem ahead of us was not general nuclear war, but limited war, either nuclear or non-nuclear. Europe, also, was on people's minds and for the first time we began to feel that unless something were done we might well lose Europe.[56]

Strategic bombardment was anathema to many scientists, more so with the prospect of thermonuclear weapons being used in that role. Gavin was an invaluable ally.

Project Vista

A lone campaigner has limited impact. What transformed the debate was the creation of a formal joint military-university study group embracing all three services, which ensured that SAC could no longer monopolize the argument. Air force planners were themselves conflicted about the allocation of nuclear resources between strategic and tactical uses. The impetus for this review came from Ivan Getting and Louis Ridenour, who it is said buttonholed Lee DuBridge, Caltech president and GAC member, in a chance meeting. Ridenour urged a series of partnership projects with leading universities, proposing that Caltech might undertake a policy study of either strategic or tactical air. A number of meetings followed, and the Caltech group, according to DuBridge, who had come under pressure to accept the project, reached the conclusion that they were neither possessed of the expertise to evaluate, nor greatly interested in, strategic air. However, the tactical air problem, particularly the problem of close support of ground troops, "was more nearly in line with our interests, and the group agreed to give the matter further thought."[57]

So was launched Project Vista, led by DuBridge, who gathered around him like-minded scientists, providing a forum for the "nuclear mafia."[58] On the GAC, DuBridge himself had opposed the hydrogen bomb, and several Caltech scientists, including Charles Lauritsen and William A. Fowler, shared strong reservations about all three aspects of thermonuclear warfare—the development of the science, the dangers of nuclear testing, and the large-scale bombing of Soviet cities.[59] Along with these critics, Robert Bacher would lead the special weapons part of the study. At a late stage, Oppenheimer, who shared these views, joined the group and became the dominant influence in what amounted to a challenge to the established air force doctrine of strategic bombardment. Oppenheimer drafted the controversial fifth chapter of the report.

Fowler served as research director for the project and, according to Getting, "immediately proceeded to alienate every air force officer who tried to help."[60] Fowler later recalled that "all of us were rather opposed to strategic bombing, that is, to a complete dependence on SAC and were determined to acquaint the DOD with the fact that there were other ways of defending Europe."[61] Another member of the team explained that by this they meant that the department "had not yet realized what the potentialities of the atomic weapon were, and hence were riding the initial horse of nothing but the strategic air use of the weapon, and failing to capitalize on other uses."[62] Another physicist, Norman F. Ramsey, a long-standing member of the Air Force Scientific Advisory Board, pointed up the key issue of "how to cut the pie":

The problem was from the Air Force point of view how can you support ground troops and again what fraction of your money should go to that kind of a weapon. The all out strategic people would argue that the only way to do [it] is by strategic bombing, and don't waste your money on tactical support.[63]

DuBridge had played the bureaucratic politics of the situation well by ensuring that the project had a base in all three services, rather than allowing it to become an air force project. This was a distinct gain for the army, which provided the resources to manage the project. It tapped into the ongoing debate about how close air support should be provided, where it had been the characteristic army view that commanders on the ground ought to be able to call in the support they needed, as and when they needed it. This position had long been opposed by Vandenberg, both as the general commanding the Ninth Air Force in Europe following D-Day and currently as air force chief of staff.[64] Vandenberg held a balanced view, opposing Project Vista's excessive emphasis on tactical air power at the expense of SAC. According to the biographer Phillip Meilinger, Vandenberg "sniffed a plot" to shift the balance of atomic power from the air force in favor of the army, and after

Vista directed that Oppenheimer be banned from participating in all future air force projects.[65]

Notwithstanding the air force–army dispute over the operation of close air support, the landscape was already changing with the possibility of lighter, low-yield weapons entering the stockpile. As early as October 1949 the GAC—under Oppenheimer's chairmanship—had urged that more attention be given to the development of smaller tactical nuclear weapons, widening the possibilities of battlefield use. For the Vista group, US superiority in the production of such weapons "may make the difference between victory and defeat in Europe during the period 1951 through 1955."[66] Robert Bacher explained that

> one of the things that could really be brought to bear on the problem of keeping [the] Russians out of Western Europe was the tactical employment of atomic weapons. We felt at that time that we had a sufficient stockpile of atomic weapons that utilization in this field was both possible and appropriate and that it would be a great advantage to our military strength to do this. . . . On the question of allocation of weapons to tactical use . . . there existed, or was about to exist . . . means by which the essential components of the bomb could be made available for one type or another quite readily.[67]

The Vista report continued, "Two main tasks are clearly foreseen. These are the use of atomic bombs in counter air operations against the airfields of the USSR in Eastern Europe and satellite countries, and the use of similar weapons in support of ground actions." The need to achieve air superiority gave targeting priority to enemy air bases where fifty airfields, mostly in East Germany, would be attacked with one hundred atomic bombs at the start of a conflict. The goal would be to offset NATO's lesser numbers in aircraft. Other targets would be forward supply depots, important command headquarters, and troop concentrations behind enemy lines. Warheads in the one-to-fifty-kiloton range were proposed, and, most provocatively, the group recommended the creation of a Tactical Atomic Air Force with priority for the procurement of aircraft personnel and equipment.[68]

In making their policy recommendations, the DuBridge group had added fuel to the interservice argument over roles and missions. The proposal in the Vista report that SAC could be placed under the operational control of commanders in the European theater was inflammatory. So too was the proposal of full partnership of the army and an expanded role for the navy. As a consequence of their forthright stand against elements in the air force, the architects of Project Vista earned the enmity of some key figures in the leadership of that service.[69] At SAC, Curtis LeMay's position was one of entrenched resistance to the diversion of atomic resources from his medium bomber force, although a further WSEG study (no. 12) would again cast doubt on SAC's ability to achieve its strategic bombardment objectives, in this case in relation to the neutralization of the Soviet bombers' retaliatory capability. On the tactical weapons issue, the air force was adamant that "the allocation of additional atomic weapons to troop targets is not warranted at the expense of weapons required to gain air superiority," and that "the outcome of the ground battle is contingent upon the outcome of the air battles."[70]

On 12 November 1951, at a Vista conference at Caltech, DuBridge presented a preliminary draft of the group's proposed report, including the summary and conclusions that Oppenheimer had written. On 21 November, Oppenheimer had lunch with Air Force Secretary Finletter, with William Burden (Finletter's special assistant for R&D) and Garrison Norton (Burden's deputy, and later assistant secretary of the navy) also in attendance. A note of the meeting recorded that

> the VISTA Group conceives of the tactical target system in the light of a campaign dedicated to the defense of Europe and in a situation in which the USSR has not undertaken strategic attack on our cities or on the cities of our allies. Under these circumstances, our strategic capability should be maintained but not applied in the initial phase of war. . . . The deterrent effect of holding our strategic attack in reserve is considered to be decisive in protecting our cities and those of our allies against atomic attack.[71]

The air force reaction was predictably hostile. In an article in *Fortune* magazine taken to reflect air force opinion (and published with no named author), Oppenheimer was portrayed as having "transformed Vista into an exercise for rewriting U.S. strategy, [with] a veiled suggestion that Air Force doctrine was based on the slaughter of civilians."[72] In December, DuBridge, Lauritsen, and Oppenheimer flew to Wiesbaden to meet Eisenhower, and followed with a meeting with his air deputy, Lt. Gen. Lauris Norstad, at his headquarters at Fontainebleau.[73] With Secretary of Defense Robert A. Lovett being quite relaxed about the visit, it was facilitated by one of his assistant secretaries, James Perkins, but when a furious Finletter learned of the visit, he recalled Norstad to Washington to brief him in advance and settle the line to be taken on Vista.[74]

The meeting in France produced a sharp polarization between Norstad, defending existing air force policy, seemingly on instruction from Finletter, and Oppenheimer, who, under pressure, was forced to do some minor redrafting of the report. The wheels had come off Ridenour's project, something he had been warned about by Vandenberg's office.[75] Yet the point of contention was limited. As Norstad recalled, DuBridge brought his core team over to France and insisted that Norstad read a précis of the Vista argument:

> I came down to one point and I screamed—I howled a bit. DuBridge said "I know exactly what you are reading." . . . I said, "Lee, you don't expect me

to accept that, go along with that do you?" He said, "No, that is why I knew you howled." Afterwards, I said, "That sounds like Oppie to me." . . . I talked to Oppie for a while. When I got through talking with him, then I asked DuBridge—and I told DuBridge I was making some progress—to come back in. I said, "Oppie said he is willing to take a crack at rewriting that paragraph. Is that all right?" He said "All right." He said, "Yes, that's a good idea. If Oppie would rewrite it, that would be good." He rewrote it and made it—not the way I would have written it, but it was still acceptable.[76]

Gavin recalled later mentioning the Vista report to Norstad, who "used strong language in his denunciation of it."[77] This was Norstad's public face and reflected air force policy, but his private view of the project was far more benign. Writing to his close friend Charles V. Murphy, an air force reserve colonel who was the author of the controversial *Fortune* article, he recalled,

> As a matter of fact, I was quite impressed with DuBridge and what I considered was an open-minded and objective approach to the study. Further, there was much in the report as I first saw it with which I was in general agreement. . . . I think that the Vista group suffered from the fact that they depended for a great deal of their information on the emotional presentations of highly opinionated experts. The result was a tendency toward extreme and exclusive positions and conclusions. . . . In my two meetings with the group, I thought they showed a great willingness to discuss the matter dispassionately and modify their stated views whenever a good case was made in opposition.[78]

Norstad's generous judgment was not echoed elsewhere. In February 1952, DuBridge, Lauritsen, and Fowler briefed the Joint Chiefs of Staff and a group of high-ranking Pentagon officers, receiving a hostile reception.[79] Finletter refused to release the report in light of the threat it posed to SAC's mission, although its existence and its general conclusions were leaked and became publicly known at the time.[80] DuBridge later recalled that security concerns about the report were such that they led to it being edited by MLC officers for internal consumption, on the grounds that other military personnel were not cleared to read some of their statements on atomic energy.[81] Ridenour's successor as chief scientist, David T. Griggs, was angered by the way that anti–nuclear bombardment scientists had been given a privileged platform. Working with Finletter, Griggs would orchestrate the counterattack to undo the damage done to doctrine by Vista.

The Vista group had found themselves living beyond scientific expertise by venturing into the larger debate on military policy. The Vista report as a whole, and specifically the controversial fifth chapter, sought to ratify policy positions already expressed publicly by Oppenheimer, Vannevar Bush, and

James Conant, although its authors were careful to eschew direct criticism of strategic bombardment.[82] Later, under repeated questioning, Lauritsen emphasized that he personally supported a strong strategic air force, a position he thought was not inconsistent with the Vista arguments, on account of the growing size of the stockpile.[83] The division of roles between tactical and strategic airpower, Lauritsen said, derived in part from the timescales of response:

> [The] important thing was to strike immediately against their tactical airfields and the immediate military targets that could attack our field forces. This had to be done within a matter of hours after hostilities, while the long range strategic operations could at best be days, and that the immediacy of the attack was not nearly as important as in the case of the ground forces.[84]

Lee DuBridge, interviewed by Martin Sherwin in 1983, recalled an exchange with Gray Board counsel Roger Robb, who presented him with one of the volumes of the Vista report on nuclear weapons. According to DuBridge's telling, the report said,

> "We conclude that the hydrogen bomb would have no use in tactical warfare. There was no tactical application," or something of the sort. Robb said, "You signed this report and Oppenheimer had something to do with it. Was that a correct statement of what you believed?" I said yes. And he said, "That's all." It only dawned on me later that he did not know what "tactical" meant. He thought this was a flat statement that we thought there was no military use for the hydrogen bomb. . . . What we meant was on the battlefield, there was no place [for it].[85]

This was a good story, one that chimed well with the predominant account of Oppenheimer's "show trial." It is hardly borne out by the later declassified portions of the hearing transcript, however. These show that DuBridge had extended discussions with Robb about nuclear weaponry in the tactical setting. DuBridge's position was quite specific: envisioning a battle between NATO armies and Russian armies in Western Europe between the Rhine and the border of the Soviet zone,

> We felt that if a thermo-nuclear weapons [sic] was available and used on armies, that its area of destruction through blast and its area of damage through radio activity would be so great that we would be destroying many civilian populations in a friendly area—Western Germany—to such a great extent that the use of such a terribly destructive weapon in Western Germany was not feasible and not desirable and would be against our interests. Therefore, we saw no tactical use for it in that kind of a battle. Therefore, we made no further study of the thermo-nuclear problem in that report.[86]

In one sense the Vista group had a winning argument. In resisting tactical nuclear weapons, the air force set its face against technological development that was to produce smaller, lighter weapons that could be delivered on the battlefield by fighter bomber aircraft. These, it was claimed, offered greater accuracy than the army's atomic artillery. Tactical atomic capability, George Lemmer notes, was coming to be seen "as a natural armament of numerically inferior but technologically superior nations." In July 1952 the Forty-Ninth Air Division, capable of delivering lightweight nuclear weapons, was deployed to Britain under US Air Force Europe. By 1955 lightweight tactical thermonuclear bombs of one-megaton yield had become feasible. By this time, Lemmer writes, "the old distinction between tactical and strategic weapons was fast disappearing and even the differences between tactical and strategic air forces were being questioned."[87]

In another sense, however, the Vista group was trapped in their own assumption that the deployment of thermonuclear weapons could occur only in the context of the strategic bombardment of the Soviet cities. By equating a process—fusion—with a massive yield, they made a fetish of the hydrogen bomb and overlooked the technological progress that would produce a wide variety of fission and fusion weapons of various sizes, shapes, and weights, with yields varying from fractions of kilotons to multiples of megatons. The trade-off between large-yield and limited-yield weapons, of which so much had been made a few years earlier, was already resolving itself with the proliferation of weapons types, weights, and sizes. Pure fission weapons, though an advance on the paradigmatic Fat Man, were still heavy. Fusion bombs were smaller, lighter, and less exposed to accidental detonation, major advantages in the field. The image of the giant and resource-costly Super that had so dominated the debate in 1949–50 had yet to fade.[88]

Project Vista, then, was the continuation of the argument that began with the 1949 controversy over the Super and continued right through the eventual Personnel Security Board hearings that removed Oppenheimer's security clearance. It achieved renewed attention for Oppenheimer's views and his record of opposition to the Super. And this was not Oppenheimer's only foray into nuclear strategy. His earlier chairmanship of the Long-Range Objectives Panel presaged some of Vista's controversial recommendations with its emphasis on the military utility of small-yield atomic weapons.

It was an obvious connection to make, for Vista's emphasis on tactical nuclear weapons—for which Oppenheimer personally argued so eloquently—could be seen as a skillful tactical diversion from the larger project of developing thermonuclear weapons for the strategic deterrent. In this way his espousal of tactical weaponry could be interpreted as a part of his larger plan to block the development of the Super, when attempts to block the continuing theoretical work had failed.[89] Oppenheimer's advocacy of small tactical nuclear weapons encouraged air force leaders to interpret it as what Ivan Getting and John Christie describe as an "end run designed to delay the hydrogen bomb and reduce the availability of fissile material for use in hydrogen bombs."[90] Charles V. Murphy was close to Finletter and recalled him as being "filled with wrath" over Oppenheimer's having shared information with the Alsop brothers. Finletter and Murphy had collaborated throughout the early 1950s, the secretary briefing the air force insider and sharing Oppenheimer's security file with him. Finletter later regretted these extensive briefings; interviewed in 1968, he confessed, "I never had much confidence in that fellow."[91]

Air force leaders had no sooner seen off Project Vista than they were forced to engage with a second diversion from their main purpose: some of the same scientists, notably Oppenheimer, mounted another attack on the reliance on strategic bombing. In this case, the ground they chose was the air defense of the United States as an alternative to what they considered undue reliance on deterrence through strategic bombing.

Scientists for Air Defense

While the air force leaders struggled to assemble an adequate air defense system, they remained, in the words of an official historian, committed to the doctrine that while defenses "could raise the threshold of uncertainty for an attacker, limit damage to critical areas, and exact a heavy price for an attacker, defenses could not in themselves deter or win wars; winning wars was clearly the province of SAC."[92] Accordingly, despite their advocacy of an elaborate system of radar belts and interceptor fighters, Generals Vandenberg and Twining opposed a recommendation being considered by the National Security Council in late 1952 for just such an extensive network.[93]

The air force and the National Security Resources Board had earlier cosponsored a study, known as East River, of the mobilization problems to be expected in the case of modern warfare. This study, which reflected army rather than air force views, moved quickly in the direction of focusing on civil defense against nuclear attack, which, said the study's authors, could not be effective without adequate air defense. Secretary of Defense Lovett, well aware of the problems of achieving such a standard of security, charged the East River group with defining a system that would repel saturation attacks. The arguments then became public, with the Alsop brothers taking the lead in arguing the possibility, through technology, of "near-total air defense." For the Alsops, the stubbornness of the Air Staff was the principal obstacle to achieving it.[94]

The air force needed a fresh start on this issue. In 1951, following strenuous urging by Ivan Getting and Louis Ridenour, the Lincoln Laboratory was established at MIT to undertake studies of air defense. That work, under the physicist George Valley, built on that of the Air Defense Systems Engineering Committee and pointed toward a system dependent on a single large computer linked to the early warning radar net. Air force leadership was still not convinced that the complex, all-interdependent system developed by Lincoln would meet the immediate need to intercept manned bomber raids; also the leadership was too heavily oriented to a future when the threat from ballistic missiles would predominate. The prospects of an air defense system exacting sufficient damage against an attack by Soviet long-range bombers was limited in any event, while the prospects for effective air defense against intercontinental ballistic missiles (ICBMs) was minimal. The RAND Corporation, asked to review the issues, criticized the air force leadership for their "distrust" of Lincoln and their failure to understand what the MIT scientists were recommending.[95]

Project Lincoln was established as, and remained, a major long-term research investment oriented to the mid-range future. Under MIT's auspices, another research exercise got under way: the Lincoln Summer Study Group on air defense, apparently prompted by Ridenour's enthusiasm for this means of obtaining a short-term study of pressing problems by gathering together very bright minds under time constraints. Headed by Jerrold Zacharias, the Summer Study Group was centered on a small number of scientists, some of them veterans of the Manhattan Project, the GAC, and the contentious Vista project. The influential presence of J. Robert Oppenheimer in an exercise that, like those that went before, confronted air force doctrine provided a continuity from opposition to the Super right through to Oppenheimer's security board hearing.

The remit of the Summer Study Group was to advise on how best to devise an early warning network with a linked interceptor force and to consider defenses against an ICBM attack. When the group held a briefing in late August 1952, it reported that distant early warning was feasible.[96] The overall rationale, however, was almost designed to antagonize the air force, and SAC specifically. Murphy's *Fortune* article charged Oppenheimer and other scientists with trying to get the government to discard or modify a strategy of "retaliatory deterrence" and replace it with a "defensive strategy," while Oppenheimer quoted an officer in Air Defense Command saying, "It was not really our policy to attempt to protect this country, for that is so big a job that it would interfere with our retaliatory capabilities."[97] Since 1947, the air force had dismissed the aspiration of an impenetrable air defense as a manifestation of the dangerous "Maginot Line" philosophy. Zacharias, Oppenheimer, and Isidor Rabi turned this argument back on SAC in an uncompromising counterdoctrine: they asserted that the Maginot Line *psychology*—a term almost calculated to antagonize with its reference to the unconscious—should be understood as exclusive reliance on a single weapon or weapons system:

> The great emphasis placed in recent years on the development of an effective "retaliatory force" in the belief that this constitutes an adequate defense is another manifestation of this psychology. Again, we put "all our eggs in

one basket. . . ." We conclude, therefore, that continued dependence on a retaliatory force as our sole defense represents the development of a dangerous Maginot Line psychology.[98]

Air force leaders were quite perturbed by passages such as this. Finletter had feared the study would get out of hand, and it now seemed to have done so. They saw in this once again the malign hand of Oppenheimer, the principal opponent of their "balanced" stance of maintaining both offensive and defensive capabilities. In the words of an official air force history,

> Once again the prominent physicist advocated a course of action that collided with Air Force policy. Besides advocating tactical atomic weapons, perhaps at the expense of higher yield bombs needed for the Strategic Air Command, and opposing the development of the hydrogen device, he had argued for a heavy investment in air defense that might draw money away from the deterrent force. Oppenheimer thus became a symbol of opposition to the Air Force and nuclear deterrence.[99]

Oppenheimer's opposition to the Super, his involvement in Vista, and now this ascription of the Maginot Line mentality to the air force amounted to an attack on the mindset of the strategic bombing offensive. The Alsop brothers reflected the approach taken by the Summer Study Group, and Oppenheimer certainly fed the conclusions of the group to the Alsops, meeting with Joseph Alsop regularly at this time.[100] The resulting similarity of the group's conclusions and the Alsops' articles did not escape the notice of air force headquarters, as chief scientist David T. Griggs indicated in testimony to the Oppenheimer hearing.[101] By this point Oppenheimer, according to the biographer Abraham Pais, had "made more powerful enemies within the Air Force who viewed his activities and advice with extreme suspicion and resentment."[102]

The Air Force Counterattacks

Not only Oppenheimer but the larger group of anti-H-bomb scientists faced uncomfortable scrutiny by the Personnel Security Board established to review the former Los Alamos leader's security clearance. The formal move against Oppenheimer was to look into accusations, originally made by the JCAE's William Borden and vigorously supported by Lewis Strauss, that he might have been a Soviet agent. Improbable as it may have seemed, there was enough in Oppenheimer's background, amplified by his evasiveness, to feed the suspicion. Working independently of this was the gathering strength of the air force's determination, if not to quash Oppenheimer, then to quash the arguments he and others—veterans of the GAC, and latterly of

Vista—were leveling against SAC's plans for strategic nuclear bombard-ment. Possibly the tenor of the argument on this issue might have been less fundamentalist had the stage not been effectively left to the air force. The more subtle and considered arguments that might have been expected from State Department testimony—what a difference in tone Acheson would have offered—were absent, as State Department witnesses were not called to testify. Paul Nitze recalled Oppenheimer's lead counsel, Lloyd Garrison, meeting him and Acheson, but on discovering their criticism of his client's position, saw no advantage in having them appear before the board.[103]

As early as 1951 there had been doubts about Oppenheimer's loyalty within the Department of the Air Force, but they were readily dealt with by the removal of his access to classified information. Absolute exclusion followed in January 1954 when, following a directive from Eisenhower, Under Secretary of the Air Force James H. Douglas gave notice of an order to "place a blank wall between Dr. J. Robert Oppenheimer and all areas of operation of the Department of Defense, whether in research projects of a sensitive nature or otherwise." Any contacts between Oppenheimer and other scientists involved in air force research and development that might violate the directive were to be reported to the secretary.[104] That left the ar-gument to rebut Oppenheimer and the Vista group still to be made, and the security board hearing was one forum in which the air force needed to have a presence. That presence took the form of two witnesses: former air force chief scientist David T. Griggs and Maj. Gen. Roscoe C. Wilson. Of these, Griggs's testimony was the more potent, much of it being redacted from the published account.[105] Indeed, it had been left to Griggs to set out the official air force line on behalf of former secretary Finletter, who refused to testify at the hearing.[106]

Griggs had joined RAND on its setup in February 1946, becoming the pro-ject's first full-time employee. As the project expanded, he was appointed head of the atomic energy section. Thereafter he consulted for a number of defense agencies, among them the Armed Forces Special Weapons Project, until appointed air force chief scientist in succession to Ridenour, serving from September 1951 through the end of June 1952. Testifying, Griggs re-called Finletter telling him at the time of his appointment in September 1951 that there were serious questions as to Oppenheimer's loyalty, a perspec-tive that Vandenberg shared. "It was clear to me," Griggs advised, "that this was not an irresponsible charge on the part of Mr. Finletter or on the part of General Vandenberg, and accordingly I had to take it into consideration in all our discussions and actions which had to do with the activities of Dr. Oppenheimer during that year." As to the progress on the Super,

> We felt at the time we are speaking of, namely, late 1951 and early 1952, the
> effort on this [Los Alamos] program was not as great as the circumstances
> required under the President's directive. . . . [It] was not large enough to be

commensurate with the need for effort in order properly to pursue the President's directive and the subsequent directives setting the rate and scale of effort.[107]

Impatient with that progress, the air force began to unilaterally pursue its proposal to establish a second laboratory dedicated to thermonuclear processes.[108] Teller had been advocating the establishment of a second laboratory at Livermore, and Finletter strongly supported him. Secretary of Defense Lovett was skeptical of the need, but was eventually persuaded by the service secretaries and the redoubtable LeBaron. Teller had the support of the ailing McMahon, and the NSC backed the proposal. In July 1952 the AEC established the second laboratory at Livermore.[109]

Griggs recalled a meeting at which the Vista report was presented in draft form to a small group of key Air Force Department officials, consisting of himself, William Burden, Garrison Norton, and Lt. Col. Teddy Walkowicz, special assistant to Vandenberg. Those who attended the briefing reacted strongly against the proposals, as did Finletter and Vandenberg when the content was reported. Pressure was applied for the "objectionable" statements in Oppenheimer's chapter 5 to be revised, as on thermonuclear weapons the report's proposals were "unfortunate from the standpoint of the Air Force."[110] The first contentious issue was the proposed division of the stockpile:

> At the time this recommendation was made, there was no allocation of the stockpile. We thus had that comparative freedom of action to use the stockpile in any way that the Department of Defense and the President saw fit. Had this decision been accepted . . . it would have reduced our freedom of action, would specifically have reduced the ability of SAC.[111]

Moreover, according to Griggs, Vista had called for the US "to give up . . . the Strategic Air Command, or more properly I should say the strategic part of our total air power." Had Vista's proposals regarding the content of the stockpile been accepted, advised Griggs, they would similarly have acted to restrict US military atomic capability.[112]

As Griggs's testimony indicated, the air force had closed its ranks against Oppenheimer and his associates at an early date, far in advance of the AEC's moves to assess his loyalty. Lee DuBridge recalled that in the fall of 1952, he was told at a meeting of the Science Advisory Committee of the Office of Defense Mobilization that the air force had its sights on Oppenheimer; presidential science adviser James Killian reportedly whispered to DuBridge, "People at the Air Force are going to be after Oppenheimer, and we have got to know about it and be ready for it." DuBridge recalled Killian mentioning that the matter was being pursued by Roscoe Wilson, who at this point held a key position at air force headquarters as assistant deputy chief of staff/operations for atomic energy.[113]

Air force attempts to isolate Oppenheimer included the encouragement of hostile press coverage of what the *Fortune* article called "the story of physicist J. Robert Oppenheimer's campaign to disarm the Strategic Air Command" via the Vista report, and linking it to the earlier opposition to the Super:

> [Oppenheimer] and his followers have no confidence in the military's assumption that SAC as a weapon of mass destruction is a real deterrent to Soviet action. On the contrary, they believe that, by generating fear in the Kremlin, it has been a goad to Soviet development of counter-atomic weapons. They argue that it has aroused misgivings in Western Europe; and that a renunciation of atomic-offensive power by both major adversaries is essential to an easement of world tension. . . . Finletter read it as a brief for disarming the nation's strongest weapon while the Red Army and its tactical air forces still held the military balance of power in Europe. Moreover, he suspected that the hold-back of the H-bomb was not unrelated to the Vista theory.[114]

Charles Murphy, author of this unsigned account, was editor of the magazine, and his appointment as air force reserve colonel had been arranged by Norstad, a close friend and fishing partner. Murphy was close to figures in the Air Staff, and he emerges time and again throughout the politics of the Super. His piece reflected the view within the air force that Oppenheimer was, according to Edwin Yoder, its "number one enemy in the scientific establishment."[115] Later, C. D. Jackson, a Time Incorporated executive, regretted that Murphy had joined with James Shepley, *Time* magazine's Washington bureau chief, to orchestrate a campaign against Oppenheimer.[116] It would prove particularly potent.

Murphy assured Norstad that he had "consulted no one presently connected with the Air Force" when researching the article.[117] He was more equivocal in his later recollection that "no uniformed officer" had assisted with the piece, hinting that Finletter, Under Secretary Roswell Gilpatric, and Assistant Secretary Garrison Norton provided him with briefings. The following year, Murphy was awarded the Gill Robb Wilson Award by the Air Force Association, an award given to writers and publishers for service to the air force.

Although Wilson was initially credited with the lead role in the air force's attack on Oppenheimer, his testimony proved to be less potent than that of Griggs. When he appeared before the board, Wilson found himself borne on the wave of innuendo generated by the security hearing's prosecutor. His position seemed ambiguous, as he made it clear at the outset that he was "appearing here by military orders, and not on my own volition."[118] Thereafter, his evidence seemed indefinite and halfhearted, exposing him to the ridicule of the Alsops.[119] Schilling found it unimpressive, and was later surprised by the man's vigor and focus when he came to interview him. "I am impressed," he wrote, "at how much better a showing the anti-JRO witnesses make in person. Wilson seems stupid and highly parochial in his testimony, and he certainly doesn't give this impression in speaking—which is not to deny the missionary zeal, it is just not so apparent. All told, a pleasant guy."[120]

The ambiguity of Wilson's testimony flowed, perhaps, from mixed feelings arising from his own personal relationship with Oppenheimer. Interviewed three decades later, he confessed,

> Oppenheimer is one of the great sorrows of my life. I was on many committees with Oppenheimer, and he was remarkably kind to me and really a great mind, an incredible mind. But he worried me because he was always suggesting that we quit building these big weapons and build small ones. The character of an atomic bomb is that the bigger you make it the more efficiently you use the fissionable material. It takes, for instance, maybe twice as much fissionable material to make a shell as it does a bomb, and you get maybe one-hundredth the effect. I got upset about this many, many times, but I liked Oppenheimer, and we were friends. I [had] been to his house many times, but I didn't know anything about his politics at all. I didn't know anything about his wife's politics. Then after the war I was called in. They were having an investigation over Oppenheimer's security clearance. They asked me all these questions. I wound up testifying against Oppenheimer. As I sat there I could see tears running down the guy's face. I know that I had a considerable hand in lifting his ticket, and it was based mostly on the testimony of the big bomb and the little bomb. This has really been on my conscience for a long time, although I don't know what I could have done about it.[121]

Wilson's testimony underlined the specific fears of the air force, not that Oppenheimer was disloyal to the United States—few serving officers believed that—but rather that his advice was unreliable and constantly opposed to policy. Inconvenient it might have been, but this propensity was easily neutralized by holding Oppenheimer at arm's length. Air force scientific and technical expertise had been growing apace, and there was arguably less need for external civilian consultants than had been the case during the immediate postwar years. Strategic Air Command had developed as a largely self-contained organization, while, as Project Vista and the air defense issues had shown, Air Force Department headquarters had grown intolerant of external criticism, using Griggs and (however remotely) Murphy to fashion the case against Oppenheimer. The scene was set for a final reckoning with him, although the air force had neither the wish nor the incentive to see him destroyed professionally.

However, the agenda of the Personnel Security Board hearing and the manner of its prosecution were set by Strauss, who had a very different set of concerns, some arising from national security considerations, others seemingly personal.[122] And there was a wider setting too. "The pall of Mc-Carthyism," as Walter LaFeber termed it, hung over the lives of scientists as much as it did the actions of the Eisenhower administration.[123] Oppenheimer was seen as an easy target for McCarthyite sentiment. When McCarthy used a television interview to allege that the development of the hydrogen bomb had been deliberately held back by Communist sympathizers among the scientists, the threat of an investigation by McCarthy was enough to propel Strauss, conscious of the AEC's own vulnerability, to proceed quickly with moves to dispose of Oppenheimer. With Eisenhower weighing in on Strauss's side, an investigation was averted and a divided commission had the authority to proceed with the security hearing.[124]

If the large implications of the Oppenheimer case as the martyrdom of a liberal hero "did not assure it a place in American consciousness," Richard Hewlett and Jack Holl observe, "the publication of the transcript surely did. . . . For those whose lives were touched directly, the case had added dimensions. No participant would ever be the same again."[125] Thomas Murray, one of the two commissioners sympathetic to Oppenheimer, would defend his eventual vote against him as dictated by "the exigencies of the moment," a clear reference to the McCarthyite threat.[126] It was a nervousness that would infect even former commission chair Gordon Dean. Strauss had driven through a vicious and in many respects extralegal inquiry. He would not escape its repercussions.

By 1954, Oppenheimer was firmly in the frame as the principal critic of air force practice and, by implication, of Eisenhower's uncompromising New Look strategy. He would be publicly targeted as the man who impeded the development of the hydrogen bomb, but the substance of the case against him, effectively ignored by popularizations, rested on his successive interventions to challenge the direction of national security policy. Moving on from initially disputing the feasibility and morality of the Super, he had led the story of its development into new areas in which he and his remaining associates were on weaker ground.

Rewriting Los Alamos

In 1945, Los Alamos scientists, under the wartime leadership of Oppenheimer, were national heroes, but the intense bureaucratic conflicts engendered by the Super proposal in the autumn of 1949 cast the laboratory in a different light. In that year, the prospect of the hydrogen bomb burst onto the political scene, calling forth an immediate reaction from members of Congress and some members of Truman's administration: why had it not been actively pursued in the period since 1945? Some, of course, saw little reason for concern. The prospects of succeeding in the search for the Super were so remote as to rightly relegate it to a low priority. For others, the answer was to be found in scientific inertia, the political unreliability or moral squeamishness of Los Alamos scientists, and the equivocal political loyalties of Oppenheimer himself.

There then began a sustained attempt to rewrite Los Alamos's history to portray the work undertaken there post-1945 as influenced by a spirit of deliberate resistance to the Super prospect, even as a conspiracy to frustrate national security interests. There was indeed a plot, but not of this nature. The moves at the Atomic Energy Commission and the Pentagon to first isolate Oppenheimer and then subject him to the security hearing that destroyed his governmental career were accompanied by sustained leaks of information designed to portray Los Alamos and its former scientific leader as attempting to subvert the Super project. This attack culminated in an opinion-shaping book by two Washington journalists, written with the private encouragement and public disavowal of AEC chair Lewis Strauss and offering a sensational critique of the Los Alamos record.

Inertia at Los Alamos?

As opinion began to swing behind the president's decision to proceed with the Super, some of the commissioners who were in place at that time became eager to ensure a positive public account of their role. In 1953 the

AEC produced an internal document recording the history of the thermonuclear debate. Strauss had rejoined the commission as chair, and the document emanated from his office. He claimed to be the author, which he was not—the initial draft was a secretariat paper and he quibbled with some of its omissions.[1] Although he claimed to have drafted the document for his own personal record and for the benefit of new commissioner Eugene M. Zuckert, at least some of the other commissioners saw a copy. Thomas Murray, a Catholic with a profound moral objection to thermonuclear weapons and a thorn in Strauss's side, passed a copy to former commissioner Henry Smyth.[2]

Smyth protested the way in which he had been represented in this "incomplete" and "misleading" document.[3] He argued that he had been opposed to the development of a thermonuclear weapon in October/November 1949 only so long as certain conditions obtained; if they were to change, then he would have been obliged to support it, as eventually he did.[4] When Sen. Bourke Hickenlooper recalled at a hearing of the JCAE that majorities of the General Advisory Committee and of the commission itself had opposed the production of a thermonuclear weapon, Smyth, who was appearing before him, demurred. Strauss, ever quick to refer to the record, challenged Smyth's "lapse of memory."[5] The disagreement with Smyth rumbled on. Smyth insisted on a meeting with Strauss to explain his position in detail, and followed up with a full memorandum of events, implicitly rebuking Strauss with his complaint about

> the tendency of the press to oversimplify into a for or against vote the complicated series of decisions on the hydrogen bomb made throughout the fall and winter of 1949–50. Such oversimplification misrepresents the facts and the reasoning of the men concerned.[6]

Smyth recalled that his November 1949 reservations had been dispelled by December, by which time he had been persuaded of the potential utility of the weapon. He accordingly felt able to change his position and join Strauss in what then became a majority view, with David Lilienthal, a lame-duck chair, the sole dissenter. For Smyth, the president had made the correct decision to authorize the Super, and had he not agreed fully with it, he "would have felt in honor bound to resign at that time from the Commission."[7]

The political climate was changing, and the AEC and its members would be called on to defend their record. In announcing his decision on the Super in January 1950, Truman had directed the AEC to "continue" work already under way. This gave a particular slant to the decision, seeming to minimize its significance as setting a new direction for atomic weaponry. At the same time it could not avoid raising the question of just what work *was* under way, and to what effect—a point that became the immediate focus of critical interest.

The source of much of the criticism that followed is traceable to air force circles, to an air force that was becoming more technically savvy. Newly appointed chief scientist Louis Ridenour fitted well, having already expressed trenchant views in favor of strategic bombardment and on the impossibility of effective defense against nuclear attack, positions that mapped exactly onto then-current air force doctrine.[8] Now, immediately prior to taking up his official air force appointment, Ridenour turned his attention to the Super, responding immediately to Truman's announcement and effectively setting the agenda for the criticism of Los Alamos and the AEC that would follow. Writing in the March 1950 issue of *Scientific American*, he argued,

> The fusion bomb is not a brand-new possibility that has suddenly burst upon the minds of men. . . .
>
> It seems a little curious that the fusion bomb should have been proposed— as it apparently was—in terms of a reply to the Soviet achievement of the fission bomb. . . .
>
> One may, for example, ask: If the decision to make the superbomb was necessary and inevitable, why has it been delayed until now? Why were the "sound proposals" mentioned by Oppenheimer in 1945 allowed to gather dust? . . .
>
> *The hydrogen bomb was not delayed because we lacked the idea. The effort to make it must, therefore, have been postponed by a deliberate policy decision.* What were the issues or facts on which such a decision was based? . . .
>
> It is conceivable that the delay was due simply to the failure of responsible officials to make the most of their opportunities and responsibilities. (emphasis added)[9]

The full tide of criticism was held back for a few years. Significantly, though, the passage emphasized above was also emphasized by Lewis Strauss, who underlined it in his own copy of the magazine.

Was the hydrogen bomb deliberately held back? Such was the assumption of the conspiracy theorists, whose day had now come. There were three strands to their criticism. The first was that little progress had been made on the Super from the time of its first conception, midway through the Manhattan Project. The second strand was that Los Alamos had been tardy in its response to the presidential directive of 31 January 1950. The third strand, linking the other two, was that this lack of progress was due to deliberate decisions, made against the United States' national security interest, by a small group of scientists led by J. Robert Oppenheimer.

The charge that fundamental work on the Super was neglected during the wartime and immediate postwar years was leveled against the laboratory, and against the AEC's oversight of it. From then on, the charge would be repeated. In 1952, AEC chair Gordon Dean testified before the JCAE, encountering the full brunt of Bourke Hickenlooper's deeply entrenched hostility to the commission. The committee's minority Republicans waxed furious at the evidence that the US possessed very few atomic bombs in 1947. Hickenlooper said during Dean's testimony,

> So the whole hydrogen project has suffered from an inertia since 1946. Based upon the limitations of the experiments and the knowledge at that time in 1946, we had two or three expositions of the feasibility of this hydrogen project and flat statements from reliable people that in their opinion the hydrogen explosion was feasible based on what they had learned up to that time. They said there were things they had to prove. That is very true. But there was a complete inertia and the General Advisory Committee was partly responsible for that, and the Commission was partly responsible for that, because both of them by majority vote advised against going into the hydrogen problem. . . . Some of the reasons were put on moral grounds, others were put on the question of feasibility, but there was that inertia, and that has contributed to us being no farther along than we are at the moment.[10]

Hans Bethe meanwhile advised Dean that "the progress of our work on thermonuclear weapons, since the first Russian bomb explosion and especially since Teller's discovery of the new approach, has been about as rapid as was technically feasible." Continuing efforts at a similar rate would assure a safe margin of advantage over any Soviet program.[11]

A known opponent of the Super during his earlier term as AEC chair, David Lilienthal was bound to face severe criticism of his record in this changing climate. When he appeared before the Gray Board reviewing Oppenheimer's security status, he found himself facing "prosecutor" Roger Robb and, unaccustomed to adversarial questioning, appeared inept:

"Q. . . . What were the details of the work which you referred to in that statement, 'to continue its work on the hydrogen bomb.' Just what was being done? . . . Precisely what were you doing? How many people had you working on it?
"A. I don't know.

"Q. How much time had they spent?
"A. I can't answer that. . . . The records are available. It was part of the work program of the Los Alamos Laboratory and it was reported from time to time.

"Q. If I told you, Mr. Lilienthal, that the record showed that there was comparatively little work that had been done or was being done, would you dispute that?
"A. No, comparatively little compared to the other programs that were approved, I am sure that is true.

"Q. I will reframe the question. If I told you that the records show that there was little work that had been done, would you dispute that?

"A. Yes, I think I would. It covers a long period of time."[12]

The physicists fought back with a defense of the laboratory. In the aftermath of the Oppenheimer hearing, Los Alamos director Norris Bradbury made a public statement giving a spirited account of the laboratory's work, pointing up the inescapable opportunity costs of Super development in the immediate postwar period and the impossibility of wholly separating fission from fusion development:

> Had the Laboratory attempted to exploit the thermonuclear field to the exclusion of the fission field in 1946, what would have happened? . . . The fission weapons stockpile would have been but a fraction of its present size. The essential fission techniques required for practical thermonuclear weapons would not have been developed. . . .
>
> Rather than delaying the actual accomplishment of thermonuclear weapons, the Los Alamos Scientific Laboratory has, by its insistence on doing necessary things first, demonstrably provided the fertile soil in which the first feasible ideas could rapidly grow, and demonstrably did develop such weapons, and probably, but not demonstrably, did so years ahead of any other course which could have been pursued with the facilities and people available. Technically, the development of fusion weapons is so inextricably allied with and dependent on the development of fission weapons, that great success in the former had to follow success in the latter.
>
> The assertion that the Los Alamos Scientific Laboratory was reluctant to work in the field of thermonuclear weapons is false.[13]

The passage of time did not soften the sense that the laboratory had been unfairly castigated. In the words of a later Los Alamos consultant writing in her doctoral dissertation, it "is easy and convenient"—though wrong—"to argue that Los Alamos Laboratory and the AEC took a long time to develop a working hydrogen weapon" and that individuals delayed the work.[14] Bradbury's colleagues came together in 1983 to vehemently rebut that charge. The laboratory, said the chemist Richard D. Baker, "was floundering as to what to do in '46, but Norris [Bradbury] was not acting that way; he was just going ahead making plans."[15] When it came to the Super, which the laboratory had been working on continuously from 1946, the mathematician J. Carson Mark said, "Truman's words didn't necessarily mean that we did anything much different from what we had been doing because we didn't really know how to make a gadget that would work as a hydrogen bomb."[16] Even Edward Teller added an uncharacteristically cautious note in retrospect, grumbling in a 1987 book that Truman's low-key order to "continue" work on the Super had given the false impression that "we could produce a hydrogen bomb simply by tightening a few more screws."[17]

Much of the criticism, in 1950 and later, was leveled at the General Advisory Committee and Oppenheimer's leadership of it, but the discussion was broadening beyond the early phase of theoretical development to address issues of national security policy. Opposition to the established air force doctrine of strategic bombardment, encapsulated in Project Vista, was now publicly cited as flowing from opposition to the Super and as a deliberate attempt to constrain US air power.

A Whiff of Conspiracy?

Any good conspiracy theory demands a secret organization, ideally concealed behind a mysterious code word. The apparent identification of a group opposed to air force strategy, operating under the acronym ZORC, provided the necessary igniter. The occasion of its emergence was a meeting under the auspices of another of Ridenour's Summer Study Group initiatives, in this case concerned with continental air defense. This study group took shape as Project Lincoln, and was responsible for examining and evaluating a series of proposals to provide the United States with some protection against Soviet air assault. Alongside the main study, Oppenheimer and a number of other figures not directly involved in Lincoln met to brainstorm more far-reaching proposals for an impenetrable defensive shield. This group was ZORC.

"ZORC takes up the fight" against the H-bomb, wrote Charles Murphy in a section heading in his anonymously published article in *Fortune*. Murphy portrayed ZORC as an entity, an organization that acted as a unit with a single objective: to prove there could be an air defense so perfect that the US might become a fortress nation with no need for an offensive atomic weapon. But why "ZORC"? The mysterious title was taken from the initials of the four principals: Jerrold Zacharias, Robert Oppenheimer, Isidor Rabi, and Charles Lauritsen. Throughout the period of the Lincoln study, alleged Murphy, these four war gamed, testing US defenses against the tactics of the Soviet long-range air force. It was what Murphy called "a shift in tactics" by a group now on the defensive over Project Vista.[18] Their shadowy activity would have been unknown to the air force had not an air force officer in civilian clothing sat in on a session at Cambridge in August 1952 and written down "ZORC" and its translation from the blackboard. He filed a report on ZORC to air force headquarters.[19]

This speculation about a dissident cabal of physicists persisted beyond the immediate impact of Murphy's popular article. When Oppenheimer and the witnesses against him appeared before the Personnel Security Board, ZORC reappeared with them. David Griggs gave conspicuous testimony on ZORC, claiming that he himself had seen the letters written at the Cambridge meeting.[20] This was specifically denied by Zacharias under prolonged questioning in which he characterized the Murphy article as a scurrilous journalistic trick.[21] Moreover, while the principals' initials could have been put on a blackboard, this would have been neither at a time nor at a place at which Griggs could have been present.[22] It seems likely that the chief scientist had formulated a false memory from reading Murphy's account of ZORC in *Fortune*, but there are reports that Griggs later regretted testifying with a "fictitious" story.[23]

The Personnel Security Board hearings were held in private, and while the transcript was unexpectedly published in the summer of 1954, it had been extensively redacted on national security grounds.[24] The classified deletions were not published for another sixty years.[25] With the publication of the redacted transcript, the controversy dramatically reentered the public domain, fueling the debate with the additional detailed information extracted from witnesses. Writing in *Newsweek* in the fall of 1954, Raymond Moley mocked the way in which Oppenheimer had been portrayed to be "at once a statesman, a moral leader, and a seer. His intrusions covered the entire range of public affairs, diplomacy, politics, and military policy." His threat to US security lay not just in his opposition to the development of the H-bomb but also in what Moley described as his strenuous attempts, over a period of years, "to frustrate the efforts of the Air Force to create the means of delivering it to its target."[26] The full force of the attack went beyond criticism of Oppenheimer's misjudgment and possible disloyalty. The earlier criticisms of lack of enthusiasm and inertia at Los Alamos were now supplanted by allegations of a full-blown campaign among scientists and their supporters. ZORC had been the mere tip of the iceberg. A larger number of "irresponsible" scientists and the leadership of the laboratory were now said to be involved.

This more sustained attack came in the form of a popular book by two Washington journalists, James R. Shepley and Clay Blair Jr. Shepley and Blair not only boosted and made more public the intense arguments over the role of Los Alamos in the period leading up to the presidential decision and the period immediately following; they made the alarming claim that there existed, as an exact counterpart to Strategic Air Command, what they dubbed "SUSAC," with equivalent capabilities.[27] It was a popularization of the air force's tendency to see the development of Soviet forces as mirroring its own—what Edward Kaplan terms the "enemy in the mirror" phenomenon.[28] In the years after the decision, this tendency generated concern about a supposed "bomber gap" in the Soviet's favor. On a visit to Moscow in 1956, air force chief of staff Nathan Twining was told by the Soviet defense minister, Marshal Georgy Zhukov, "I think you have the reports too high in estimating our strength," but the air force and other US officials chose to disregard the remark as purposely misleading.[29]

Shepley and Blair's book spread concern and sharpened and perpetuated what was already a highly polarized controversy. The two journalists enjoyed privileged access to the defense establishment. Shepley, a former aide to Gen. George Marshall, had become chief of the Washington bureau of Time Incorporated. Blair, a former submariner, was an accomplished author and Pentagon correspondent for *Time* magazine, where he specialized in atomic weapons policy. Later, as a chosen, trusted collaborator, he would coauthor Omar Bradley's autobiography.[30]

Shepley and Blair previewed their book with a lengthy excerpt in *U.S. News and World Report* in September 1954, under the title "The Hydrogen Bomb: How the U.S. Almost Lost It." The publicity, then and later, tended to simplify even further their crude and vivid representation of the Super story; the magazine's introduction to the excerpt extolled the research done by Shepley and Blair and said, "Most of the nation's H-bomb troubles can be traced back to one man—Dr. J. Robert Oppenheimer. The authors say that Dr. Oppenheimer, almost singlehandedly, stopped the H-bomb program in its tracks."[31]

Lewis Strauss made many appearances in their sensationalist narrative, which described his 5 October 1949 memorandum calling for a "quantum leap" on the Super as "the one reaction that altered history and truly set the stage to keep free men abreast of their fate."[32] They claimed that by Los Alamos's own supposed admission, "nothing had, in fact, been done" on the Super between June 1946 and 31 January 1950.[33] The implication was that this neglect was due to Bradbury's being in thrall to Oppenheimer:

> The extent to which Oppenheimer influenced his onetime physics student, Bradbury, is a matter of controversy as yet unresolved. It seems clear that Bradbury owed his appointment to Oppenheimer. Moreover, it is clear that . . . Oppenheimer could . . . have caused the removal of a weapons-laboratory director who opposed him.[34]

Shepley and Blair reflected the air force view that the nuclear physicists were largely ignorant of air power, making the ZORC group a threat to national security by undermining Strategic Air Command.[35] Their overall verdict took the Personnel Security Board findings and popularized them with their own translation into heated prose:

> The plain fact was that on a question of overriding importance Dr. Oppenheimer was wrong, tragically and frightfully wrong. Repeatedly the point was made in Dr. Oppenheimer's behalf that it is not criminal to be wrong. That is undebatable. It is not criminal to be wrong about the weapons of the atomic age, only fatal. Whether Oppenheimer was guided or misguided would have been of no importance had the West learned that Communist Russia possessed the ultimate weapon, after the U.S. had decided not to build it. The Kremlin would have been free to dictate its terms to the world. . . .

It was an accident bordering almost on the miraculous that the nation had working in its atomic weapons laboratory, where he could pit both his knowledge and his determination against Dr. Oppenheimer, a man like Edward Teller. It is remarkable at the very least that the man who had the genius to build the hydrogen bomb was also a man impelled by the belief it should be built.[36]

The book, published on 30 September 1954, was widely reviewed, overwhelmingly favorably.[37] *Newsweek* celebrated the lessons that most readers would draw from it: the book "tells us how far beyond the proper province of scientific competence Oppenheimer and other scientists went in their efforts to prevent the United States from having the hydrogen bomb."[38] Yet Henry Luce, publisher of *Time* and *Fortune*, was upset at what he saw as the impropriety of his bureau chief publishing such a book without his knowledge.[39]

Despite the blizzard of favorable reviews from writers who were not well placed to judge Shepley and Blair's accuracy, rebuttals and refutations quickly established that it was the authors themselves who were wrong, tragically and frightfully wrong, in the account they offered to the American public. Hans Bethe, in an article written in 1954 and not made public for some years, first looked at the *Fortune* article characterizing it as painting a "highly biased and inaccurate picture of H-bomb development and of the efforts of many American scientists to establish a more adequate air defense system for this country." Of the information and opinions presented in the Shepley and Blair book, Bethe said,

have obviously been obtained from persons holding extreme views on a number of matters. Whoever these persons may have been, they were extreme in their dislike and/or distrust of Oppenheimer, extreme in their certainty of the malfeasance of Los Alamos, extreme in their conviction that anyone who expressed misgivings or raised questions concerning the wisdom of committing ourselves to the H-bomb program was ipso facto subversive. As a result, the book is full of misstatements of fact, and so phenomenally biased as to retain little contact with the events that actually occurred.[40]

On behalf of Los Alamos, a furious Bradbury protested that

the imputation of disloyalty to that now large group of scientists and technicians who are fundamentally responsible for every nuclear weapon, fission and fusion, that the United States has in its stockpile, who are responsible for the atomic weapons leadership that this country presently enjoys, and who are dedicated to the continuance of this leadership, is a tragic, if not malevolent, thing. The motives behind these accusations of Los Alamos are unclear; their bases are faulty and irresponsible information necessarily obtained from those who do not and cannot know the classified facts.[41]

Schilling's interviews, conducted while *The Hydrogen Bomb* was still enjoying some currency, often touched on views of its merits. None praised it; almost all deplored it. For some, the wounds were still raw. Meeting with Norris Bradbury and his chief classification officer in December 1956, Schilling was quizzed for his view on Shepley and Blair; he replied judiciously that he was convinced he could do a better job.[42] In a 1958 draft introduction of the book he started to write following his interviews, Schilling declined to elevate the differences between his own account and that of Shepley and Blair "to the stature of an academic dispute," but promised that his account would differ significantly from theirs with respect to "the detail of the content, the form of the analysis, and the character of the conclusions."[43]

Meanwhile, the ongoing reputation of Shepley and Blair's book would rest largely on whether it could be shown that they possessed hard factual material and, if so, how it came into their possession. It was well known that their argument, according to a report on it in *Saturday Review* published at the end of October, had been denied "by almost every other Government official familiar with the atomic program except Admiral Strauss, who comes off very well in the Shepley-Blair book and who has been suspected of being one of their sources."[44]

Former AEC chair Gordon Dean, outraged by the draft manuscript he had seen, was unsparing in his criticism: "This is no time for mincing of words. This is a vicious book. And it is an untrue book. If it is accepted by the public as a true account of America's struggle to achieve a thermonuclear weapon, it will be nothing short of a tragedy."[45] Dean remonstrated about the way his own role was portrayed by the authors, holding their account challengeable both in libel law and on security grounds. Moreover, he strongly suspected that Strauss himself was the source for much of what was said there, pointing out to him, "You are quoted at great length throughout the book—daily movements, conversations with all kinds of people, etc." Dean's feelings ran high, and his representations to his former ally now became more formal in tone:

> In view of the numerous false references to my participation in the thermonuclear program, and in view of your key position [as chair] from which to refute these, I feel very strongly that you have a duty either to see that the book is not published or that the false statements concerning me are corrected.[46]

Strauss gave little quarter on the history, conceding only that Dean had abandoned his own initial opposition to "eventually [come] round to my point of view."[47] This continued to be his position, and it did nothing to allay Dean's suspicions. Dean made far-reaching inquiries to establish who the authors had talked to, concluding that they did not gather information from the AEC commissioners "with one possible exception," a clear allusion to Strauss. Dean wrote to Acheson, lambasting Shepley and Blair for the "worst kind of reporting" and asking whether they had consulted him. The secretary of state replied that he had no recollection of any meeting with Clay Blair, and "so far as I can recall, I do not know him." His records showed two encounters with Shepley as part of a program of off-the-record briefings with groups of newspapermen, but the subject of these meetings was not thermonuclear development but current policy on NATO and the German forces.[48] Dean made no headway in setting the record straight, and with the support of *Time* and *Fortune,* and despite fierce criticism as to its accuracy, Shepley and Blair's book continued for many years to be read as an enthralling inside-dopester account of the H-bomb decision.

During April 1954, prior to the publication of *The Hydrogen Bomb,* Dean had been incensed by press articles that portrayed Strauss as "completely alone in fighting for the development of the greatest weapon of all time." Dean protested that this claim was "quite untrue and places me in a very bad light." He appealed to Strauss, his successor as chair of the AEC, to release the documents that had reported the commissioners' individual recommendations to the president, adding with a glance over his shoulder at the McCarthyite threat that "*my instinct for self-preservation* requires that by one device or another these . . . implications be rebutted" (emphasis added).[49]

In early September, *Life* magazine published an article on Edward Teller, repeating the claim that Strauss had been the commission's only dissenter from the GAC's advice.[50] Dean again took the opportunity to respond vigorously prior to publication, pointing out that from the very outset he had been

opposed to the views of the General Advisory Committee along with Lewis Strauss. In fact, while Mr. Strauss was in Beverly Hills in the Fall of '49 I was the only person present arguing for a strenuous thermonuclear program at a specially called meeting of the General Advisory Committee's Weapons Subcommittee.

His role had been to

spearhead, along with Mr. Strauss and Senator McMahon, the drive for a high priority program in the Fall of '49 and [I] had primary responsibility [as chair] for three years thereafter to keep it as a high priority and see it through to its conclusion.[51]

Strauss's own recollection was that Dean, someone whom he had regarded from the outset as a natural ally, and whose reliability McMahon had assured him of, had been wobbly to begin with and had come over to his side

143

only in December. Nevertheless, he grudgingly stepped in to protect Dean's reputation with his own letter to the editors of *Life*.[52]

On 8 July 1954, President Eisenhower, urged by Strauss, awarded a presidential citation to the laboratory for its momentous success in the field of fission weapons and its equal accomplishments in the fusion field.[53] The award did little to neutralize the sore feelings, although the nuclear chemist George Cowan recalled that when Strauss visited Los Alamos in the wake of the Oppenheimer hearings to face the "caustic" and critical comments of the "indignant" scientists, he was "so skillful in flattering everybody that he had us eating out of his hand in about ten minutes. As soon as he left, people turned to each other and said, 'What happened?'"[54] Strauss's influence could be felt by even the most strong-minded individuals. He was determined that Luis Alvarez would testify against Oppenheimer at the Personnel Security Board hearing. The physicist did not wish to do so, but Strauss insisted, and Alvarez's resistance collapsed—much to his discredit in the eyes of his fellow scientists.[55]

Schilling encountered the smooth, courteous Strauss in the first of two interviews with him. His responses were anodyne and, Schilling wrote, "could equally as well have been directed to the local Rotary Club," with "no trace of Strauss the villain."[56] At a second interview, however, "his temper and claws showed when I asked him about the stuff Souers had told me. He wanted to know who said this; I said why I couldn't say. . . . This dege[ne]rated into an impasse, on which he stood firm that I could not expect him to comment on conversations without his knowing where I had heard these things."[57] Schilling retrieved the situation, but felt forced to breach his undertaking to Souers.[58]

Whose Breach of Trust?

The question of Shepley and Blair's journalistic practice was raised in the sharpest form by those key players in the story who denied having met them. The Alsop brothers challenged the book's list of sources, noting that it contained the names of only three scientists: Lauritsen, DuBridge, and Smyth, the first two of whom had no recollection of meeting the authors.[59] Smyth, the sole AEC commissioner to vote against the withdrawal of Oppenheimer's security clearance, would hardly have subscribed to their conclusions. He told Schilling that it was "a horrible book. Just not true."[60] That broad judgment appears to have been shared by all of those taking part in Schilling's interview program who had seen the book.[61]

In the authors' defense, the book's publisher put out a four-page press statement claiming that Shepley and Blair "collected an enormous quantity of research in the field of the atom in strategy and politics," but, significantly, not in dedicated interviews for the book. In their reporting of US strategy on atomic affairs, the publisher maintained, they had "literally thousands of conversations, both privately *and in company with other news men*, with practically every top-level governmental official concerned with atomic energy or military strategy from the years 1945 to 1954" (emphasis added). The list of people from whom information had been acquired in this way was indeed impressive, and included four secretaries of state, three defense secretaries, AEC members, and members of staff of the JCAE. Among the military establishment, the authors claimed as informants former secretaries of all three services as well as three successive chiefs of staff for the army and three chiefs of naval operations. The list was rounded off by members of the White House staffs of both Truman and Eisenhower.[62] Yet this defense was clearly a smokescreen. The authors had listed all of the officials and military officers *who had spoken to the press in their presence*. Many of those cited had never met Shepley and Blair. Their inclination to claim as an interview source anybody whose press conference they attended was risible and did nothing to deflect the criticism of their method.[63] Shepley and Blair would not have gained classified information from attending press conferences, nor would AEC scientists at Los Alamos and elsewhere—much less military officers—have readily revealed it. Yet Dean was not alone in protesting that the published manuscript contained classified information.

The most telling protests came from Norris Bradbury. In September 1954, referring to an earlier telephone conversation, Strauss wrote to Bradbury to discuss Shepley and Blair's book, denying any influence over the publication. But Bradbury's concerns were too serious to be readily brushed aside. The following month Bradbury wrote Strauss to complain that Shepley had claimed that when the text of the book was "reviewed" by the AEC, certain portions deemed "even more damaging" to Bradbury had been removed. Bradbury assumed that any such deletions would have been made on the grounds of classification. He was not to know that the passages concerned were those marked by Strauss in a private, unofficial review. The AEC's own official security review had done little more than to ask for the manuscript to be referred to the Department of Defense and the CIA for further scrutiny.[64] As to what remained in the text, Bradbury's objection concerned the inclusion of classified material that had escaped whatever scrutiny the manuscript had been put through. "Most of their statements in the classifiable areas are untrue," he argued to Strauss, "but occasional ones such as [redacted] matter, and the [redacted] matter are close to the truth and classified." In particular, he was alarmed by the extensive discussion of the test of the "boosted" weapon.[65]

So who were Shepley and Blair's informants? And who leaked classified information to them? For the scientists and AEC commissioners, the finger pointed clearly to Strauss himself, not least for the inclusion of details known only to him. If proved, such intentional planting of a story, including classified information, would have been scandalous, whether the explanation was his overweening vanity or a relentless desire to bury Oppenheimer's reputation. He certainly had experience with this type of operation, having in the past planted stories with his close friend Arthur Krock, the Pulitzer Prize–winning journalist, who had published Strauss's material unchanged.[66]

Circumstantial evidence of Strauss's complicity abounds. He and his family had a long-lasting, affectionate, and intimate friendship with Charles Murphy, Shepley and Blair's forerunner in putting the air force's case against Oppenheimer into the public domain.[67] In the interval between the Personnel Security Board report and the (far more critical) recommendation to the commission, authored by Kenneth Nichols, Murphy lunched with Strauss and sought a meeting with board chair Gordon Gray, mentioning that he knew "what L.S. is thinking."[68] Strauss also maintained a close connection with Clay Blair that involved shared business interests, and Blair arranged for Strauss's own book, *Men and Decisions*, to be extensively edited by his publishing colleagues prior to Strauss's finalizing the text.[69] While Strauss claimed not to know Shepley well, they became friends and regular correspondents during the late 1950s and 1960s; the Shepley family received a birthday gift of a silver cup from him in the fall of 1963.[70] With all three authors, Strauss would from time to time revisit the Oppenheimer affair in correspondence in which there are, among other things, hints that the AEC chair warned newly appointed commissioners against hoping that the Oppenheimer files would be reopened.

The most bizarre aspect of this episode was the intervention of Strauss to buy the manuscript of *The Hydrogen Bomb* from the authors so as to block its publication. He was at this point surely mindful of the seriousness of his breach of trust and aware that it would be seen as reflecting poorly on him if his involvement became public knowledge. His failed attempt to block publication of the book was revealed by Shepley in a television appearance on NBC's *Comment* program. Recollecting that Strauss offered to buy the manuscript and lock it away, he announced that Strauss was acting on the "highest" motives, "to shield his scientists from public controversy." Yet this was itself a staged revelation, as Strauss and Shepley had earlier conferred over how best to go public on this offer. Strauss approved a lengthy draft statement, written by the journalist with help from the ubiquitous Murphy, recalling how Strauss, tortured by political pressures and protective of the scientists, had turned to him in sadness with the proposal.[71] If there were indeed a genuine intention to buy and thereby suppress the manuscript—and it may have been an empty gesture—it argues for Strauss's culpability, as much of what had been written could be traced to him, as well he knew.

Circumstantial evidence of a conspiracy is not enough to convict the AEC chair of acting against the statutory duties of his own organization, and the Strauss papers at the Hoover Presidential Library contain no correspondence between him and the journalists who would cover the period when the book was being researched. There is, however, some more direct evidence of his having successfully concealed the record of his duplicity in loudly deploring the publication of a manuscript to which he had given covert assistance. In June or July 1954, Shepley privately passed the manuscript to Strauss. Strauss read it carefully, and in a lengthy handwritten note suggested as many as sixty-six specific corrections, changes of emphasis, or different angles on the treatment of the material. A small number of these indicated possible security violations to be edited out, which had the effect of confirming that the authors had been given access to classified material.[72] Most of the comments represented issues of judgment where Strauss felt the text could be altered to strengthen the thrust of the story.[73] On 10 July, the manuscript was returned to him so that he could verify the corrections made by the authors.[74]

The "Last Straws"

"Very smart and very vain" was Oppenheimer's characterization of Strauss in an unconscious mirror image of Strauss's view of the scientist. Nemesis follows hubris, and Strauss, a man judged equally quick to crush an enemy and to uplift a friend, was no exception. By 1959 his atomic energy career was over and he was fighting for confirmation to the cabinet post of secretary of commerce, to which Eisenhower had nominated him in the face of hostile congressional opinion. Old scores would be settled in the confirmation hearings, in particular by Sen. Clinton Anderson of New Mexico—a premier "atomic" state. Anderson had long feuded with Strauss, who had declined a mooted appointment as permanent chair of the AEC in the knowledge that his old enemy Anderson was likely to inherit the chairmanship of the JCAE, making the AEC job politically untenable.[75]

His entire reputation was now at stake as Senate opponents of the confirmation sought to disparage his record on nuclear issues and so block the nomination. In this they succeeded, bringing Strauss's career in public service to a close.[76] Alluding to the hydrogen bomb, Anderson publicly mocked Strauss's characteristically grandiose stance in a television interview, objecting to what he said was Strauss's insistence that "I instituted it, I developed it."[77] Mockery was the least of Strauss's problems. By now, his veracity was in question, with his reputation as a braggart and his combative style threatening to terminate his career. His maneuverings on the AEC, his implacable defense of the much-criticized Dixon-Yates contract, and his autocratic style of chairmanship now provided further sticks with which to beat him in the course of the confirmation hearings.[78]

The hearings put his standing with Truman under the spotlight, and to his great disadvantage. As the hearings opened, Anderson warned Truman that "we are probably going to have a little trouble with the Admiral Strauss when he comes up for confirmation as Secretary of Commerce." *Newsweek* was running a story lauding the veteran atomic advocate, praising Strauss's judgment that the United States should develop the H-bomb in the face of intense opposition and concluding that "in the end, after several months of argument, Mr. Truman decided that Strauss was right. But for this decision, which was due largely to the fight made by Strauss, the Soviet atomic arsenal might now be far more powerful than ours."[79] Support of this kind would do Strauss more harm than good. It impelled Anderson to ask the former president a direct question: "whether Strauss persuaded you or had anything to do with your final decision?"

Truman's account in his reply was opaque. He began by claiming mysteriously that "the order for the hydrogen bomb was issued before anyone had made any approach to me on the subject. No one influenced me in this decision." He continued,

> At that time however, all was theory and assumption, and even the scientists and the AEC were divided on the subject of continuing work on the hydrogen bomb. I was asked about this first by the chairman of the AEC, David Lilienthal, whom I told that investigations were proceeding and that whatever results might be obtained would work only for the welfare and benefit of the country.
>
> Because of this division of opinion, however, I set up a special committee of the National Security Council to advise me. . . . With the support of that recommendation, I ordered the AEC to continue the work already begun.

Continuing in friendly tone, he encouraged Anderson "to give the gentleman you mentioned in your letter of the 13th a good cross-questioning, and I hope that you will do it," for which purpose he should feel free to paraphrase Truman's own recollection "for your own approach to the situation."[80] Anderson did more than this, briefing Drew Pearson, who broke the story of the former president's supposed chicanery in a radio broadcast on 21 March 1959, claiming that "Harry Truman has written a letter [to Anderson] . . . flatly and categorically denying that Admiral Strauss, now up for confirmation as Secretary of Commerce, had anything to do with the decision to develop the hydrogen bomb. The truth is not in that fellow, Truman added."[81]

With some bitterness, Strauss complained to his old ally Louis Johnson that "ex-President Truman has written [Anderson] a letter to say that I had nothing to do with the decision to make a thermonuclear weapon. . . . It has hurt me that he should turn against me in order to provide my opponents with ammunition."[82] Anderson returned to the attack following Strauss's testimony to the Senate committee. In his opening statement Strauss recounted his actions as a member of the AEC, recalling that he had begun the movement to initiate development of the thermonuclear bomb "against respectable and substantial opposition within the commission." He chose his words unwisely in claiming in front of the hearing that "President Truman concurred with my recommendation" in ordering the AEC to develop such weapons, allowing him to "resign in good conscience" from the AEC.[83]

Anderson went back to Truman:

> Did [Strauss] ever make any direct recommendation to you about the hydrogen bomb? If he did, did you concur with his recommendation, or did you follow the advice of the special committee of three: Mr. Acheson, Louis Johnson and Mr. Lilienthal? Was his resignation of April 15, 1950 tied in any way to your action on what was called the super-bomb? If not, what was the reason which he gave, publicly or privately, if your records reveal that?

Anderson warned, "I have been a little disturbed at his claim that he began the movement to initiate development of the thermonuclear bomb."[84]

Strauss could have no recourse to the former president at this delicate stage in his career. Protocol demanded that any approach should await the results of his confirmation hearing. He instead wired Sidney Souers, who had been his intermediary with the president in October 1949 and who had arranged for Strauss's urgent representations to be laid before him. Souers had continuing access to Truman and obtained a copy of the letter, assuring Strauss that there was in it "no basis whatever to justify the statement made by the commentator—'the truth is not in that man.'" Souers then relayed what was clearly Truman's own position, carefully framed for Strauss's apparent benefit:

> Mr. Truman does maintain, and has always maintained, that he made the decision with respect to the development of the hydrogen bomb without the help of anyone. . . . I presume his feeling is correct because he is the only man who could make it. He would probably admit that you were for it and that I was for it and that quite a few others were against it, such as many of the scientists, but I do not believe that it made any particular difference to him who was for it or who was against it. He never had any doubt in his own mind that it should be developed if that were possible.[85]

With Souers as his mouthpiece, Truman minimized the offense with studied neutrality.[86] Indeed, his position was not even privately attributable, with Souers referring only to information received from his "friend." In a further letter, however, Souers took less trouble to shield his identity, writing that "the letter from our friend here was in response to one written to him by one of the senators."

When the wounded Strauss forwarded copies of his memoranda and correspondence from October 1949 as a reminder, Souers confirmed his recollection of events, but pointed out gently to his old associate that

I think you know that I have always given you credit for being a strong advocate of going ahead with the Super Bomb and felt that you were entitled to full credit for that. I think you know that in my own way I was just as strongly for it. But, even in view of that, I cannot quarrel too much with the position of the President that he did make the decision himself and he was always proud of having made it, in spite of the very strong advice he received from many others who were against it.[87]

None of this satisfied Strauss, who wrote in injured tones to Truman, querying the withdrawal of the former president's support and seeking a meeting.[88]

Strauss's failure to win the vote on his confirmation was virtually unprecedented at that time. Arthur Krock deplored it as a "poignant" misery, taking four pages in his memoirs to detail the horse trading that had taken place on the Senate floor to provide the crucial negative votes that tipped the scale.[89] The outcome gave satisfaction to many of the enemies Strauss had made in the course of a long career.

The condemnation of Oppenheimer had provoked fury among many scientists. The Manhattan District veteran Robert R. Wilson recollected the period in some detail, criticizing the Oppenheimer hearings as "a complete and utter disgrace and national disgrace. I am still ashamed of my country that those hearings were held at all." He was surprised not to see mass resignations. There were none, but concerned scientists did lobby against Strauss: "A group from Brookhaven and a group particularly at Cornell and a group in Washington of physicists, scientists in Washington, DC," according to Wilson, wittily termed themselves the Last Straws Committee in mockery of Strauss's curious affectation in which the preferred pronunciation of his surname was given as "Straws" rather than the familiar Germanic form. "I was so outraged," recalled Wilson,

and the other people were so outraged. . . . We were so outraged, that we decided that we would do whatever we could to prevent him from becoming the Secretary of Commerce. . . . We worked as a pretty effective lobby against him. . . . I think in part it was just anger about what had happened to Oppenheimer and an attempt to get even. It came down to those simple matters. It was lashing out and doing something, but certainly it was done in that case. . . . Perhaps it did add one more straw to the last straws.[90]

Conclusions

Most accounts of attempts to shape Truman's decision on the Super focus on the scientific imperatives, tempered by personal animosities between the powerful personalities among the nuclear scientists. This book assumes a different angle of attack, portraying the conflicts that arose over the Super as rooted in the distinct interests of the several institutions through whose channels the politics flowed, notably the AEC itself, the Military Liaison Committee, and the Departments of Defense and the Air Force. That pattern of conflict—naturally enough, given its origins— persisted through the years that followed Truman's January 1950 decision and encompassed successive disputes over nuclear weapons policy. While dissent continued, it shifted focus opportunistically. The Super controversy did not end in that month, but became displaced onto arguments about tactical nuclear warfare and comprehensive air defense. The major players and their characteristic postures continued in place, until and indeed beyond Oppenheimer's exclusion from government decision making in 1954.

The pace of change in weapon design was rapid. In both technical and political terms, the ground was shifting under the dissenters' feet. For some time they continued to contest decisions that had already been overtaken by technological development. Meanwhile, events unfolded in ways that were forecast—the Super decision accelerated, rather than triggered, the Soviet thermonuclear program, a development on which the expectations of both dissenters and advocates were not far apart. Neither group had been able to argue convincingly the effect that decisions made in Washington might have on those in Moscow. And there was some further vindication for Oppenheimer, who, the ill-judged GAC report aside, was ahead of the game during these years, anticipating lightweight weapons and tactical usages while heaping well-deserved scorn on the misconceived nuclear-powered bomber.

Interpreting the Politics of Advice

The course of developments as mapped out in this book reflects a rearview-mirror image of events. Yet however neat and progressive—and indeed predictable—the story of the Super might seem from the vantage point of today, it could not have seemed more different at the time, as Schilling discovered. Even six years or so after the events he explored in his interviews, the business of advising first the AEC and then the president was still characterized by the rancorous politics of a tunnel-vision debate. To sense this atmosphere we need only turn to the overall impressions that Schilling set down when he shared them with special lecture audiences at the University of Wisconsin in 1964 and King's College London in 1965, and with Harvard's Richard E. Neustadt in connection with a seminar given there in 1966.[1]

Schilling was not one to oversimplify the essentially political activity of pressures and counterpressures, bargaining and compromise, alliance and counteralliance that characterize the politics of policy. Even so, he was taken aback by some of what he encountered in the contest between advocates and opponents of the Super, as he reflected, a decade later, on what he had learned from interviews or correspondence with almost all of the identifiable (and living) participants in the events of 1949–50.

The "kaleidoscopic" character of the case. It looked like a wholly different decision (and policy process) depending on whose eyes were looking at it and through which of the institutional vantage points it was being seen. The views of the people at the State Department about what went on were quite different from those of the people in Congress, which were quite different from those of the people in the Department of Defense, which were different again from the views of the people at Los Alamos, and so on. Some of the reasons for this are explained by the next three points. It is worth noting that during his interview program, Schilling outlined his interpretation of the kaleidoscopic nature of the case to Paul Nitze, who conceded that, as far as he could tell, all of the points were a fair reflection of the realities of that time.[2]

Partial views. Each of these institutional views of the decision and the decision-making process was not only different, one from the other, but also partial. All institutional perspectives were missing a large amount of the action and some of the central actors. For instance, Los Alamos and the State Department had very little interaction.

The sense of isolation expressed by many of the participants. Each seemed to feel that he was alone, surrounded by enemies or by massive indifference to the needs of the occasion. And there were people who were on the same side of the argument but did not seem to be aware of the fact that they had allies. Strauss professed that at key moments he worried about his position of isolation, had no sense of the supporting views of Edward Teller and Ernest Lawrence, and was also unaware of support from the JCAE until a chance meeting with Senator McMahon at a Beverly Hills hotel. Teller spoke of having no contact with the State Department, the military, or the MLC, and little with the AEC or JCAE, during all or most of the decision period. Nichols felt he and the other military people involved had been frozen out by the AEC and had trouble finding out exactly what the GAC and AEC reports even said.[3] A prime case of people failing to find they were allies were George Kennan and the GAC on the anti-Super side.

The egocentric views of the participants. The members of the major institutions involved in the decision all seemed to see themselves as its heroes. They cast themselves at the center of the action and saw others as peripheral to it. In some note cards and outlines, Schilling imagined how each institution would have collectively judged the period in retrospect. GAC: We fought the good fight against the people who just wanted a bigger weapon without thinking through the rationale. AEC: Scientists here, scientists there, we straightened this out, we got others to face up to their responsibilities. Department of State: Commissioners and military in a big hassle; we made the decision from Olympian heights and straightened it out. JCAE: Executive branch all tied up in knots—we pushed and pushed and got the H-bomb. Military: We got the civilians to make a bomb. Los Alamos: Big bureaucratic hassle in Washington; we just kept on working; we made the bomb in spite of everyone. Truman: I made the tough call.

The intensity and the bitterness of the personal animosities that the political debate engendered. The major product of the decision-making process in this instance was not policy but heat. A nice, dedicated, personable, intelligent, balanced person A would find himself in opposition to what he saw as a bad, stupid, biased, petty person B. The wheels of government do not turn without friction, and this case took a great toll on some personal relationships, something that the interview subjects acknowledged. Henry Smyth said that the chief trouble with the whole case had been too many "emotional" people involved, with Teller in particular being so emotional about the matter as to be unstable.[4] For his part, in his 1956 interview with Schilling, Teller stated that he had still never discussed the GAC report with any of its authors, saying he had been so mad at the time that to do so would have risked permanently rupturing relationships with the others, and now expressing real regret that he would never be able to talk about it with Enrico Fermi, who had died two years earlier.[5]

A notecard written by Schilling following the conclusion of the interview program mused, "If I repeated all the critical things that I have heard about each of these participants: re how stupid, conniving, double-dealing, unstable, etc—impression would be created that the Gov't was staffed by a bunch of knaves, dupes, madmen, juveniles, and dopes. But this not my personal experience—nor is it plausible that there be so many." The notecard then reasoned that if you involve N nice people of relatively normal psychological temperament and above-average intellect and imagination in a decision where different positions are assumed in a situation of imperfect communication and somewhat irrational proceedings, then all participants begin to look like ogres. This perspective reflects conflict, not reality, in the sense that if you take these people out of this context, an observer would make quite a different judgment. But in a conflict situation, personal quirks grate and become causally associated with what you do not like in the other's intellectual position.

And these were big issues, disputed with a passion appropriate to the matter at hand. In his notes on the subject, Schilling imagined two psychological perspectives. From one perspective, you would get mad too if a bunch of people seemed intent on fixing it so that Russia got the H-bomb and you did not, and in their argument came up with lot of debatable points regarding technical possibilities and military use. This would be especially infuriating given that these same people had not been swayed by any of these points a few years earlier during A-bomb development. From the other perspective, you would likewise get mad if you confronted a group of people who could not see any further into the future than the idea that we could improve our security by making bigger and better blasts. Here was an opportunity to take a new turn in the direction the world had been going in since 1945; it certainly seemed worth a try, especially since the H-bomb did not look like it would add much to US power even if it could be made.

Complexity. A wealth and variety of conversations, contacts, meetings, and documents occasioned the making of a decision that, on its face, was rather restricted in the number of people who knew what was going on and had a part in its doing. An illustrative example is a single day from the diary of John Manley, physicist and GAC secretary. On 1 November 1949 he saw three AEC commissioners: Lilienthal, Smyth, and Pike; talked with the acting head of the Military Applications Directorate, Admiral Russell; had a phone conversation with Teller; talked with LeBaron, chair of the MLC; and had dinner with Volpe, general counsel to the AEC.[6] Nor was the complexity always hidden from public view. As a point of comic relief to illustrate the amount of leaking going on, Kennan related a time during the decision process in which a leading dowager asked him, Joint Chiefs chair Omar Bradley, economic adviser Leon Keyserling, and a number of other important Washington figures to dinner. After the meal she dismissed the servants and then proceeded to ask her guests all sorts of embarrassing questions about secret high-policy matters.[7]

Informality. Much more business took place interpersonally and informally than through formal, neutral channels of communication. These actions far exceeded the formal processing of papers along bureaucratic lines of procedure.

Confusion regarding the issues: What are we trying to decide? It was remarkable how confused the participants managed to get over just what were the issues that they were in fact debating. There was confusion on questions regarding producing tritium in the crash program and the possible trade-off in plutonium production for fission use—was the creation of tritium for experimental, test, or production use, in new or old reactors, in parallel or sequential production? There was confusion on questions regarding the shortage of scientific talent—was progress on the Super at Los Alamos being held back by lack of talent, and if so, did the talent have to be reallocated from the fission program or could new talent be found elsewhere? There was confusion over the H-bomb as symbol or substance. Kennan thought the real concern was US policy regarding whether nuclear weapons would only be used for deterrence and for second-strike retaliation, or whether possible first use would be incorporated into the US defense posture. The GAC's reservations really had to do with the morality of strategic bombardment, a reservation that would continue in the minds of H-bomb opponents, as this book has demonstrated. These questions were not resolved in the minds of the people concerned.[8] Nevertheless, it should not be thought that there were no clear issues in the debate; there were. As Schilling observed in another note card written after the interviews, "These problems are no more solvable just because they are real."

Distorted views of the motives and positions of others. As one might expect, there was a difference between how people saw themselves and how others saw them, resulting in grossly distorted views that the participants had of each other's purposes and positions. No one seemed to take anyone else at their declared value. For example, David Lilienthal was surprised and concerned when he found out how dependent the United States had become on nuclear weapons, and he convinced himself that a greater need than the H-bomb was a strengthened conventional weapons force and a more flexible response strategy. But to the military, Lilienthal's statements were a case of "good reasons for real reasons"—cover for the fact that Lilienthal simply did not like nuclear weapons. Teller believed that Oppenheimer opposed H-bomb development largely out of personal vanity, the sense that no one could improve on what he had done with A-bomb development.[9] Regarding Truman's decision, those who saw the H-bomb as a much more powerful weapon, and therefore as obviously needed, portrayed Truman as a man who had common sense. Conversely, those who saw the focus on a weapon as missing larger issues of security and policy saw Truman as a person of limited imagination or as someone caught in a political vice. And then from the vantage point of the White House staff, Sidney Souers had a view of a sober, responsible Truman seeing all angles of the decision.

The "hangover effect." The way people lined up in favor of or opposed to certain issues often seemed much more a reflection of alignments based on preceding policy debates than of the debate currently at hand. Illustrations of this effect include lingering antagonisms between Oppenheimer and the Berkeley group of scientists led by Lawrence, which dated to Oppenheimer's having left Berkeley after the war and was followed by Lawrence's role in the security travails of Oppenheimer's brother Frank. Past feuds between the AEC and the Department of Defense regarding A-bomb requirements—wherein the DoD did not think the AEC was willing to make bombs and the AEC did not think the DoD had any reasoning behind its bomb requests—affected the H-bomb debate. Just as the DoD did not believe Lilienthal had the nation's defense interests at heart and thus looked askance at his A-bomb opportunity costs and conventional warfare points, so, too, did the AEC not really believe that the DoD request for the H-bomb had any real analytical substance to it but rather reflected an instinctive response—to acquire a more powerful weapon—without any thought to need, cost, or alternatives. Strauss had bad relations with the GAC dating back to a 1947 controversy over the exporting of radioisotopes for medical purposes, something the GAC supported but Strauss opposed, leaving the GAC with a low opinion of Strauss.[10] There had been recurring conflict between the JCAE and Lilienthal that had become especially severe earlier in 1949, with Sen. Bourke Hickenlooper leading an investigation of the AEC chair with the goal of having him removed over several allegations of poor management. Although the JCAE's final report exonerated him, the episode left Lilienthal tired and politically weakened.[11] The ordeal no doubt had an impact on the judgments and actions Lilienthal would take during the H-bomb debate.

Kennan and the Policy Planning Staff had been involved in bruising episodes with Congress and others during 1947 regarding how the United States would continue to maintain access to nuclear raw materials overseas, and over the state of the information-sharing agreements with Britain. Kennan believed that the antagonism (and overt warning) that Hickenlooper and Strauss showed him during the H-bomb decision was in part due to the residual feelings from these earlier issues.[12] Teller began his interview with Schilling by saying that you cannot understand later events unless you first know something about earlier days, going back to 1945 and what Teller said was Oppenheimer's conscience about using the A-bomb against Japan only bothering him after the drop, not before.[13] All of these background matters contributed to the heat and antagonisms of the H-bomb debate, and these issues and antagonisms carried forward past the Truman decision.

Handicaps of secrecy. There were considerable effects that the requirements of secrecy imposed on the ability of some of the participants to comprehend the issues involved. In particular, there was great confusion over who in the State Department knew the current size of the US atomic stockpile, which had been quite small following World War II and was a key piece of information in being able to formulate nuclear strategy. In May 1949,

McMahon said publicly that only about twenty-four people in the whole country knew the size of the stockpile—the president; the secretary of state; the secretary of defense; the secretaries of the air force, navy, and army; the four members of the Joint Chiefs; the five AEC commissioners; the seven MLC members; and the heads of the major laboratories involved in atomic work. Neither he nor anyone else in Congress knew.[14] Yet interviews revealed doubt that even all of these people did, especially where the State Department was concerned. While Dean Acheson maintained that he had access to stockpile data and that Gordon Arneson had too, Arneson said no one in State had that information, maybe not even Acheson, and that when representatives of State had requested it, they were refused.[15] The problem had been endemic. In early 1947, when asked to provide recommendations for atomic-materials production rates, James Forrestal, secretary of the navy, said he did not know the size of the stockpile, but that the chief of naval operations did. However, when the chief was asked the same thing, he said he did not know but thought Forrestal did.[16] And in 1954 when John Foster Dulles announced the policy of massive retaliation, he did not know the stockpile size. According to the JCAE staffer Kenneth Mansfield, many people did not *want* to know; there was too much responsibility attached to knowing, and people were afraid they would talk in their sleep. When the JCAE was finally informed, not all members went to the briefing.[17] And when the JCAE finally got clearance to look into the matter, they discovered that annual production was determined by low-level bureaucrats in the Raw Materials Division of the AEC.[18]

This security effect had definite costs. Lilienthal attributed his surprise at learning of the United States' dependence on nuclear weapons to a lack of communication from the DoD to the AEC that was part of the excessive classification that permeated much of the atomic energy area.[19] Kennan shared many of the same concerns, but due to secrecy barriers the Lilienthal and Kennan sides were never joined.

Weapons and morality. One reason for the amount of heat in the debate was that the GAC's point about the immorality of the H-bomb, and how its use would be inconsistent with US objectives, was flawed. To be consistent, the objection should have been extended to the A-bomb as well and, arguably, to all weapons. One can recognize that some GAC members may have felt it better to try to stop H-bomb development—which seemed possible— than to strike at A-bombs, or at strategic bombing as a whole, which seemed less likely to succeed. But because the weapon and not strategic bombing was made the point of objection, it became difficult to reconcile this with Oppenheimer's A-bomb efforts during the war, or with the opponents' continued support of the boosted fission program. As a result, the debate focused on technical objections and the ensuing reactions.[20]

AEC tactics and why Lilienthal lost. To win, Lilienthal had to do two things: divide the enemy (the DoD) and ally with State. He accomplished neither. Regarding the first, the Defense Department had little trust in his arguments. Furthermore, what sidelined Lilienthal, at least in part, was the shift in the definition of the problem, from a question of how large the production program should be to the question of research and development. The services were all agreed regarding the need for research and development, whereas they might have fought over the size of a production program. Thus the Weapon Systems Evaluation Group conception of the problem was not one to raise interservice differences.[21] Regarding the second, Acheson and others within State grew to resent Lilienthal's putting forth arguments, such as those doubting the political-strategic wisdom of being dependent on nuclear weapons and thus urging an increase in conventional arms, that they viewed as outside the AEC's proper area of concern. In addition, Arneson felt that Lilienthal's level of troubled feeling about the issue prevented him from presenting his case well. Arneson mentioned in particular his having witnessed an hour-long plea from Lilienthal to Acheson that resulted only, once Lilienthal had departed, in Acheson saying, "I just don't get the point to his thinking."[22] A comparison can be seen with Oppenheimer, who stopped fighting this decision as soon as he saw he could not persuade Acheson (although, as this book makes clear, he continued to fight in other contexts).[23]

The role of international relations premises. This is a point where there was a clear division of opinion regarding consequences. There was a school of thought that held that nuclear weapons were the Western nations' best defense. To those in this school—including Teller and Strauss—the breaking of the nuclear monopoly was a catastrophic event. There was another school who had never been happy about the West's reliance on nuclear weapons. To them—including Kennan and Oppenheimer—this event was less consequential in one particular sense, in that it showed that they were right all along in not pinning policy to this monopoly. And to them it was also of consequence in another direction—now something must be done about the overreliance on atomic weapons. These two approaches to atomic weapons and international relations led to two interpretations of the meaning of the Russian A-bomb, and these led in turn to two different approaches to the Super issue. To the first school, the Super was clearly needed; the nuclear weapons position must be maintained, and opposition to the Super seemed perverse. But to the second, the Super project looked like making an old mistake all over again.

Views on this divide were often related to a second point of view regarding international relations: the question of capability versus intent in threat perception. Should you plan on the basis of the likely intent of an adversary, or should you base all your plans on the capabilities of an adversary and assume that it will do whatever bad things it can to you? For most of those involved in the H-bomb decision, the guiding philosophy was clearly capability oriented. This caused Kennan great frustration, since he saw no desire on the part of the Soviets to try to overrun Western Europe; they had already had "their belly full" of war after World War II, which had been far more destructive for them than for the other Allies, and they were not about to start another war, nuclear weapons or not. Kennan said he tried hundreds of times to convince DoD officials that the Soviet leaders did not want to lose their industrial plant, which was the only thing they had to show for all their revolutionary sacrifices (and which would have been a primary target of any US strategic bombing campaign).[24] As Kennan detected and Acheson admitted, a pattern in international relations is for the search for security to reach the most reliable or lowest-common-denominator solution available, one that revolves around the capabilities of armed forces. So it is possible to believe that, regardless of one's conclusions about the H-bomb decision itself, it was unfortunate that the Kennan-type perspective was so weakly voiced within the governmental decision-making process.

Another instance of international relations premises having an effect was the question of whether the H-bomb decision point could be used to break the stalemate on the international control of atomic energy, a question that arose not just in 1949 but also in 1952 during the drive by Vannevar Bush and the State Department Panel of Consultants to reach an agreement with the Soviets to forego testing of the H-bomb. Acheson's position was simple: the Russians did not operate in this kind of "deliberate way." There were times when you could negotiate with the Russians and times you could not. The time between 1949 and 1952 was a time when you could not.[25]

The bitterness Schilling noted perhaps accounts for his finding that the participants had grossly distorted views of each other's purposes and positions. And in one particular respect, the archival record throws a rather different light on Schilling's finding of the "isolation" of the participants. At various stages, but most notably in the period after Truman's initial decision, when the arguments were moving on, some of these individuals formed their own potent coalitions against the dissenters, coordinating their actions while being less than forthcoming about their purposes, both to Schilling and to the public record. In that art, Lewis Strauss was supreme.

If such a complex, contradictory, and inconsistent picture emerged from Schilling's interviews, it is because they mapped the way the arguments went at the time of the original events. The passage of a few years failed to impose greater rationality on the recollections of those involved. Schilling, ever keen to make sense of the confused story of the Super, put a question to Lt. Gen. Alvin Luedecke that he had not asked previously:

> I asked if at the time he thought these people were really questioning strategic bombing rather than the H-bomb, in terms of morality. He agrees that this is what they logically should have done, but he doesn't think they saw it this way.[26]

This was one of those occasions when Schilling pushed beyond the protocol of his study to pose what would have seemed to some of the participants a tangential issue and to others a central concern. With all the evidence now available, not least regarding Project Vista, the Lincoln Summer Study, the formerly redacted passages of the Security Board hearing, and the additional archival sources, it is apparent that Schilling's question had identified the crucial thread of continuity in H-bomb dissidence: the strategic bombing posture of Strategic Air Command.

Opposing—and Supporting—"Strategic" Bombing

The H-bomb dissidents opposed the proposal to continue thermonuclear research, rightly anticipating that to determine feasibility would require a test, with all its attendant dangers. A test would also bring adoption for use that much closer. They were appalled by the prospect of using a weapon of such massive and necessarily indiscriminate destructiveness against cities and their civilian populations. Yet to maintain a firm distinction between the consequences of thermonuclear and atomic bombing required as great a degree of casuistry as maintaining the distinction between World War II's mass city bombing and atomic assault. However much they struggled to draw meaningful lines, opposition to developing the Super was inseparable from a rejection of the SAC doctrine of strategic bombing.

What was that doctrine? The final months of World War II saw the virtual abandonment of the US Army Air Forces practice of selective precision targeting. True, the accuracy achieved had been variable, but in the Pacific, the Twentieth Air Force was pressed into the service of a policy of indiscriminate area bombing with incendiaries. The argument was still conducted in terms of the broad goals of "strategic bombing," but the term was too elastic. This was *area bombing*, or what, in the later nuclear age, became known euphemistically as countervalue targeting, or more bluntly as population targeting—that is, the targeting of a civilian population per se.[27] It provided an accepted baseline for the use of the atomic bomb against Hiroshima and Nagasaki, and it was this understanding of what "strategic bombing" meant that Oppenheimer and his associates opposed. Kenneth Mansfield believed that Oppenheimer objected to strategic bombing because it was "clumsy and heavy-handed. It is using the sledgehammer rather than the surgeon's scalpel; it takes no great imagination or sophistication."[28] How true this was of the bombings of Japan. How much more so it would have been of a thermonuclear conflict, in which even in the early stages of H-bomb deployment the Soviet Union would be estimated to suffer sixty million fatalities and lose 118 of its 134 major cities.[29]

The response of the air force in defense of its central doctrine of strategic bombardment had the effect of aligning the conflict in a sharply polarized fashion. The proposal to have Oppenheimer lead a review of the efficacy of the strategic bombing plans was decisively rejected by Air Force Secretary Thomas Finletter and chief of staff Hoyt Vandenberg, spilling over into a rejection of the man himself as a trusted consultant and marking the beginning of a period in which scientific advice—and scientific advisers—would come to be treated with suspicion. When Secretary of Defense Robert Lovett asked James Perkins, deputy chair of the Defense Research and Development Board, to look at the troubled relationship between the Pentagon and the Atomic Energy Commission, Perkins reported a belief within the higher ranks of the air force that the GAC was under the control of people who were opposed not only to the H-bomb but also to the strategic use of A-bombs.[30]

By the time Project Vista got under way, the air force and to a lesser extent the Defense Department were monitoring developments in order to head off any proposals that might run counter to the prevailing doctrine. Lovett was relaxed about the Vista authors presenting their proposals to Eisenhower and Lauris Norstad, although when Perkins arranged the trip for them, Finletter was furious, feeling his service was being undermined. Initially the Vista proposals were greeted with mild interest, especially by Norstad, although the official line then hardened.

The follow-on to Project Lincoln saw Oppenheimer and other dissidents developing a forceful argument in favor of comprehensive air defense as a viable alternative to a strategy of deterrence. They turned back the "Maginot Line" accusation against the air force, exposing SAC's "all eggs in one basket" posture as rooted in a deeply embedded organizational conservatism. Faced with such a fundamental critique, the air force closed ranks. Vandenberg's successor as chief of staff, Gen. Nathan Twining, later published his conviction that this civilian-scientific "weakness of purpose" aimed to erode the United States' reliance on nuclear deterrence.[31]

Today it is generally accepted that there is no real evidence that the Soviets ever considered launching a "bolt from the blue" against the United States.[32] Air force leaders' conviction that this threat was real through 1950–54 may indeed have been a misperception, but it arose from the inescapable—and surely understandable—tendency of military men to perceive threat in terms of the adversary's capabilities, given that his real intentions were unknowable.[33] Capabilities loomed large in the calculus, eclipsing geopolitical rivalries as a trigger for conflict, and creating a climate in which, Francis Gavin remarks in a penetrating analysis, "the weapons themselves—their lethality, their numbers, their deployments—drove the politics, not the other way around." It is, Gavin observes, "an extraordinary way of viewing international relations."[34]

Nevertheless, issues in international relations are often represented in terms of "frames"—and often in terms of competing frames. That tendency becomes especially marked when issues reach the public arena, with the mass media looking for simple, coherent stories to tell. Frames, or the process of framing, provide ways of making sense of complexity, categorizing and storytelling for purposes of public representation, often in vivid, polarized terms.[35] The Soviet threat, both then and later, provided an opportunity for contesting frames, with seemingly significant effects on public opinion.

Competing frames in relation to the several aspects of the Super prevailed throughout the period covered in this book. How do they bear on the divisions that so polarized the advocates and opponents of the Super? The answer advanced here is twofold. First, there are the organizational alignments that, on the military side, shaped responses to the prospect of the Super and to its development, testing, production, and entry into service. Second, there are the factors that made this conflict one of fundamental beliefs, of deeply held values.

To take the first point, the well-worn adage "where you stand depends on where you sit" is often (but wrongly) attributed to Morton Halperin or Graham Allison. Coined by Edward Miles, who formulated it while serving in the Bureau of the Budget in 1947, it is almost a platitude, yet the ongoing patterns of conflict between the Department of Defense, the air force, and the MLC on the one hand and the AEC (under both Lilienthal's and Dean's chairmanships) on the other are entirely understandable in those terms.[36] Organizational interests are dominated by the desire to maintain the autonomy of the organization in pursuing what its members view as the essence of the organization's activity.[37] It is easy to claim too much for the power of this insight, for, as the policy analyst Edmund Beard points out, while policies are undoubtedly "influenced to a greater or lesser degree by organizational and personal interests, which operate generally within a broad set of shared images or constraints," there is a danger that the Halperin/Allison organizational politics perspective has become "all-inclusive"— capable, objects Beard, of "explaining any policy, or for that matter any action, in retrospect."[38]

Importantly, though, the originators of the organizational politics perspective did warn that to view organizations—even military organizations— as monoliths is to miss the reality of divisions within them.[39] Henry Smyth exemplified this point, summarizing his views on the Oppenheimer case as "a campaign by certain Air Force zealots against Oppenheimer and presumably this arose from violent opposition to some of the advice that Oppenheimer gave which was contrary to the views of a faction of the Air Force."[40] But while there were such factions, the most powerful of them, Strategic Air Command, was strong enough to be able to overwhelm any internal doubters and set the orthodoxy. Its doctrine, which had been shaped—with remarkable freedom from interference—by Curtis LeMay, appeared to the dissidents to be fatally mistaken.

It is important to understand how this "mistake" arose, and this is the second point. Strategic bombardment was more than what Michael Oakeshott would have dismissed as a "bright idea," following his famous declaration in his essay on political education that "freedom, like a recipe for game pie, is not a bright idea" to be deduced "from some speculative concept of human nature. . . . [It] is not an 'ideal' which we premeditate independently of our political experience, it is what is already intimated in that experience."[41] By that reckoning, the doctrine of strategic bombardment is something best understood as arising from what Oakeshott would have termed the "intimations of a particular *military* experience."

Henry S. Rowen surely gets this absolutely right:

> Characterizing *the* doctrine of a Command or Service is a tricky business. Within these organizations there are people who have a considerable variety of values, attitudes and expectations—almost as large a variety as is held in American society. Nevertheless, within a Command certain values and operational codes tend to dominate and strongly affect perceptions, attitudes and actions of its members. *These are created in large measure by learned experiences and interpretations of experience. Doctrine is, among other things, a codification of learning.*[42]

US Air Force officers put their trust in the experiences of the Army Air Forces' campaigns in World War II, and in the learning—on which the bombing of Japan put a seal—they derived from them. That propelled their opposition to the scientific advice channeled through the AEC, and their subsequent effective maneuvers to neutralize Projects Vista and Lincoln. The conflict may have been experienced as vicious, but it was an expression of situational rationality, and driven by the simplest of organizational logics.

It does not belittle the position taken by the air force advocates of strategic bombing to describe it in these terms. However it originated, the doctrine was founded on deeply held values and beliefs, "intimations of experience" as deep and as genuine as those that drove Oppenheimer and his fellow dissidents. That these values and beliefs were so deep-rooted explains the intensity of the polarization that Schilling encountered in his interviews. The conflict was vicious because the feelings were visceral.

A conflict between two opposed coalitions of players, advocating respectively for and against thermonuclear weapons, provides a framework for understanding the working of "policy entrepreneurship" among these networks of participants as they negotiate and bargain with a view to changing attitudes and beliefs within and beyond government.[43] From this perspective, policy beliefs can be seen as hierarchically organized. At the surface level, advocacy coalitions (and their countercoalitions) are dealing with *policy specifics*, programs supported (or opposed) by bureaucratic or political interests but open to change by determined leaders. Examples would be particular technologies, deployments, or practices. At a deeper level they may well encounter the *policy core* of fundamental governmental values—the taken-for-granted world of public policy inviting (but unlikely to respond to) fundamental challenge. At this level we might find conflicting values about how best to secure US security interests: through deterrence, negotiation, or arms control. These difficult-to-change values may themselves be rooted in the *deep core* of fundamental and ontological axioms—resilient, deep-seated, and impervious to challenge and change. When we drill down to this level, we encounter opposed views on the acceptability of engaging in nuclear warfare against civilian populations, rooted in the value placed on innocent lives. From this perspective, argument over a specific proposal (to develop the Super) triggered deeper-seated, fundamental beliefs in conflict, even when the argument appeared to be expressed superficially at the surface level of military policy.

The passionate advocacy of the dissenting coalition (Oppenheimer, Conant, DuBridge, Kennan, Lilienthal, and many other scientists and churchmen) arose from a deep belief that to use a thermonuclear weapon against a civilian population would be an act of evil, even of genocide. Although they were on the losing side, they showed remarkable resilience in shifting their advocacy onto other specific areas of policy in attempts to shift policy away from the reliance on strategic bombing, while steering around the obvious deep-core controversy that underlay it. For the opposing coalition of the Pentagon, the Military Liaison Committee, and the US Air Force, supported by McMahon and Strauss (and in time by a majority of Strauss's fellow commissioners) and by a few scientists such as Teller and Alvarez, the deep-core beliefs centered on the primacy of US security and the need to counter the threat posed to that security by a nuclear-armed Communist aggressor. It was obviously the more powerful alignment, and during 1949–54 there could be no reconciliation or compromise between these opposing coalitions.

Many advocacy coalitions are loosely organized or even transient. In this case, the prevailing ideas about US security in the nuclear age were set down and elaborated by Strategic Air Command, which, under LeMay, assumed the prerogative of judging how that security could be maintained. It is difficult to overstate the personal significance of LeMay in setting what has been described as the "organizational culture" of SAC. That term is widely and loosely used, and rarely brings enlightenment. In the case of SAC, however—that "Air Force within an Air Force," as Melvin G. Deaile aptly calls it—the term is justified.[44] SAC was dominated by a charismatic leader who understood the importance of exemplary leadership, the potency of symbols, and the routes to establishing a shared mentality among aircrew. It provides a rare example of a virtually closed, monovalent organization. The nuclear dissidents stood little chance against so formidable an opponent.

Now Thrive the Armorers

Today, Truman's reputation still rides high. His ready grasp of a situation and his distaste for unnecessary complication enabled him to keep abreast of the Super proposal without getting distracted by the scientific or moral debate. There was, he confided, really no decision to make, confounding Barton Bernstein's puzzle as to whether the president was responding to bureaucratic pressures, a technological-scientific imperative, congressional and domestic political pressure, his sense of international needs, or a demanding military and their congressional supporters.[45] As matters presented themselves to Truman, there was no acceptable alternative. If the Russians could achieve the Super, then the United States must endeavor to stay ahead and not delay.

There are critics who contend that Truman's decisions over the course of his presidency intensified the US-Soviet conflict due to his alleged lack of insight, his supposed inability to "see beyond his immediate decision or visualize alternatives," as Arnold Offner puts it.[46] Unquestionably, his decision to proceed with the hydrogen bomb could only have the effect of raising the stakes in the great power conflict. Was decisive action in that instance less to his credit than would have been extended mature consideration, made with the benefit of the scientific advice that he had effectively foresworn? Surely not. Such advice might not have differed from that provided indirectly through the GAC, or would have been inconclusive. More reliable intelligence might have helped but, had it been available, would likely have confirmed the Soviet interest in thermonuclear development. Like the Soviet leadership, Truman had to contend with a fog of scanty information and a horizon clouded by supposition.

In reality Truman was faced with no alternative to making a decision that took account of unsupported speculation about Soviet thermonuclear potential. It happened that those speculations were correct, and that Soviet nuclear science did pose a threat to the United States. While Truman could have held back, Soviet developments were subject to the same relentless logic of iterative decisions that propelled them forward; weapons of mass destruction had taken on a life of their own in both countries.[47] The claim put forward by the dissidents that refraining from Super development would have constrained the Soviet program was never more than a perilously slim hope.

Forebodings about the crippling cost of a thermonuclear weapons program proved to be misplaced, the actual weapon costs being dwarfed by those of the massively expensive delivery vehicles, even before the missile age got fully under way.[48] In another respect, the dissenters' skepticism proved well founded. Between 1945 and 1996, the United States produced some seventy thousand nuclear weapons; a Brookings study concluded that the allocation of resources to these weapons "sometimes had little discernible relationship to the levels of threat these weapons were supposed to counter."[49]

Was the buildup of nuclear arms that followed stabilizing or destabilizing? It is often argued that the development of thermonuclear weapons so raised the stakes in international conflict that both superpowers were bound to shy away from it in mutual limitation. The common claim is that, as Kenneth Waltz has argued, the United States and the Soviet Union "constrained each other," that they "held each other in check."[50] Luis Alvarez had no doubts on this score:

> I have difficulty understanding why so many people see nuclear weapons as mankind's greatest threat. Not one of them has been used since World War II, and without question they have prevented World War III, which would otherwise almost certainly have been fought by now with enormous loss of life.[51]

Skeptics of this notion of mutual restraint can cite an important counterfactual: that the notion implies that in a nonnuclear world, the United States and the Soviet Union would have gone to war.[52]

These things are unknowable. So too is the future of world politics. Schilling closed his 1961 article on the Super with these words:

> Both the Soviet Union and the United States would no doubt have preferred a world in which neither had the H-bomb. Each, however, wished to avoid a world in which the other had the H-bomb and it did not. Both rushed to make it, and they ended in a worse position than that in which they had begun.[53]

That judgment stands. What we have presented here, then, is a story of hopes and fears, hopes largely dashed and fears, mercifully, not yet realized.

Notes

Preface

1. Quoted in Ambrose, *Eisenhower*, 484–85.
2. "Columbia Founds War-Peace Study."
3. Guilhot, *Invention of International Relations Theory*, esp. 156, 183. Guilhot's contributors, reviewing the discussions of half a century earlier, are dismissive of what they term the "anti-liberal, anti-scientific" distortions of an academic approach that they consider to have been designed primarily to sustain "American hegemony."
4. Internal memorandum, Fox to Rabi, 2 May 1956, WRS personal papers.
5. Fox, *Institute of War and Peace Studies*, 5.
6. Schilling, "Scientists, Foreign Policy, and Politics." An expanded version appeared as a chapter in the book *Scientists and National Policy Making*.
7. Schilling, "H-bomb Decision," 30n.
8. Schilling, "H-bomb Decision," 30n. The cover letter of the initial contacts that Schilling made to obtain these interviews stated that "any discussion would be treated after the usual academic custom for such case studies: no quotations or citation." References to this crop up repeatedly in the interview notes: some subjects are very anxious about the point, some moderately so, while some seem content if what they say goes on the record. When asked about this decades later, Schilling said that the "customary" language was a dodge used by several institute studies, in the sense that both he and the interviewee were sometimes aware that questions and answers were edging into (what was then) classified material, and saying there would be no quotation or citation gave an "out" in the discussion. It is also relevant that the interviews were conducted only a few years after the Oppenheimer hearing, and the "no quotations or citation" promise may have had as much to do with the political, and in some cases personal, sensitivity of the subject matter as with concerns about classified information. In any case, Schilling later said (and an abandoned early draft confirms) that direct citations were always supposed to be included in the book that he intended to write. And certainly with the passage of time since then, there is no reason not to include them, and that is what this book does. (Explicit quotations from the interviews are infrequent, since Schilling kept very detailed notes of the interviews rather than transcriptions.)
9. Young, "Hydrogen Bomb."
10. Young, "Revisiting NSC-68."

11. On page 829, note 45, of "Hydrogen Bomb," Young states that Schilling could not recall interviewing Strauss. This Schilling in fact did, on two occasions; his reticence probably derived from his regret at not having completed the study.

Introduction

1. Bundy, *Danger and Survival*, 197–98.
2. Hewlett and Duncan, *Atomic Shield*.
3. Anders, *Forging the Atomic Shield*; Defense Threat Reduction Agency, *Defense's Nuclear Agency*; Rosenberg, "American Atomic Strategy."
4. McMahon to Truman, 30 May 1952, in US Department of State, *Foreign Relations of the United States, 1952–54*, pt. 2, 955–57.
5. Ferrell, *Harry S. Truman and the Cold War Revisionists*, 80; Donovan, *Tumultuous Years*, 148–57; Truman, *Memoirs*, 308–9; Rhodes, *Dark Sun*, 404, 407–8. The scant two pages that Truman devotes to the matter should not be assumed an accident or an oversight committed by collaborating writers, as Truman was heavily involved in the writing of his memoirs. See Alperovitz, *Decision to Use the Atomic Bomb*, 540–42.
6. Broscious, "Longing for International Control," 37–38.
7. Offner, *Another Such Victory*, 362–63, is critical of what is portrayed as Truman's willful self-isolation from nuclear weapons advice. Herken, *Cardinal Choices*, 29–33, 37–38, 54–60, makes a similar case on the basis of deeper research.
8. Bernstein, "H-bomb Decisions," 327–28.
9. Bernstein, "Truman and the H-bomb," 17.
10. York, *Advisors*, 45–46.
11. Davis, *9/11 Commission Recommendations*, 14.
12. Bernstein, "Four Physicists"; Galison and Bernstein, "In Any Light."
13. Herken, *Cardinal Choices*, chaps. 3–4.
14. Smyth correspondence with Hamilton Fish Armstrong, 26 May 1959 through 2 August 1960, "History of the H-bomb #2" folder, series 7, Henry DeWolf Smyth Papers, American Philosophical Society.
15. Book outline, box 2, folder 9, Robert LeBaron Papers, Hoover Institution, Stanford University. The outline, prepared for consideration by a publisher, was alternatively titled *Decision at H-day*.
16. Truman, *Memoirs*, 295, 306, 308, 310; Ferrell, *Harry S. Truman and the Cold War Revisionists*, 80; Donovan, *Tumultuous Years*, 152–56.
17. More specifically on Truman's decision to use the atomic bomb, see Ferrell, *Harry S. Truman and the Bomb*. The leading critical account of that decision in a wealth of literature is Alperovitz, *Decision to Use the Atomic Bomb*.
18. Warner R. Schilling (hereafter WRS) interview with Dean Acheson, 24 October 1956, 8. Each interview was typed up by Schilling shortly after its completion, and the page numbers cited here for each interview refer to those notes. (For certain interview subjects, Schilling also kept separate notes for questions pertaining to scientist-military relations in general. If those notes are referenced, they will be so indicated.)
19. The suspension of Oppenheimer's security clearance, and its removal following a four-week AEC Personnel Security Board hearing, has been extensively covered elsewhere. See Bird and Sherwin, *American Prometheus*, chaps. 33–37; Hewlett and Holl, *Atoms for Peace and War*, chaps. 3–4. Particularly useful is Bernstein, "Oppenheimer Loyalty-Security Case Reconsidered." An unclassified but redacted record of the hearing is in US Atomic Energy Commission, *In the Matter of J. Robert Oppenheimer: Transcript of Hearing before Personnel Security Board*; subsequently, the Department of Energy released *In the Matter of J. Robert Oppenheimer: Transcript of Hearing before Personnel Security Board, Record of Classified Deletions*.
20. In an unfinished draft of an introductory chapter, composed after the completion of his interviews, Schilling wrote, "The Oppenheimer hearings have been much discussed. This

study is not intended to be a statement on Oppenheimer in that context; that is not its purpose, and no evidence is supplied in that regard." Postinterview introduction draft, 5, WRS personal papers.

21. Schilling, "H-bomb Decision," 24.

22. Quoted in Bernstein, "Four Physicists," 258.

23. J. H. Manley, "Military Worth," 15 December 1949, 20, "History of the H-bomb #1" folder, series 7, Smyth Papers.

24. WRS interview with Rear Adm. T. B. Hill, 1 May 1957, 2. Citations refer to military interview subjects by their rank at the time of the interview, which may be different from their rank at the time of the events described in the narrative.

25. WRS interview with Maj. Gen. Alvin R. Luedecke, 3 May 1957, 7.

26. An important treatment of nuclear testing is Blades and Siracusa, *History of U.S. Nuclear Testing*.

27. WRS interview with Maj. Gen. Alvin R. Luedecke, 3 May 1957, 6.

28. Galison and Bernstein, "In Any Light," 284.

29. Galison and Bernstein, "In Any Light," 283–84, 315.

30. See for example Haynes, *Awesome Power*, 151 and index.

31. WRS notes on conversation with Kenneth Mansfield, 15 December 1955, 1.

32. This passage summarizes the perspective set out by Hilsman in "Foreign-Policy Consensus," esp. 362–63, elaborated in Tarr, "Military Technology," 138–39.

33. This and other observations drawn by Schilling are expanded on in the conclusion.

34. WRS interview with Harry S. Truman, 14 September 1957, 2.

1. The Shock of the "New World"

1. Hewlett and Anderson, *New World*.

2. "MLC Comments concerning H-bomb Developments," 16 June 1954, AEC Secretary's files, RG 326, National Archives and Records Administration (hereafter NARA).

3. Lilienthal, *Change, Hope and the Bomb*, 142–43.

4. Dean Acheson, interview by William Hillman and David Noyes for the preparation of Truman's memoirs, 16 February 1955, Post-Presidential Papers, Harry S. Truman Presidential Library.

5. Siracusa, "NSC 68," 7–8; Hammond, *NSC-68*, 289–92.

6. Young, "Revisiting NSC 68," 23–25.

7. Nitze, *From Hiroshima to Glasnost*, 87.

8. Schilling's own work on the budgetary process in this fiscal year, *Politics of National Defense*, is highly pertinent to this point.

9. Gordin, *Red Cloud at Dawn*, 183–89.

10. Gordin, *Red Cloud at Dawn*, 189–90.

11. Ziegler, "Waiting for Joe-1," 198–201.

12. Bush, advice to the Joint Planning Staff, 22 August 1945, cited in Schnabel, *History of the Joint Chiefs*, 65. On Bush's role more generally, see Zachary, *Endless Frontier*, 292–309, 349–51.

13. Ziegler, "Waiting for Joe-1," 201–2; Wolk, *Planning and Organizing*, 180, 221–22.

14. Ziegler, "Waiting for Joe-1," 215.

15. Gordin, *Red Cloud at Dawn*, 195–283.

16. Condit, *History of the Joint Chiefs*, 279.

17. "An Interim Report on British Work on JOE," 22 September 1949, President's Secretary's Files, HST.

18. Hewlett and Duncan, *Atomic Shield*, 362–65; Ziegler, "Waiting for Joe-1," 216.

19. Chief of Naval Research, "Analysis of Sample of Airborne Material," 26 September 1949, President's Secretary's Files.

20. Meilinger, *Hoyt. S. Vandenberg*, 151.

21. Condit, *History of the Joint Chiefs*, 279.

22. Johnson to Truman, 27 February 1950, "Public Relations Reference the H-bomb Decision," President's Secretary's Files. Johnson was urging views put to him by David Sarnoff of the Radio Corporation of America, a reserve brigadier general.

23. Gordin, *Red Cloud at Dawn*, 223–38.

24. Symington, memorandum to Johnson, 8 November 1949, President's Secretary's Files.

25. Bradley, "This Way Lies Peace," quoted with a few discrepancies in Futrell, *Ideas, Concepts, Doctrine*, 282, 353n38.

26. Schnabel, *History of the Joint Chiefs*, 129.

27. "General LeMay Calls AAF Custodian of World Peace," War Department press release, 19 July 1946, box 5, press releases 1945–46, Eben A. Ayers Papers, HST.

28. Schnabel, *History of the Joint Chiefs*, 65.

29. Quoted in Defense Threat Reduction Agency, *Defense's Nuclear Agency*, 47; see also Bundy, *Danger and Survival*, 177, 662n106, for the quotation's origins as found by David Holloway.

30. WRS interview with Paul Nitze, 27 February 1957, 2.

31. WRS interview with Robert Tufts, 13 March 1956, 2.

32. Steury, "How the CIA Missed Stalin's Bomb," 22.

33. Condit, *History of the Joint Chiefs*, 280.

34. US Atomic Energy Commission, *In the Matter of J. Robert Oppenheimer: Transcript of Hearing before Personnel Security Board, Record of Classified Deletions*, 6.

35. Testimony of Rabi, in US Atomic Energy Commission, *In the Matter of J. Robert Oppenheimer: Transcript of Hearing before Personnel Security Board* (hereafter *Oppenheimer Personnel Security Board Transcript*), 467.

36. WRS interviews with Kenneth Pitzer, 14 December 1956, 1; William Borden, 10 October 1956, 4; and Gordon Arneson, 27 March 1957, 3.

37. WRS interview with George Kennan, 14 September 1956, 2.

38. Nitze, *From Hiroshima to Glasnost*, 86–87.

39. US Department of State, Policy Planning Staff PPS/58, "Political Implications of the Detonation of Atomic Bomb by the USSR," 16 August 1949, in US Department of State, *Foreign Relations of the United States* (hereafter *FRUS*), 1949, 514–15.

40. Department of Defense, Appendix C, "The Military Implications of Thermonuclear Weapons," Annex 1, in "Report by the Special Committee of the National Security Council to the President," 31 January 1950, *FRUS*, 1950, 520–21.

41. WRS interview with Maj. Gen. Leslie Groves, 6 August 1956, 9.

42. "D.C. Nominees Sought to Take Atom Courses."

43. Report by the Director, Joint Staff, to the Joint Chiefs of Staff, on the strategic implications of Soviet possession of atomic weapons, 8 November 1949, 471.6 USSR (11-8-49) S.1, box 88, JCS Geographical File 1948–50, RG 218, NARA.

44. Proposed amendments to JIC 502 by Director of Naval Intelligence, Enclosure B, n.d., ca. 12 January 1950, box 88, RG 218, NARA.

45. JIC 502, Appendix B, "Implications of Soviet Possession of Atomic Weapons," 20 January 1950, 11–12, 17, 19, box 88, RG 218, NARA.

46. In-flight refueling technology was widely known, and the AAF was an early adopter. It was not an unreasonable expectation that Soviet strategic bombing practice would follow a similar path. In fact Soviet interest was limited, and it is believed that by 1952 just a small number of Tu-4s had been converted to supplier/receiver roles. JIC 502, Appendix B, 26–27; Zaloga, *Kremlin's Nuclear Sword*, 20.

47. JIC 502, Appendix B, 42.

48. JIC 502, Appendix B, 17, 24.

49. Mitrovich, *Undermining the Kremlin*, 52–58.

50. Maj. Gen. C. P. Cabell, Director of Intelligence, US Air Force, Commanders Conference, Ramey Air Force Base, Puerto Rico, 25–27 April 1950 (hereafter Commanders Conference), 2–14, National Security Archive, https://nsarchive2.gwu.edu/nukevault/special/doc03a.pdf.

51. Beisner, *Dean Acheson*, 243.

52. Symington, memorandum to Johnson, 8 November 1949. The complexities of the successive war plans from Pincher to Dropshot are covered in Ross, *American War Plans*.

53. Quoted in Schilling, *Politics of National Defense*, 128; for analysis of the force goal, see 71–79.
54. McCullough, *Truman*, 741.
55. Symington, memorandum to Johnson, 8 November 1949.
56. Barlow, *Revolt of the Admirals*, chaps. 5, 8–9.
57. Schilling, *Politics of National Defense*, 168–73.
58. Deaile, *Always at War*, 75–76.
59. Schnabel, *History of the Joint Chiefs*, 130.
60. Schaffel, *Emerging Shield*, 53–56.
61. Kaplan, *To Kill Nations*, 79.
62. Monks, "Soviet Strategic Air Force," 214–15.
63. Friedman, "Soviet Bomber Force," 169–70; Baker, "Long-Range Bomber."
64. Schaffel, *Emerging Shield*, 62–67, 69.
65. Schaffel, *Emerging Shield*, 89.
66. Schaffel, *Emerging Shield*, 68.
67. Schaffel, *Emerging Shield*, 76.
68. Schaffel, *Emerging Shield*, 95–102.
69. Schaffel, *Emerging Shield*, 89.
70. Futrell, *Ideas, Concepts, Doctrine*, 285–86.
71. Quoted in Condit, *History of the Joint Chiefs*, 286.
72. Minutes of the meetings of the Joint Chiefs of Staff, JCS 2084, 16 November 1949, Liddell Hart Centre for Military Archives (hereafter Liddell Hart).
73. Minutes of the meetings of the Joint Chiefs of Staff, JCS 2084, 23 November 1950, Liddell Hart; Condit, *History of the Joint Chiefs*, 286.
74. Minutes of the meetings of the Joint Chiefs of Staff, JCS 2084/1, 1 December 1949, Liddell Hart.
75. Condit, *History of the Joint Chiefs*, 288.
76. Schaffel, *Emerging Shield*, 197–98.
77. Lt. Gen. Curtis E. LeMay, CINCSAC, Commanders Conference, 518, https://nsarchive2.gwu.edu/nukevault/special/doc03b.pdf.
78. Cabell, Commanders Conference, 4, https://nsarchive2.gwu.edu/nukevault/special/doc03a.pdf. Cabell explicitly rejected CIA advice on Soviet intentions, regarding military intelligence as better founded.
79. Cabell, Commanders Conference, 9, https://nsarchive2.gwu.edu/nukevault/special/doc03a.pdf.
80. Maj. Gen. S. E. Anderson, Commanders Conference, 43, 46, https://nsarchive2.gwu.edu/nukevault/special/doc03a.pdf.
81. McMullen, *History of Air Defense Weapons*, chap. 6, n.p.
82. York, *Race to Oblivion*, 18–21. York was the sometime US director of defense research and engineering.
83. Atomic Energy Commission, *Draft Chronology, Atomic Energy Commission Thermonuclear Program*, Appendix: Expansion Program 1949, 131, box 465, Lewis L. Strauss Papers, Herbert Hoover Presidential Library.
84. WRS interview with John Ohly, 20 May 1957, 1.
85. Ohly to Johnson, 7 October 1949, box 8, entry 184, RG 330, NARA.
86. "Report to the President by the Special Committee of the National Security Council on the Proposed Acceleration of the Atomic Energy Program," 10 October 1949, President's Secretary's Files. Also reproduced in *FRUS*, 1949, 559–63.
87. Truman to Sidney Souers, 26 July 1949, *FRUS*, 1949, 501–3.
88. "Report to the President by the Special Committee."
89. Nichols to Gen. Omar Bradley, 7 October 1949, box 8, entry 184, RG 330, NARA.
90. "Report to the President by the Special Committee."
91. Leffler, *Preponderance of Power*, 327.
92. This summary is based on a detailed chronology of events submitted by McMahon to Truman on 30 May 1952, and passed to the NSC's special committee on atomic energy on 12 June of that year. President's Secretary's Files.
93. McMahon to Johnson, 14 July 1949, *FRUS*, 1949, 482–84; Truman, *Memoirs*, 297.

94. Marks, "Washington Notes," 327; *Investigation into the United States Atomic Energy Commission*, 87.

95. Hickenlooper to McMahon, January 1950, box 21, JCAE series, Bourke B. Hickenlooper Papers, Herbert Hoover Presidential Library.

96. Dingman, "Atomic Diplomacy," 51–55.

97. Hewlett and Duncan, *Atomic Shield*, 525–29; James S. Lay, Executive Secretary, NSC, to Truman, 2 October 1950, approved 9 October, President's Secretary's Files.

98. "Charge of 'Reluctance' on H-bomb Is Denied," *US News and World Report*; Joint AEC-DOD report to McMahon, 2, 17 January 1952, box 387, RG 330, NARA.

99. McMahon to Secretary of Defense, 2 April 1952, box 387, RG 330, NARA.

100. York, *Advisors*, 26.

101. Hawkins, *Project Y*, 14–15. This volume reproduces the earlier *Manhattan District History*, completed by the Los Alamos Scientific Laboratory in 1947 and first made available in 1961. *Project Y* modifies the *District History* with the addition of declassified material and some other revisions, including stylistic changes in the wording of several passages, made in 1983.

102. Hawkins, *Project Y*, 87.

103. Hammel, interview by Sherwin. One minor transcription error corrected by comparison to recording.

104. WRS interview with Hans Bethe, 17 May 1957, 1. On the failure to anticipate the damage at Hiroshima, see also Fermi, *Atoms in the Family*, 242.

105. WRS interview with Hans Bethe, 17 May 1957, 2.

106. Hammel, interview by Sherwin.

107. Hawkins, *Project Y*, 87–88.

108. WRS interview with Maj. Gen. Leslie Groves, 6 August 1956, 6.

109. Hewlett and Anderson, *New World*, 356.

110. Quoted in Herken, *Cardinal Choices*, 36.

111. Truslow and Smith, *Project Y*, 307–8.

112. Moody, *Building a Strategic Air Force*, 322.

113. Pfau, *No Sacrifice Too Great*, 112–13; Strauss to Commissioners, 5 October 1949, box 176, Strauss Papers. Strauss's "quantum jump" language came from an earlier letter to him from his staff assistant William Golden; see Bundy, *Danger and Survival*, 204, 665n18.

114. A measurement of the subdued impact of the Johnson disclosure is that a major newspaper story on it left the superbomb aspect out of the headline; see Friendly, "*New A-Bomb.*" A detailed description of the attention to the disclosure is in "President Orders Exploration." The 1947 revelation occurred in an *Infantry Journal* article and was noted by some newspapers, but gained no lasting attention. See Associated Press, "Hydrogen-Helium Use."

115. Alsop and Alsop, "It's Not So Funny, Really."

116. Pike to Truman, 7 December 1949, President's Secretary's Files.

117. Galison and Bernstein, "In Any Light," 285; York, *Arms and the Physicist*, 114.

118. Nitze, interview by Dick and Hasdorff, 235–36. In his memoirs, conscious perhaps of the niceties of protocol, Nitze records that he first approached LeBaron, who referred him to the "atomic colonels" for his briefing. Nitze, *From Hiroshima to Glasnost*, 88.

119. Rhodes, *Dark Sun*, 387.

120. WRS interview with Maj. Gen. Roscoe C. Wilson, 23–24 April 1958, 6.

121. Testimony of Vandenberg to JCAE, 14 October 1949, quoted in testimony of R. C. Wilson, *Oppenheimer Personnel Security Board Transcript*, 682–83.

2. Advising on the Super

1. Acheson, memorandum of telephone conversation with Sidney Souers, 19 January 1950, Dean Acheson Papers, Harry S. Truman Presidential Library. Also reproduced in US Department of State, *Foreign Relations of the United States*, 1950, 511–12.

2. Directive, Military Liaison Committee, 12 April 1948, AEC box 20, Bourke B. Hickenlooper Papers, Herbert Hoover Presidential Library.

3. AEC, Office of the Secretary, General Correspondence Relating to Weapons, 1946–51, box 99, RG 236, National Archives and Records Administration (hereafter NARA).

4. WRS interview with Robert LeBaron, 29 March 1957, 2–4.

5. Pfau, *No Sacrifice Too Great*, 112–13. Some years later, Strauss argued that the work to develop the Super should have been put in hand in 1946, rather than left to 1950. Strauss to Congressman Sterling Cole, 23 November 1953, box 465, Strauss Papers.

6. Pfau, *No Sacrifice Too Great*, 113; Rhodes, *Dark Sun*, 381; Hewlett and Duncan, *Atomic Shield*, 374; Galison and Bernstein, "In Any Light," 285. The memorandum itself is Strauss to Commissioners, 5 October 1949, box 176, Strauss Papers.

7. WRS interview with Sidney Souers, 8 October 1957, 3–4.

8. Rhodes, *Dark Sun*, 381; Pfau, *No Sacrifice Too Great*, 119; Hewlett and Duncan, *Atomic Shield*, 362–410.

9. WRS interview with Robert LeBaron, 1 May 1957, 2.

10. For an examination of the underlying attitudes on both sides of the divide as they related to the planning of postwar military research, see Sherry, *Preparing for the Next War*, 120–58.

11. WRS interview with Maj. Gen. Alvin R. Luedecke, 3 May 1957, 3.

12. WRS interviews with Maj. Gen. Kenneth Nichols, 22 April 1957, 3; Maj. Gen. Roscoe C. Wilson, 23–24 April 1958, 8, 11.

13. Schilling, "H-bomb Decision," 33.

14. WRS interview with Joseph Volpe, 2 May 1957, 6.

15. Robert LeBaron to Robert A. Lovett, 7 January 1952, box 387, RG 330, NARA.

16. WRS interview with Maj. Gen. James McCormack Jr., 21 June 1956, 4.

17. WRS interview with Maj. Gen. Alvin R. Luedecke, 3 May 1957, 2.

18. WRS interview with Robert LeBaron, 29 March 1957, 4.

19. Bradley and Blair, *General's Life*, 517.

20. WRS interview with Maj. Gen. Herbert B. Loper, 20 May 1957, 1.

21. WRS interview with Gordon Dean, 9 July 1956, 3. It is not clear whether the anecdote—which, at the time, Dean did not want to appear in print—refers to Johnson or one of the three later secretaries of defense that Dean served with during his time as AEC chair.

22. Hewlett and Anderson, *New World*, 643–52.

23. Feaver, *Guarding the Guardians*, 134–63.

24. Lilienthal, *Journals*, 2:627.

25. A general account of the three-day meeting is in Hewlett and Duncan, *Atomic Shield*, 381–85. For the second-morning incident, see Pitzer, *Chemist and Administrator*, 105.

26. WRS interview with Kenneth Pitzer, 14 December 1956, 5.

27. Testimony of Pitzer, in US Atomic Energy Commission, *In the Matter of J. Robert Oppenheimer: Transcript of Hearing before Personnel Security Board*, 697–709.

28. Pitzer, *Chemist and Administrator*, 105–7.

29. General Advisory Committee report, 30 October 1949, US Atomic Energy Commission Historical Document no. 349, US Department of Energy. The report is reproduced in Cantelon, Hewlett, and Williams, *American Atom*, 116–23; parts 1–3, quotations, 120; minutes of the three-day meeting, 113–15. For an account that includes the drafting done on the second night, see Rhodes, *Dark Sun*, 395–402.

30. General Advisory Committee report, 30 October 1949, Majority Annex. See Cantelon, Hewlett, and Williams, *American Atom*, 121–22.

31. General Advisory Committee report, Minority Annex, "An Opinion on the Development of the 'Super.'" See Cantelon, Hewlett, and Williams, *American Atom*, 122–23. The caveat about Soviet behavior is in the main portion of the report; see *American Atom*, 120.

32. Anders, *Forging the Atomic Shield*, 59.

33. WRS interview with Maj. Gen. Leslie Groves, 6 August 1956, 5.

34. WRS interview with Gordon Dean, 9 July 1956, 7.

35. WRS interview with Henry Smyth, 7 August 1956, 5, 8.

36. WRS interviews with Adm. James S. Russell, 27 February 1956, 3; Carroll Wilson, 23 November 1956, 3.

37. WRS interview with Kenneth Pitzer, 14 December 1956, 5.

38. Bundy, *Danger and Survival*, 219. Barton Bernstein has also been severely critical of the GAC's thinking, especially that of Fermi and Rabi. He concluded that the committee was, in the main, one of men who had been deeply implicated in the atomic bomb project and were now being asked to reexamine matters that were "near the core of their assumptions, careers and beliefs." It was a "formidable challenge" and "one they could not fully meet." Bernstein, "Truman and the H-bomb," 14.

39. Nichols, *Road to Trinity*, 273–75.

40. Col. Carl F. Fischbein, Office of the Secretary for Defense, memorandum for the record, 23 January 1950, box 9, RG 330, NARA.

41. WRS interview with Luis Alvarez, 15 December 1956, 4. Alvarez asked for this recollection not to be published, but with the passage of six decades that request seems outweighed by the historical importance of conveying the participants' feelings during this process.

42. WRS interview with Adm. Arthur C. Davis, 21 June 1957, 2.

43. Galison and Bernstein, "In Any Light," 290; WRS interview with Oliver Buckley, 13 September 1956, 5.

44. WRS interview with Sidney Souers, 8 October 1957, 5.

45. WRS interview with Lee DuBridge, 11 December 1956, 4.

46. WRS interview with Lee DuBridge, 11 December 1956, 4.

47. WRS interview with J. Robert Oppenheimer, 11 June 1957, 13. Per Oppenheimer's request, Schilling's notes of this interview were given to him afterward. Left behind in Oppenheimer papers, they have been cited by other scholars in the years since.

48. Recollected in WRS telephone conversation with John Manley, 16 December 1956, 3, WRS personal papers.

49. Compton to Truman, 9 November 1949, box 7, RG 330, NARA.

50. WRS interview with Lt. Gen. David M. Schlatter, 24 May 1957, 6.

51. WRS interview with Hans Bethe, 17 May 1957, 11.

52. Galison and Bernstein, "In Any Light," 287.

53. Manley interview with Herken, 1985, in Herken, *Cardinal Choices*, 236n52.

54. Atomic Energy Commission, *Draft Chronology, Atomic Energy Commission Thermonuclear Program*, p. 37, box 465, Strauss Papers.

55. WRS interview with Isidor Rabi, 7 May 1956, 2.

56. WRS interview with Cyril Smith, 17 December 1956, 5.

57. WRS interview with Lee DuBridge, 11 December 1956, 6.

58. WRS interview with Oliver Buckley, 13 September 1956, 4.

59. WRS interview with Cyril Smith, 17 December 1956, 1.

60. WRS interview with Lee DuBridge, 11 December 1956, 5.

61. WRS interview with J. Robert Oppenheimer, 11 June 1957, 13.

62. WRS interview with Oliver Buckley, 13 September 1956, 5.

63. Farber, "Conant Discusses Student Activism."

64. Strauss to Conant, 10 March 1970, box 432, and secretarial note, Strauss Papers. Conant confirmed the accuracy of the quotation of his views in Conant to Strauss, 30 March 1970.

65. Galison and Bernstein, "In Any Light," 286, 295.

66. WRS interview with Glenn Seaborg, 15 December 1956, 3. AEC executive secretary Luedecke thought Seaborg ineffective in his later role as chair, and, uncomfortable, soon felt compelled to resign his own post. Luedecke, interview by Anderson, 108.

67. Luedecke, interview by Anderson, 61.

68. WRS interview with Maj. Gen. Herbert B. Loper, 3 April 1957, 2.

69. WRS interview with Maj. Gen. Kenneth Nichols, 22 April 1957, 5.

70. Wilson, letter to Schilling, 2 June 1958, WRS personal papers.

71. WRS interview with Robert LeBaron, 29 March 1957, 3.

72. WRS interview with Maj. Gen. Roscoe C. Wilson, 23–24 April 1958, 8.

73. WRS interview with Vannevar Bush, 19 February 1958, 4.

74. Dean to Roswell L. Gilpatrick (undersecretary of the air force), 14 April 1952; LeBaron to William C. Foster (undersecretary of defense), 28 April 1952; Dean to Gilpatrick, 15 May 1952, box 387, RG 330, NARA.

75. Memorandum by LeBaron, 9 November 1953, folder 45, box 3, Robert LeBaron Papers, Hoover Institution, Stanford University.

76. WRS interview with Henry Smyth, 7 August 1956, 2.

77. WRS interview with Gordon Dean on topic of scientist-military relations, 9 July 1956, 1.

3. A Decision Reached

1. James Webb, interviewed in Donovan, *Tumultuous Years*, 152.

2. WRS notes from Manley Diary, 16 December 1956, 5, WRS personal papers.

3. McMahon to Truman, 1 November 1949, President's Secretary's Files, Harry S. Truman Presidential Library (hereafter HST).

4. McMahon to Truman, 21 November 1949, in US Department of State, *Foreign Relations of the United States* (hereafter *FRUS*), 1949, 588. According to the former JCAE staff member Kenneth Mansfield, McMahon's letter was drafted by William Borden and signed by his chair. WRS interview with Kenneth Mansfield, 18 August 1956, 5.

5. WRS interview with Henry Smyth, 7 August 1956, 14. The Alsop papers at the Library of Congress contain notes of a number of revealing conversations, not least with Maj. Gen. Sam Anderson. The usefulness of the Alsop papers is noted in Parrish, "Behind the Sheltering Bomb," chaps. 10, 12–14.

6. WRS interview with Sidney Souers, 8 October 1957, 4; WRS interview with Arthur Krock, 24 April 1958, 2.

7. Alsop and Alsop, "Pandora's Box I"; Alsop and Alsop, "Pandora's Box II"; McMahon correspondence with Truman, 3 January, 5 January 1950, President's Secretary's Files.

8. Bernstein, "Truman and the H-bomb," 15–16.

9. Arneson, interview by Johnson, 62–63.

10. WRS interview with George Kennan, 14 September 1956, 2–4.

11. Quoted in Talbott, *Master of the Game*, 53.

12. Gaddis, *George Kennan*, 378.

13. WRS interview with George Kennan, 14 September 1956, 4.

14. The following summary is taken from Atomic Energy Commission, *Draft Chronology, Atomic Energy Commission Thermonuclear Program*, box 465, Lewis L. Strauss Papers, Herbert Hoover Presidential Library.

15. Hewlett and Duncan, *Atomic Shield*, 386–88; Pfau, *No Sacrifice Too Great*, 117–18; Atomic Energy Commission, *Draft Chronology*, 32.

16. Strauss to Roy B. Snapp (AEC secretary), 3 November 1949, box 465, Strauss Papers.

17. WRS telephone interview with Maj. Gen. James McCormack Jr., 23 January 1958, 2.

18. Pearson, "Crusade against H-bomb Planned."

19. "Memorandum for the President by the United States Atomic Energy Commission," 9 November 1949, *FRUS*, 1949, 576–85.

20. Lilienthal, *Journals*, 2:623–33.

21. Strauss to Truman, 16 January 1950, box 465, Strauss Papers.

22. Bradley to Johnson, 13 January 1950, *FRUS*, 1950, 503–11.

23. Robert LeBaron, Office of the Secretary of Defense, memorandum for the record, 11 January 1950, box 9, RG 330, National Archives and Records Administration (hereafter NARA).

24. Acheson, memorandum of telephone conversation with Souers, 19 January 1950, Dean Acheson Papers, HST. Also reproduced in *FRUS*, 1950, 511–12.

25. Memorandum by Rear Adm. Robert L. Dennison, 18 November 1949, President's Secretary's Files. LeBaron claimed authorship of this useful device, which had of course been used before to consider the fission bomb expansion program. WRS interview with Robert LeBaron, 1 May 1957, 3.

26. WRS interview with Louis A. Johnson, 20 June 1957, 2–3.

27. WRS interview with Robert LeBaron, 1 May 1957, 3.

28. WRS interview with Sidney Souers, 8 October 1957, 9.

29. Alsop and Alsop, "Indecisive Decision."

30. Offner, *Another Such Victory*, 361; Acheson, *Present at the Creation*, 348–49, 373–74.

31. Lilienthal, *Journals*, 2:613–14.

32. WRS telephone interview with Maj. Gen. James McCormack Jr., 23 January 1958, 1.

33. Nitze, *From Hiroshima to Glasnost*, 90–91.

34. Thompson, *Hawk and the Dove*.

35. "Memorandum by the Director of the Policy Planning Staff (Nitze) to the Secretary of State," 17 January 1950, *FRUS*, 1950, 13–17, in particular point (a).

36. Leffler, *Preponderance of Power*, 329–30.

37. Quoted in Gaddis, *George Kennan*, 379.

38. Gaddis, *George Kennan*, 380.

39. "Memorandum by the Counselor (Kennan)," 20 January 1950, *FRUS*, 1950, 22–44.

40. Kennan, *Memoirs*, 474–75. Interviewed by Schilling, Paul Nitze commented that with the passage of time he found Kennan's position still more difficult to understand. WRS interview with Paul Nitze, 1 May 1957, 2.

41. WRS interview with Dean Acheson, 24 October 1956, 5.

42. Notes from meetings diary, Acheson Papers. This was the same count given by Acheson when referring to his diary during WRS interview, 24 October 1956, 5.

43. Nitze, interview by Hammond, 1.

44. WRS interview with J. Robert Oppenheimer, 11 June 1957, 14.

45. Galison and Bernstein, "In Any Light," 309.

46. WRS interview with Sidney Souers, 8 October 1957, 10.

47. "The Atom: The Loaded Question," *Time*, 30 January 1950, quoted in McCullough, *Truman*, 762.

48. Hewlett and Duncan, *Atomic Shield*, 404–5. In subsequent years, Smyth became somewhat defensive about his switch; he kept in his files drafts of letters to newspapers and clippings of congressional testimony in which he said he had maintained a consistent thought process throughout. See "Extract from JCC Hearing Jan. 27, 1950" and "Letter to the Editor of the Washington Post," n.d., "Hydrogen Bomb Development in the U.S. Chicago, IL" folder, series 6a, Henry DeWolf Smyth Papers, American Philosophical Society.

49. Hewlett and Duncan, *Atomic Shield*, 406.

50. US Atomic Energy Commission, *In the Matter of J. Robert Oppenheimer: Transcript of Hearing before Personnel Security Board, Record of Classified Deletions* (hereafter *Personnel Security Board, Classified Deletions*), 30–43, presents an extended account of the 31 January committee meeting, identified as Lilienthal's note of the discussions dated 31 January 1950 and dictated later that afternoon, following the meeting with Truman. The quotes of drafts and positions taken are from these notes. See also Hewlett and Duncan, *Atomic Shield*, 407–8; Lilienthal memorandum, "Development of a Thermonuclear Weapon," 15 February 1950, box 7, RG 330, NARA (at least part of which is reproduced in *FRUS*, 1950, 539–40).

51. Lilienthal notes, *Personnel Security Board, Classified Deletions*, 42; "Development of Thermonuclear Weapons," report by the Special Committee of the National Security Council to the President, 31 January 1950, *FRUS*, 1950, 513–17; Lilienthal memorandum, "Development of a Thermonuclear Weapon."

52. Arneson, "H-bomb Decision," 27.

53. Testimony of Lilienthal, *Personnel Security Board, Classified Deletions*, 52.

54. Arneson, "H-bomb Decision," 27; Lilienthal, *Journals*, 2:623–33; WRS interview with Dean Acheson, 24 October 1956, 8.

55. Truman to Lilienthal, 31 January 1950, President's Secretary's Files.

56. Galison and Bernstein, "In Any Light," 306.

57. Ayers, diary for 1950, entry for Saturday, 4 February 1950, Eben A. Ayers Papers, HST.

58. WRS interview with Harry S. Truman, 14 September 1957, 1–2, 4–5.

59. Tris Coffin to Strauss, relaying information from Sidney Souers, 22 February, 27 April 1950, box 429, Strauss Papers.

60. US Atomic Energy Commission, *In the Matter of J. Robert Oppenheimer: Transcript of Hearing before Personnel Security Board*, 307.

61. Lilienthal, *Journals*, 2:633.

62. WRS interview with David E. Lilienthal, 23 August 1957, 5.

63. Manual annotation by Strauss on Atomic Energy Commission, *Draft Chronology*, 108.

64. WRS interview with David E. Lilienthal, 18 June 1957, 2.

65. Reston, "H-Bomb Decision." This publication has possibly been conflated with a separate episode, where Lilienthal's 9 November 1949 memorandum to Truman was shown to Arthur Krock, the *New York Times* journalist who enjoyed particularly close relations with Lewis Strauss, leading Lilienthal to comment in his diary about the hypocrisy of the H-bomb advocates' secrecy concerns. See Lilienthal, *Journals*, 3:498; Stern and Green, *Oppenheimer Case*, 255–56.

66. Lilienthal to Acheson, 28 February 1964; Acheson to Lilienthal, 5 March 1964, doc. 163, Acheson Papers. Also available in Merrill, *Documentary History*, 808–9.

67. When Acheson was interviewed by Schilling, his recollection remained one of unanimity among the three. WRS interview with Dean Acheson, 24 October 1956, 7. In a second interview, when Schilling pressed for clarification, Acheson recalled Lilienthal insisting on making a statement on a "related matter," which would have been his condition for agreement with the recommendation—the wide-ranging review of US defense policy that resulted in NSC-68. WRS interview with Dean Acheson, 21 June 1957, 2.

68. Acheson, *Present at the Creation*, 349.

69. Loper, memorandum to LeBaron, "A Basis for Estimating Maximum Soviet Capabilities for Atomic Warfare," 16 February 1950, President's Secretary's Files. Also available in Merrill, *Documentary History*, 393–95.

70. Johnson to McMahon, 5 May 1950, quoted in "Policy and Progress in the H-bomb Program: A Chronology of Leading Events," Joint Committee on Atomic Energy, 1 January 1953, RG 128, NARA. On 20 February, LeBaron commended the Loper memorandum to Johnson, who referred it immediately to the Joint Chiefs. Rosenberg, "American Atomic Strategy," 84n88.

71. Herken, *Cardinal Choices*, 51.

72. WRS interview with Lt. Gen. Alvin R. Luedecke, 3 May 1957, 7.

73. Rosenberg, "American Atomic Strategy," 84n88.

74. WRS interview with Maj. Gen. John E. Hull, 29 March 1957, 1.

75. Herken, *Cardinal Choices*, 50–51.

76. Johnson to Truman, 24 February 1950, President's Secretary's Files.

77. "Report to the President by the Special Committee of the National Security Council on Development of Thermonuclear Weapons," 9 March 1950, President's Secretary's Files. Also available in Merrill, *Documentary History*, 444–46.

78. James Lay, Executive Director, National Security Council, to Secretaries of State and Defense and Acting Chairman, AEC, with draft approved by the president, 19 June 1950, President's Secretary's Files. Also available in Merrill, *Documentary History*, 466–71.

79. James Lay, Executive Director, National Security Council, to Secretaries of State and Defense and Acting Chairman, AEC, enclosing draft letter to president from AEC, 29 May 1950, box 7, RG 330, NARA.

80. Support for the second laboratory was announced as part of a package of measures to accelerate the thermonuclear program. Gordon Dean to William C. Foster (deputy secretary of defense), 9 June 1952, box 14, RG 330, NARA.

81. York, *Arms and the Physicist*, 121.

82. The Berkeley Laboratory, formally known as the University of California Radiation Laboratory, was renamed the Lawrence Radiation Laboratory in 1958 after Ernest Lawrence died. During this time the weapons laboratory at Livermore was designated as the Livermore Branch of the UCRL and then of the LRL. In 1971, in response to campus protests, the two laboratories were administratively split and became the Lawrence Berkeley Laboratory and the Lawrence Livermore Laboratory, and in 1980 the LLL became the Lawrence Livermore National Laboratory.

83. York, *Arms and the Physicist*, 123–25.

84. Memorandum for the president, 11 June 1952, President's Secretary's Files, which contains excerpts from NSC 30 and several remarks by Truman. Also available in "Staff Study Prepared by Representatives of the Special Committee of the National Security Council on

Atomic Energy," 11 June 1952, *FRUS*, 1952–54, pt. 2, 973–80. For the full text of Truman's April 1949 remarks, see "Remarks to a Group of New Democratic Senators and Representatives," 6 April 1949, *Harry S. Truman* [. . .] *1949*, 199–200.

85. Buck, *History of the Atomic Energy Commission*, 2; O'Neill, "Building the Bomb," 66n68; Beisner, *Dean Acheson*, 378–79.

86. Donovan, *Tumultuous Years*, 155.

4. Moral and Political Consequences

1. Batchelder, *Irreversible Decision*, 225–69.
2. Tannenwald, *Nuclear Taboo*. A more pragmatic assessment is Botti, *Ace in the Hole*. A National Security Archive briefing book details the extent of the acknowledgment of the taboo by US political and military leaders: William Burr, ed., *U.S. Presidents and the Nuclear Taboo*, Briefing Book 611, 30 November 2017, National Security Archive, https://nsarchive.gwu.edu/briefing-book/nuclear-vault/2017-11-30/us-presidents-nuclear-taboo.
3. Gwertzman, "U.S. Papers Tell of '53 Policy."
4. Tannenwald explores the conditionality of the taboo in *Nuclear Taboo*, 148.
5. Nye, *Nuclear Ethics*, 4–5, 10–13, passim; Doyle, "Reviving Nuclear Ethics," 289–90.
6. Galison and Bernstein, "In Any Light," 284.
7. WRS interview with Hartley Rowe, 23 November 1956, 3.
8. Laurence, "Atomic Bombing of Nagasaki."
9. Kristof, "Problem of Memory," 45–46.
10. Sagan and Valentino, "Revisiting Hiroshima in Iran," 42–43.
11. Lifton and Mitchell, *Hiroshima in America*, 307, 313.
12. Thorpe, "Disciplining Experts," 539–40.
13. Bernstein, "H-bomb Decisions," 335.
14. WRS interview with Maj. Gen. James McCormack Jr., 21 June 1956, 1.
15. Thorpe, "Disciplining Experts," 540.
16. General Advisory Committee report, 30 October 1949. See Cantelon, Hewlett, and Williams, *American Atom*, 120.
17. Galison and Bernstein, "In Any Light," 291, records that the phrase "on moral grounds" was deleted from Lilienthal's diary on publication, but remains in the manuscript version.
18. General Advisory Committee report, 30 October 1949, Majority Annex, Minority Annex. See Cantelon, Hewlett, and Williams, *American Atom*, 121, 122.
19. Atomic Energy Commission, *Draft Chronology, Atomic Energy Commission Thermonuclear Program*, p. 37, box 465, Strauss Papers.
20. DuBridge to Lilienthal, 5 December 1949, box 8, entry 184, RG 330, National Archives and Records Administration (hereafter NARA).
21. Galison and Bernstein, "In Any Light," 273.
22. Bernstein, "Four Physicists," 241–44.
23. Bernstein, "Four Physicists," 257.
24. Allison et al., "Let Us Pledge"; Winslow, "12 Scientists Bid U.S. Declare It Won't Use Super-Bomb First."
25. Blackett, *Fear, War and the Bomb* (first published in Britain as *Military and Political Consequences of Atomic Energy*). In 1958, after years of contention, the UK Labour Party called for the international banning of thermonuclear weapons as a step toward general disarmament, and there were significant factions within the party that advocated unilateral nuclear disarmament entirely. See John Strachey, *Scrap All the H-bombs*, and Young, *American Bomb in Britain*, 122–26.
26. "The Hydrogen Bomb," BBC Third Programme, 14 March 1950, https://genome.ch.bbc.co.uk/6084b5acced64e77a2dba77c7dab053e; Thomson, "Hydrogen Bombs," 469 (publication of address given at Chatham House, 4 July 1950).
27. Cockcroft to Thomson, 12 May 1950, GPT FI72–2, Sir George Thomson Papers, Trinity College Cambridge Library.

28. W. G. Marley, Ministry of Supply, to Thomson, 30 June 1950, GPT FI72–3, Thomson Papers.

29. Bethe, "Hydrogen Bomb: II," 21.

30. Lerner, "'Naked Question.'" Lerner's column had visibility overseas; see Cooke, "Support for Senator McMahon."

31. Flynn, "Mark Women's Day"; Pettus, "Seattle Pastors Favor Effort." Clippings or summaries of these *Daily Worker* pieces were kept by Strauss; see box 465, Strauss Papers.

32. Dugan, *"Stassen Proposes Church Bomb Talk."*

33. Memorandum by the Counselor (Kennan), 20 January 1950, in US Department of State, *Foreign Relations of the United States* (hereafter *FRUS*), 1950, 39; Gaddis, *George Kennan*, 380, 729n13; Beisner, *Dean Acheson*, 233–34. Gaddis casts doubt on Acheson's outburst ever having taken place, and Beisner characterizes it as an "ex post facto embellishment" due to Acheson's differences with Kennan becoming worse over time.

34. WRS interview with Dean Acheson, 24 October 1956, 4–5.

35. Seitz, "Physicists and the Cold War," 87.

36. Joint Chiefs of Staff, "Request for Comments on Military Views of Members of General Advisory Committee," *13 January 1950, in Etzold and Gaddis, Containment, 373.*

37. Lewis L. Strauss (questions for discussion), 3 November 1949, box 465, Strauss Papers.

38. McMahon to Truman, 21 November 1949, *FRUS*, 1949, 591. McMahon's figure for fatalities in the multi-day-and-night, British-American bombing of Hamburg in 1943 is three times that of the best modern estimates, but his point remains.

39. For an insightful argument about the special place nuclear weapons have in Western belief systems, see Heuser, *Nuclear Mentalities?*, esp. 1–2, 143–44, 266–67.

40. Biddle, *Rhetoric and Reality*, chaps. 4–5.

41. Griffith, *Quest*, 57–90.

42. Hansell, *Strategic Air War*, 138–40.

43. Werrell, *Blankets of Fire*, 137–39. The full account of this painful decision is in Norstad, interview by Ahmann, 541–48.

44. Werrell, *Blankets of Fire*, 133–42; Deaile, *Always at War*, 55–59.

45. Quoted in Coox, "Strategic Bombing," 319.

46. Zachary, *Endless Frontier*, 247–51.

47. Griffith, *Quest*, 204.

48. Heuser, *Bomb*, 34.

49. Werrell, *Blankets of Fire*, 199.

50. US Strategic Bombing Survey, *Summary Report*, 24.

51. Lefever, "Why Agonize over Hiroshima?"

52. Heuser, *Bomb*, 183.

53. Bernstein, "American Conservatives."

54. McGhee, *On the Front Line*, 88. In the course of an exhaustive bibliographical essay, Kenneth P. Werrell comments on the literature's neglect of the conventional bombing of Japan. Werrell, *Blankets of Fire*, 336–41.

55. Bird and Sherwin, *American Prometheus*, 291.

56. Barlow, *Revolt of the Admirals*, 115–16.

57. See Schilling, *Politics of National Defense*, 169–70, for the congressional testimony.

58. WRS interview with J. Robert Oppenheimer, 11 June 1957, 5, 6, 7, 11, 12, 17.

59. *The National Defense Program—Unification and Strategy: Hearings before the Committee on Armed Services*, US House of Representatives, 81st Cong., 1st Sess., 522. Quoted (with variances) and discussed in Barlow, *Revolt of the Admirals*, 260–61, 360n65, 66.

60. WRS interview with Maj. Gen. David Schlatter, 24 May 1957, 9. The remark is paraphrased in these interview notes. But it is given as a verbatim quote (albeit anonymously) in Schilling, *Politics of National Defense*, 170 (but is misdated there as 27 May 1957).

61. Grayling, *Among the Dead Cities.*

62. WRS interview with Dean Acheson, 24 October 1956, 6.

63. WRS interview with Dean Acheson, 21 June 1957, 2.

64. Strauss to Truman, 25 November 1949, quoted in Strauss, *Men and Decisions*, 219–20.

65. DuBridge to Lilienthal, 5 December 1949, box 8, entry 184, RG 330, NARA.

66. Lewis L. Strauss, questions (for discussion), 3 November 1949, box 465, Strauss Papers.

67. Strauss to Truman, 25 November 1949, box 465, Strauss Papers.

68. Urey, "Should America Build the H-bomb?," 72.

69. Seitz, "Physicists and the Cold War," 86.

70. Leffler, *Preponderance of Power*, 330.

71. Morgenthau, "H-bomb and After."

72. Morgenthau, "H-bomb and After," 79.

73. Bethe, "Hydrogen Bomb: II," 22.

74. Compton to Truman, 9 November 1949, box 7, RG 330, NARA.

75. Hansen, *Swords of Armageddon*, II-51.

76. WRS interview with Robert Bacher, 11 December 1956, 4.

77. Atomic Energy Commission, *Draft Chronology*, 37.

78. J. H. Manley, "Military Worth," 15 December 1949, 21, "History of the H-bomb #1" folder, series 7, Henry DeWolf Smyth Papers, American Philosophical Society.

79. Allison et al., "Let Us Pledge."

80. Testimony of Oppenheimer, in US Atomic Energy Commission, *In the Matter of J. Robert Oppenheimer: Transcript of Hearing before Personnel Security Board*, 80.

81. WRS interview with Paul Nitze, 27 February 1957, 4.

82. York, *Arms and the Physicist*, 135–41.

83. Central Intelligence Agency, Joint Atomic Energy Intelligence Committee, "Status of the Soviet Atomic Energy Program," 4 July 1950, President's Secretary's Files.

84. Holloway, *Stalin and the Bomb*, 204–5, 295–97. A Soviet source assesses the significance of Fuchs's work: Goncharov, "American and Soviet H-bomb Development Programmes."

85. Hirsch and Mathews, "H-bomb." Hirsch and Mathews returned to their speculation in a letter published in the *Bulletin of the Atomic Scientists* 53, no. 4 (July/August 1997): 3, 58.

86. Holloway, *Stalin and the Bomb*, 312.

87. Holloway, *Stalin and the Bomb*, 299, 319.

88. Sakharov, *Memoirs*, 99–100.

5. Dissent and Development

1. Henry M. Jackson, speech at University of Michigan Law School, Ann Arbor, MI, 28 June 1952. Incorporated on 5 July 1952 into Proceedings and Debates of the 82nd Congress, 2nd Session, Cong. Rec. 98, pt. 11 app., A4472–74.

2. WRS interview with John Walker, 24 October 1956, 1.

3. Galison and Bernstein, "In Any Light," 281.

4. General Advisory Committee report on the Super, 30 October 1949, part 2, US Atomic Energy Commission Historical Document no. 349, US Department of Energy. See Cantelon, Hewlett, and Williams, *American Atom*, 118–19.

5. Notes on talk by Cmdr. N. E. Bradbury, 1 October 1945, quoted in Hansen, *Swords of Armageddon*, II-23. There are slight differences between the wording here and in Truslow and Smith, *Project Y*, app. 1.

6. Report of the Conference on the Super, quoted in Hansen, *Swords of Armageddon*, II-35.

7. J. Carson Mark, quoted in Rhodes, *Dark Sun*, 306; for the circumstances of Mark's remarks, see 633n, 697n.

8. Truslow and Smith, *Project Y*, 307.

9. Testimony of Alvarez, in US Atomic Energy Commission, *In the Matter of J. Robert Oppenheimer: Transcript of Hearing before Personnel Security Board* (hereafter *Oppenheimer Personnel Security Board Transcript*), 773.

10. Pitzer, *Chemist and Administrator*, 35.

11. Bradbury to Atomic Energy Commission, 14 November 1946, in Truslow and Smith, *Project Y*, 438.

12. Hansen, *Swords of Armageddon*, II-54–56.

13. Quoted in Hansen, *Swords of Armageddon*, II-56.

14. Quoted in Hansen, *Swords of Armageddon*, II-70.

15. Quoted in Hansen, *Swords of Armageddon*, II-79.

16. Hansen, *Swords of Armageddon*, II-88.

17. Bacher, "Hydrogen Bomb: III," 13.

18. On the computational demands of the Super project, and how early digital electronic computers replaced the electromechanical machines used during the Manhattan Project, see Harlow and Metropolis, "Computing and Computers."

19. Condit, *History of the Office*, 478.

20. The distribution of credit between Teller and Ulam for the breakthrough has been a matter of controversy. In any case, Teller's pursuit of an unproductive path until that point did not harm the Super project, as no one else had a usable alternative idea. Rhodes, *Dark Sun*, 460–72; Galison and Bernstein, "In Any Light," 315–16, 322.

21. Galison and Bernstein, "In Any Light," 323.

22. State Department Panel of Consultants, quoted in Herken, *Cardinal Choices*, 58–59.

23. Rearden, *History of the Office*, 455. For a full account of the history of US testing, see Blades and Siracusa, *History of U.S. Nuclear Testing*.

24. Zachary, *Endless Frontier*, 370.

25. "Memorandum by the Panel of Consultants on Disarmament," n.d., in US Department of State, *Foreign Relations of the United States* (hereafter *FRUS*), 1952–54, pt. 2, 994–1008.

26. "Memorandum by the Director of the Policy Planning Staff to the Secretary of State," 9 June 1952, *FRUS*, 1952–54, pt. 2, 958–63.

27. Condit, *History of the Office*, 479–82; Herken, *Cardinal Choices*, 54–65. Rhodes, *Dark Sun*, 482–512, gives a full account of the actual test.

28. Bernstein, "Crossing the Rubicon."

29. "Report to the President by the Special Committee of the National Security Council on Development of Thermonuclear Weapons," 9 March 1950, President's Secretary's Files, Harry S. Truman Presidential Library (hereafter HST). Also available in Merrill, *Documentary History*, 444–46.

30. Condit, *History of the Office*, 473; Truman to Sen. Burnet R. Maybank, 28 May 1952, box 7, RG 330, National Archives and Records Administration (hereafter NARA).

31. Truman to Maybank, 28 May 1952. The letter was published the following day and is available as "Letter to Senator Maybank on the Atomic Energy Program. May 29, 1952," *Harry S. Truman [. . .] 1952–53*, 384–85.

32. Robert A. Lovett, Secretary of Defense, to Kenneth McKellar, Chairman, US Senate Committee on Appropriations, 4 June 1952, RG 330, NARA; O'Neill, "Building the Bomb," 99.

33. O'Neill, "Building the Bomb," 99–103.

34. WRS interview with Lt. Gen. David M. Schlatter, 24 May 1957, 2.

35. Defense Threat Reduction Agency, *Defense's Nuclear Agency*, 74.

36. Defense Threat Reduction Agency, *Defense's Nuclear Agency*, 74.

37. Pike to Truman, 26 May 1950, Annex A, box 7, entry 184, RG 330, NARA.

38. "Report to the President."

39. Galison and Bernstein, "In Any Light," 318.

40. Galison and Bernstein, "In Any Light," 299–300.

41. WRS interview with Lt. Gen. David M. Schlatter, 24 May 1957, 8.

42. WRS interview with Carroll L. Wilson, 23 November 1956, 3.

43. Robert LeBaron, memorandum for Secretary of Defense, "Hydrogen Bomb Status Report," 1 March 1950, box 8, entry 184, RG 330, NARA.

44. Robert LeBaron, memorandum for Secretary of Defense, "Hydrogen Bomb Development," 1 March 1950, box 8, entry 184, RG 330, NARA.

45. WRS interview with Robert Bacher, 11 December 1956, 2.

46. Galison and Bernstein, "In Any Light," 313–14.

47. "Charge of 'Reluctance' on H-bomb Is Denied."

48. Strauss to Roy B. Snapp (AEC secretary), 3 November 1949, box 465, Lewis L. Strauss Papers, Herbert Hoover Presidential Library.

49. Lewis L. Strauss (questions for discussion), 3 November 1949, box 465, Strauss Papers.

50. Knaack, *Encyclopedia of U.S. Air Force Aircraft*, 77–78.

51. LeMay to Nathan F. Twining, 6 June 1955, box 205, LeMay Papers, US Library of Congress. "High yield" was conventionally defined as in excess of six hundred kilotons; Office of the Assistant to the Secretary of Defense (Atomic Energy), *History of the Custody*, 39.

52. International News Service, "'H-bomb Not Too Valuable.'"

53. Bacher, "Hydrogen Bomb: III," 13.

54. DuBridge to Lilienthal, 5 December 1949, box 8, entry 184, RG 330, NARA.

55. "Request for Comments on Military Views of Members of General Advisory Committee," memorandum for the Secretary of Defense, 13 January 1950, HST. Also available as "Memorandum by the Joint Chiefs of Staff to the Secretary of Defense (Johnson)," *FRUS*, 1950, 503–11. An earlier manifestation of this document, which shared at least some of the same language, was a letter from General Bradley to Johnson on 23 November 1949; see Hewlett and Duncan, *Atomic Shield*, 395, 644n69.

56. Department of Defense, Appendix C, "The Military Implications of Thermonuclear Weapons," Annex 1, in "Report by the Special Committee of the National Security Council to the President," 31 January 1950, *FRUS*, 1950, 520–22. This was substantially the same as "Memorandum Circulated by the Defense Members of the Working Group of the Special Committee of the National Security Council," n.d. but before 16 December 1949, *FRUS*, 1949, 605–9. Though not explicitly authored by the Joint Chiefs, this analysis made many of the same arguments as the Joint Chiefs' memorandum of 13 January; see Hewlett and Duncan, *Atomic Shield*, 398, 644n76.

57. WRS interview with Lt. Gen. John E. Hull, 29 March 1957, 3–4.

58. Department of Defense, Appendix C, "Military Implications," 521–22.

59. Kaplan, *To Kill Nations*, 45–46.

60. J. H. Manley, "Military Worth," 15 December 1949, 1–2, "History of the H-bomb #1" folder, series 7, Henry DeWolf Smyth Papers, American Philosophical Society.

61. Manley, "Military Worth," 3, 6, 11.

62. Manley, "Military Worth," 7–8.

63. Manley, "Military Worth," 20.

64. Oppenheimer to Conant, 21 October 1949, as read during testimony of Oppenheimer, *Oppenheimer Personnel Security Board Transcript*, 242.

65. Testimony of Norman F. Ramsey, *Oppenheimer Personnel Security Board Transcript*, 447, and US Atomic Energy Commission, *In the Matter of J. Robert Oppenheimer: Transcript of Hearing before Personnel Security Board, Record of Classified Deletions*, 58.

66. WRS interview with Lt. Gen. David M. Schlatter, 24 May 1957, 1–2, 7.

67. Campbell, *Silverplate Bombers*, chap. 2.

68. Knaack, *Encyclopedia of U.S. Air Force Aircraft*, 111–12n9.

69. Knaack, *Encyclopedia of U.S. Air Force Aircraft*, 167.

70. Young, *American Bomb in Britain*, 26–28.

71. WRS interview with Maj. Gen. Herbert B. Loper, 3 April 1957, 4.

72. Quoted in Brig. Gen. A. R. Luedeke, Military Liaison Committee, "Memorandum for the Record: Briefing of Mr Lilienthal re Consideration of the Military Use of a Thermonuclear Weapon," 20 January 1950. See also Hansen, *Swords of Armageddon*, II:74–75.

73. Maj. Gen. D. L. Putt to Robert LeBaron, 22 December 1949, box 8, entry 184, RG 330, NARA.

74. Hansen, *Swords of Armageddon*, II-262, V-367.

75. Ford, *Building the H Bomb*, chap. 14. A diagram of this flask appears in Rhodes, *Dark Sun*, 491.

76. Quoted in Ford, *Building the H Bomb*, 159.

77. Ford, *Building the H Bomb*, 159–60; Hansen, *Swords of Armageddon*, V-373–76; Polmar and Norris, *U.S. Nuclear Arsenal*, 44.

78. Polmar and Norris, *U.S. Nuclear Arsenal*, 44–45; Hansen, *Swords of Armageddon*, V-382–83.

79. Putt to LeBaron, 22 December 1949.

80. Gunston, *Bombers of the West*, 216.

81. Hansen, *Swords of Armageddon*, V-371; Knaack, *Encyclopedia of U.S. Air Force Aircraft*, 23–24.

82. Knaack, *Encyclopedia of U.S. Air Force Aircraft*, 157; Hansen, *Swords of Armageddon*, V-82.

83. Polmar and Norris, *U.S. Nuclear Arsenal*, 44–47; Rhodes, *Dark Sun*, 541–43.

84. Polmar and Norris, *U.S. Nuclear Arsenal*, 44.

85. Lemmer, *Air Force and Strategic Deterrence*, 12.

86. Lemmer, *Air Force and Strategic Deterrence*, 13.

87. "Carrier for H-Bomb," Memorandum for LeBaron by Brig. Gen. R. C. Wilson, 10 March 1950, box 8, entry 184, RG 330, NARA.

88. Maj. Gen. Sam Anderson to LeBaron, 27 December 1949, box 8, entry 184, RG 330, NARA.

89. Maj. Gen. Sam Anderson to LeBaron, 27 December 1949, box 9, RG 330, NARA.

90. Knaack, *Encyclopedia of U.S. Air Force Aircraft*, 126n40.

91. For a good summary of Brass Ring, see Knaack, *Encyclopedia of U.S. Air Force Aircraft*, 125–28.

92. Knaack, *Encyclopedia of U.S. Air Force Aircraft*, 126–27.

93. Alsop and Alsop, "Pandora's Box II."

6. Tactical Diversions

1. Greer, *Development of Air Doctrine*, 11.

2. Greer, *Development of Air Doctrine*, 14–44.

3. McFarland, *America's Pursuit of Precision Bombing*, 76–77.

4. Eden, *Whole World on Fire*, 69–70.

5. McFarland, *America's Pursuit of Precision Bombing*, 77.

6. Eden, *Whole World on Fire*, 70.

7. Quoted in Hone, "Strategic Bombardment Constrained," 469.

8. Hansell, *Air Plan That Defeated Hitler*, 304–5.

9. Biddle, *Rhetoric and Reality*, 3–10, 296–97.

10. Overy, *Bombers and the Bombed*, 218–30.

11. Testimony of Kennan, in US Atomic Energy Commission, *In the Matter of J. Robert Oppenheimer: Transcript of Hearing before Personnel Security Board, Record of Classified Deletions* (hereafter *Personnel Security Board, Classified Deletions*), 28–29.

12. Quoted in Steiner, *Bernard Brodie*, 114.

13. Rearden, *History of the Office*, 402–5.

14. Rearden, "U.S. Strategic Bombardment Doctrine," 396–97, 406–9.

15. Deaile, *Always at War*, 68, 91–93.

16. As commander in chief of SAC, Curtis LeMay claimed that his operational plans were developed in Omaha, without interference from higher levels. This was broadly correct. SAC Emergency War Plans were framed to fit within the Joint Strategic Capabilities Plan, which established US objectives in time of war. SAC had one target system and one strike plan, but a multitude of timing variations or options to fit any condition that might arise. By the late 1950s, the main target was declared to be the enemy's retaliatory capability. "History of the Strategic Air Command, SAC Targeting Concepts," Historical Study 73A, Historical Division, Office of Information, Headquarters Strategic Air Command, n.d. [1959?], National Security Archive, https://nsarchive2.gwu.edu/nukevault/ebb336/doc01.PDF.

17. Knaack, *Encyclopedia of U.S. Air Force Aircraft*, 77–78.

18. McFarland, "Air Force in the Cold War," 7.

19. Presentation by Strategic Air Command, US Air Force, Commanders Conference, Ramey Air Force Base, Puerto Rico, 25–27 April 1950 (hereafter Commanders Conference), 208–211, and separate document with briefing materials, 6–8, National Security Archive, https://nsarchive2.gwu.edu/nukevault/special/doc03b.pdf and doc03c.pdf.

20. Vandenberg to LeMay, 15 February 1949, box 45, Hoyt S. Vandenberg Papers, US Library of Congress.

21. In June 1948 there were only fifty atomic bombs available to SAC; Rosenberg, "U.S. Nuclear Stockpile," 26. The former air force officer Harry Borowski dubbed the SAC presence at this time "a hollow threat." Borowski, *Hollow Threat*.

22. The Harmon report, "Evaluation of Effect on Soviet War Effort Resulting from the Strategic Air Offensive," 12 May 1949, is reproduced in Ross and Rosenberg, *America's Plans for War*, 5–6. It is reprinted in Etzold and Gaddis, *Containment*, 360–64. A summary of the report's findings is in Rearden, *History of the Office*, 407.

23. Rearden, *History of the Office*, 407–8.

24. Ponturo, *Analytical Support*, 53–59.

25. Rosenberg, "American Atomic Strategy," 83–84.

26. Young, *American Bomb in Britain*, 72–75; Rearden, *History of the Office*, 409.

27. For his course lecture that discussed the Harmon and Hull reports, Schilling calculated a combination of their estimates. Harmon's range of a .3–.4 reduction in Soviet industrial capability (assuming total success in delivering atomic weapons) can be multiplied by Hull's .7–.85 rate of bombers reaching their targets and multiplied again by Hull's .5–.67 rate of the bombers hitting the targets accurately enough to cause unrepairable damage. The lower and upper bounds of the factors indicate that SAC would destroy somewhere between .11 and .23 of Soviet industry. By comparison, by November 1941, following Germany's invasion of the Soviet Union that year, one-third of the capital stock of Soviet industry had been captured or destroyed.

28. Barlow, *Revolt of the Admirals*, 97–99; Rosenberg, "Origins of Overkill," 14–16.

29. Presentation by Strategic Air Command, Commanders Conference, separate document with briefing materials, 9–11, https://nsarchive2.gwu.edu/nukevault/special/doc03c.pdf.

30. Rearden, "U.S. Strategic Bombardment Doctrine," 408–9.

31. "Comments on WSEG 10 for General Twining," n.d., ready file, 1954 folder, box 120, Nathan F. Twining Papers, US Library of Congress.

32. Getting, *All in a Lifetime*, 238.

33. Tubbs, *Establishing Air Research and Development Command*, vi, 2–3, 7–9, 21. Schlatter had nominated Lawrence Hafstad, a reactor expert and later GAC chair, as a suitable choice for this appointment. Schlatter to Robert LeBaron, 30 January 1951, box 9, RG 330, National Archives and Records Administration (hereafter NARA). For a vivid account of the establishment of the air force's research capabilities, see Kohn, *Reflections on Research and Development*, 37–41.

34. Getting, *All in a Lifetime*, 238–39.

35. Paul H. Nitze, "Memorandum by the Director of the Policy Planning Staff to the Secretary of State," 12 January 1953, in US Department of State, *Foreign Relations of the United States* (hereafter *FRUS*), 1952–54, pt. 1, 202–5.

36. Converse, *Rearming for the Cold War*, 459.

37. Leighton, *History of the Office*, 152–53, 195–96.

38. Bernstein, "Eclipsed by Hiroshima and Nagasaki," 150–52, 165, 167–69, passim.

39. "Report to the President by the Special Committee of the National Security Council on the Proposed Acceleration with Atomic Energy Program," 10 October 1949, esp. 2, President's Secretary's Files, Harry S. Truman Presidential Library. Available in Merrill, *Documentary History*, 321–32. Also available as Annex to "Memorandum by the Executive Secretary of the National Security Council (Souers)," *FRUS*, 1949, 559–63.

40. "Report to the President by the Special Committee of the National Security Council on the Proposed Acceleration with Atomic Energy Program," esp. 8.

41. WRS interview with Lt. Gen. James M. Gavin, 26 June 1958, 2.

42. WRS interview with Lt. Gen. James M. Gavin, 26 June 1958, 3.

43. WRS interview with Lt. Gen. James M. Gavin, 26 June 1958, 1.

44. WRS interview with Lt. Gen. James M. Gavin, 26 June 1958, 1, 3. Gavin, "LTG James M. Gavin," 21.

45. General Advisory Committee report on the Super, 30 October 1949, US Atomic Energy Commission Historical Document no. 349, part 1, para. 2.

46. Anderson to Robert LeBaron, 27 December 1949, box 8, entry 184, RG 330, NARA.

47. Young, *American Bomb in Britain*, 40–43.

48. Hewlett and Duncan, *Atomic Shield*, 548; Condit, *History of the Office*, 469–70. "Lightweight" was defined as less than half the weight of the 9,700 lb. Little Boy weapon used against Hiroshima. See Gibson, *Nuclear Weapons*, 91.

49. Lodge, speaking on strategic use of the atomic bomb, 11 October 1951, 82nd Congress, 1st Session, Cong. Rec. 97, pt. 10, 12938.

50. Millis, *Arms and Men*, 285–86; Rearden, *History of the Office*, 393–97.

51. Gwertzman, "U.S. Papers Tell of '53 Policy."

52. Gavin, "Tactical Use," 11.

53. Gavin, "We Can Solve Our Technical Difficulties," 65. The characterization of SAC's plan is described in Rosenberg, " 'Smoking Radiating Ruin,' " 11, wherein Rosenberg quotes a report by W. B. Moore, a naval officer, on a SAC briefing.

54. WRS interview with Lt. Gen. James M. Gavin, 26 June 1958, 1.

55. Gavin, "Tactical Use," repr. *Bulletin of the Atomic Scientists* 7, no. 2 (February 1951): 46–47, 50.

56. Gavin, *War and Peace*, 132.

57. Elliot, "Project Vista," 165.

58. Getting, *All in a Lifetime*, 236.

59. McCray, "Project Vista," 348.

60. Getting, *All in a Lifetime*, 236.

61. Quoted in Elliot, "Project Vista," 169.

62. Testimony of Walter G. Whitman, *Personnel Security Board, Classified Deletions*, 66.

63. Testimony of Norman F. Ramsey, *Personnel Security Board, Classified Deletions*, 58.

64. Meilinger, *Hoyt S. Vandenberg*, 50–52.

65. Meilinger, *Hoyt S. Vandenberg*, 197.

66. Vista report, quoted in Elliot, "Project Vista," 169.

67. Testimony of Bacher, *Personnel Security Board, Classified Deletions*, 91–92.

68. Elliot, "Project Vista," 171–73.

69. Gilpin, *American Scientists*, 120–21.

70. Rosenberg, " 'Smoking Radiating Ruin.' " The air force's defense of the allocation of atomic weapons to the strategic air battle is on pp. 36 and 37.

71. "VISTA," "Summary and Conclusions by Dr. Robert Oppenheimer," noted by Garrison Norton, 3 December 1951, 3, Eyes Only—folder 15, box 41, Lauris Norstad Papers, Dwight D. Eisenhower Presidential Library (hereafter DDE).

72. [Murphy], "Hidden Struggle," 109–10.

73. Elliot, "Project Vista," 174–75.

74. Watson, *Office of the Secretary*, 119–20.

75. Lt. Col. T. F. "Teddy" Walkowicz, Special Assistant to the Air Force Chief of Staff, to Ridenour, 6 November 1951, box 5, Louis N. Ridenour Papers, US Library of Congress. This letter indicated the close interest of Gen. Jimmy Doolittle, who had played the original role of providing scientific advice to the air force.

76. Norstad, interview by Ahmann, 433–34.

77. Gavin, *War and Peace*, 134.

78. Norstad to Murphy, 22 May 1953, Eyes Only—folder 8, box 41, Norstad Papers.

79. McCray, "Project Vista," 363.

80. Baldwin, "Experts Urge Tactical Air Might."

81. WRS interview with Lee DuBridge, 11 December 1956, 1.

82. McCray, "Project Vista," 341.

83. Testimony of Lauritsen, in US Atomic Energy Commission, *In the Matter of J. Robert Oppenheimer: Transcript of Hearing before Personnel Security Board* (hereafter *Oppenheimer Personnel Security Board Transcript*), 585–86; *Personnel Security Board, Classified Deletions*, 87.

84. Testimony of Lauritsen, *Personnel Security Board, Classified Deletions*, 88.

85. DuBridge, interview by Sherwin.

86. Testimony of DuBridge, *Personnel Security Board, Classified Deletions*, 72–76 (quotation on 76).

87. Lemmer, *Air Force and Strategic Deterrence*, 15.

88. Cochran, Arkin, Norris, and Hoenig, *Nuclear Weapons Databook*, 18.

89. Bird and Sherwin, *American Prometheus*, 443.

90. Getting and Christie, *David Tressel Griggs*, 123.

91. Interviewed in Newman, "Oppenheimer Case," 75.

92. Schaffel, *Emerging Shield*, 176.

93. Schaffel, *Emerging Shield*, 172.

94. Alsop and Alsop, "Air Defense Ignored."

95. Schaffel, *Emerging Shield*, 150–51, 199–200. On 202–7, Schaffel outlines the continuing poor relationship between air force headquarters and MIT scientists, while the army and air force contested control of the air defense system.

96. Schaffel, *Emerging Shield*, 174–76.

97. Quotations in Pike, Blair, and Schwartz, "Defending against the Bomb," 273–75. Oppenheimer, "Atomic Weapons and American Policy," 531.

98. Summer Study Group final report, quoted in Schaffel, *Emerging Shield*, 176–77.

99. Moody, Neufeld, and Hall, "Emergence of the Strategic Air Command," 56–57.

100. Pais, *J. Robert Oppenheimer*, 191. Pais's source for this was the Oppenheimer Papers at the Library of Congress.

101. Testimony of Griggs, *Oppenheimer Personnel Security Board Transcript*, 751.

102. Pais, *J. Robert Oppenheimer*, 192.

103. WRS interview with Paul Nitze, 27 February 1957, 9.

104. Douglas to Lauris Norstad, 5 January 1954, Eyes Only—folder 43, box 42, Norstad Papers. For Eisenhower's order to US Attorney General Herbert Brownell, which used similar language, see Rhodes, *Dark Sun*, 534–35, 663n. For argument that Strauss was behind this order, see McMillan, *Ruin of J. Robert Oppenheimer*, 302n7.

105. *Oppenheimer Personnel Security Board Transcript*, 743–70. Ridenour's predecessor as scientific adviser to the secretary of the air force was Ivan Getting, who would later write a warm appreciation of Griggs's achievements. See Getting and Christie, "David Tressel Griggs," 122–23, passim.

106. Getting, *All in a Lifetime*, 39–40.

107. Testimony of Griggs, *Oppenheimer Personnel Security Board Transcript*, 746, 749, 755.

108. Prior to this point, the air force had been supporting Teller in continuing his work at the University of Chicago, secretly redirecting an existing Army Ordnance study of machine guns in aerial combat to a contract for thermonuclear research. Kohn, *Reflections on Research and Development*, 45–46.

109. Condit, *History of the Office*, 477–79.

110. Testimony of Griggs, *Oppenheimer Personnel Security Board Transcript*, 747–48.

111. Testimony of Griggs, *Personnel Security Board, Classified Deletions*, 100.

112. Testimony of Griggs, *Oppenheimer Personnel Security Board Transcript*, 747, 749.

113. DuBridge, interview by Sherwin.

114. [Murphy], "Hidden Struggle," 109.

115. Yoder, *Joe Alsop's Cold War*, 136.

116. Newman, "Oppenheimer Case," 79, cited in Bird and Sherwin, *American Prometheus*, 468. Jackson also served as a presidential adviser on psychological strategy.

117. Murphy to Norstad, 21 April 1953, Eyes Only—folder 8, box 41, Norstad Papers.

118. Testimony of Wilson, *Oppenheimer Personnel Security Board Transcript*, 680.

119. Alsop and Alsop, *We Accuse!*, 22.

120. WRS interview with Lt. Gen. Roscoe C. Wilson, 23–24 April 1958, 1.

121. Wilson, interview by Smith, 83–84. It is worth noting that in five hours of talking with Schilling in 1958, Wilson never conveyed this sense of regret, despite having the chance several times when he talked about aspects of Oppenheimer's personality and actions. WRS interview with Lt. Gen. Roscoe C. Wilson, 23–24 April 1958, 6, 8, 11. The perspective of his 1983 comments may have been a personal function of the passage of time, or the lessening of the anti-Oppenheimer fervor in the political climate. Schilling had noted during the middle of his interview program the publication by a prominent anti-Communist voice of a long and patronizing invective against Oppenheimer. So attacks against Oppenheimer were not just something that had taken place a few years before the interview program; they were still continuing right in the middle of it. Evans, "Open Letter to Dr. Oppenheimer."

122. For a penetrating analysis of the hearing, see Bernstein, "Oppenheimer Loyalty-Security Case Reconsidered."

123. LaFeber, *America, Russia, and the Cold War*, 178–80.

124. A fully detailed account of the moves made by the AEC and others leading up to and beyond the hearing is given in the third volume of the commission's history: Hewlett and Holl, *Atoms for Peace and War*, 73–112.

125. Hewlett and Holl, *Atoms for Peace and War*, 110.

126. Quoted in LaFeber, *America, Russia, and the Cold War*, 180.

7. Rewriting Los Alamos

1. "A Chronology of the Thermonuclear Weapon Program to November 1952," draft, 14 August 1953, folder 7, box 465, Lewis L. Strauss Papers, Herbert Hoover Presidential Library.

2. For an account of the divisions within the AEC during the 1953–54 period, see McMillan, *Ruin of J. Robert Oppenheimer*, 183–84, 233–35.

3. Smyth to Strauss, 21 September 1953, box 535, Strauss Papers.

4. Smyth to Strauss, 21 September 1953, box 535, Strauss Papers. Smyth began drafting the reply to Strauss on 13 August, a process significant enough that Smyth's wife, Mary, recorded it in her diary. See "AEC Dates 1949–1954 from M's Diary (compiled April 1959)," "AEC—Lewis L. Strauss—Confirmation" folder, series 3, Henry DeWolf Smyth Papers, American Philosophical Society.

5. Strauss to Hickenlooper, 18 April 1952, box 465, Strauss Papers.

6. Smyth to Strauss, 21 September 1953.

7. Memorandum for files, 16 September 1953, box 487, Strauss Papers. As Lilienthal's replacement on the NSC special committee, Smyth endorsed a program of H-bomb production in February 1950.

8. On strategic bombardment, see Ridenour, "Bomb and Blackett." On 15 February 1946, Ridenour testified before the Senate Committee on Atomic Energy on behalf of the Federation of American Scientists, arguing that a nuclear attack was unlikely to be survivable.

9. Ridenour, "Hydrogen Bomb," 13–15.

10. Quoted in US Department of Energy, *In the Matter of J. Robert Oppenheimer* (hereafter *Personnel Security Board, Classified Deletions*), 23.

11. Bethe to Dean, 23 May 1952, box 387, RG 330, National Archives and Records Administration.

12. Testimony of Lilienthal, *Personnel Security Board, Classified Deletions*, 49. It is pertinent that Hans Bethe estimated that work on the Super occupied about 20 percent of the theoretical division's time, and a similar proportion of the experimental division's. These were not negligible amounts. WRS interview with Hans Bethe, 17 May 1957, 1.

13. Bradbury, "Los Alamos Laboratory," 359.

14. Fitzpatrick, "Igniting the Light Elements," 4–7.

15. "Bradbury's Colleagues," 33.

16. "Bradbury's Colleagues," 36.

17. Teller, *Better a Shield*, 76.

18. [Murphy], "Hidden Struggle," 110, 230.

19. Shepley and Blair, *Hydrogen Bomb*, 185–86. The FBI investigated this claim, but was unable to identify any such individual. Hewlett and Holl, *Atoms for Peace and War*, 47–48, 600n37.

20. Testimony of Griggs, in US Atomic Energy Commission, *In the Matter of J. Robert Oppenheimer* (hereafter *Oppenheimer Personnel Security Board Transcript*), 750, 769–70.

21. Testimony of Zacharias, *Oppenheimer Personnel Security Board Transcript*, 927–32.

22. Stern, *Oppenheimer Case*, 343n.

23. McMillan, *The Ruin of J. Robert Oppenheimer*, 219; Newman, "Oppenheimer Case," 130.

24. *Oppenheimer Personnel Security Board Transcript*.

25. *Personnel Security Board, Classified Deletions*.

26. Moley, "On Tap, Not on Top."

27. Shepley and Blair, *Hydrogen Bomb*, chap. 20.

28. Kaplan, *To Kill Nations*, 78–79.

29. Pike, Blair, and Schwartz, "Defending against the Bomb," 280n29.

30. Bradley and Blair, *General's Life*.

31. Shepley and Blair, "Hydrogen Bomb," 58.

32. Shepley and Blair, *Hydrogen Bomb*, 20–21.

33. Shepley and Blair, *Hydrogen Bomb*, 94n. The note gives 1951 as the end date, which must be an error.

34. Shepley and Blair, *Hydrogen Bomb*, 94–95.

35. Shepley and Blair, *Hydrogen Bomb*, 171, 183–86.

36. Shepley and Blair, *Hydrogen Bomb*, 228.

37. A positive review by Peter Kihss in the *New York Times Book Review* on 3 October was significantly entitled "The Triumph of Mr. Teller."

38. Moley, "On Tap, Not on Top."

39. Correspondence in Eisenhower Presidential Library, cited in Newman, "Oppenheimer Case," 171.

40. Bethe, "Comments on the History," 43. Bethe wrote two different internal accounts, one in 1952 that was highly technical and intended for senior officials with high security clearances. That paper was partly declassified following a request by Daniel Hirsch and William G. Mathews and is mentioned in their paper "The H-bomb." The second paper of 1954 was prompted by the Oppenheimer hearing and the publication of *The Hydrogen Bomb*, although it was not published until 1982, a withholding from contemporaneous publication that Smyth had urged; WRS interview with Smyth, 7 August 1956, 1. When interviewed by Schilling, Bethe referred to a classified history of the Super that he had prepared; WRS interview with Bethe, 17 May 1957, 1.

41. Bradbury, "Los Alamos Laboratory," 359.

42. WRS interview with Norris Bradbury, 10 December 1956, 2.

43. WRS postinterviews draft introduction, 10, WRS personal papers.

44. Haverstick, "Thermonuclear Cabal," 14.

45. Dean, press release, 28 September 1954. Also published as Dean, "Hydrogen Bomb."

46. Dean to Strauss, 10 September 1954, box 465, Strauss Papers.

47. Strauss, interview by Mason, 137.

48. Dean to Acheson, 23 September 1954; Acheson to Dean, 24 September 1954, Dean Acheson Papers, Harry S. Truman Presidential Library (hereafter HST).

49. Dean to Strauss, 28 April 1954, box 465, Strauss Papers. In January 1950, Dean had produced his own account of the sequence of events leading to the decision on the Super, apparently from his diary. Eventually included in the commission files as a formal paper, it is reproduced in Anders, *Forging the Atomic Shield*, 57–64.

50. Coughlan, "Dr. Edward Teller's Magnificent Obsession," 69.

51. Dean to Robert Coughlan, *Life* magazine, 2 September 1954, box 465, Strauss Papers. Dean was correct in so arguing, from the evidence of a memorandum dated 3 November 1949, probably originally a diary entry, calling for rejection of the GAC's advice. Anders, *Forging the Atomic Shield*, 49–50.

52. Strauss to the editors, *Life*, 24 September 1954, box 436, Strauss Papers. The 27 September issue of the magazine, page 11, did not publish a letter from Strauss, but rather one from a reader stating that Dean had been slighted. That was followed by a statement from the editor that relayed Dean's assertion and added praise for his tenure as chair of the AEC. In his published memoirs, Strauss elides the actual stage in the process at which Dean "later changed his opinion and concurred with me," wrongly implying that it was later than mid-November. Strauss, *Men and Decisions*, 218–19.

53. "Citation from the White House."

54. "Bradbury's Colleagues," 44.

55. Alvarez, *Alvarez*, 179–80.

56. WRS interview with Lewis L. Strauss, 20 May 1957, 1.

57. WRS interview with Lewis L. Strauss, 2 May 1958, 1.

58. Throughout the interview program, Schilling declined to tell interview subjects who else he had interviewed or to attribute to subjects what they had told him. In this case he felt guilty and confessed his "transgression" to Souers, but Souers replied that he did not mind. Letter, Schilling to Souers, 20 May 1958; letter, Souers to Schilling, 23 June 1958, WRS personal papers.

59. The Alsop brothers charged Shepley and Blair with having produced a dishonest, inaccurate, and unfair account. Yoder, *Joe Alsop's Cold War*, 136–38.

60. WRS interview with Henry Smyth, 7 August 1956, 1.

61. For example, WRS interviews with Lee DuBridge, 11 December 1956, 1; Dean Acheson, 24 October 1956, 2; Sidney Souers, 8 October 1957, 10; Joseph Volpe, 3 December 1956; and Edward Teller, 14–15 December 1956, 3. Volpe told Schilling his success in obtaining interviews was *because* of the book. Teller's comment was that the best thing to do with the book was to burn it, which is especially notable given that Teller was the *hero* of the Shepley and Blair account.

62. Press release, statement of sources, David McKay Company, publishers, 6 October [1954], box 348, folder 2 Clay Blair Papers, American Heritage Center, University of Wyoming.

63. Blair left no record of the duo's research in his papers at the American Heritage Center at the University of Wyoming. The files do contain a large number of press reviews of the book, few of them annotated by date and publisher.

64. Bradbury to Strauss, 1 October 1954, folder 25, box 511, Strauss Papers; Shelby Thompson, Acting Director of Information Services, AEC, to Shepley, 13 August 1954, folder 25, box 511, Strauss Papers, Shepley. (Due to archives renumbering, some documents in box 511 were previously in box 196; both citations are used here.)

65. Bradbury to Strauss, 1 October 1954, folder 25, box 511, Strauss Papers.

66. Young, "Cold War Insecurities," 901.

67. See correspondence with Charles J. V. Murphy, box 510 (AEC era) and box 304 (later era), Strauss Papers.

68. Newman, "Oppenheimer Case," 149.

69. Correspondence among Blair, Strauss, and Robert MacNeal, 2 January 1962 through 16 July 1962, box 192, folder 2, Blair Papers. MacNeal was president of the Curtis Publishing Co., for whom Blair worked as a correspondent and editor.

70. Shepley to Strauss, 5 October 1963, box 196, Strauss Papers.

71. Shepley to Strauss, with attachment, 24 September 1954, box 196, Strauss Papers. Shepley's statement on the television program, which took place on 26 September, is given in Strauss, *Men and Decisions*, 445–46.

72. This was precisely the point argued by Bradbury in calling for the AEC to refrain from commenting on externally authored manuscripts by uncleared personnel. Bradbury to Strauss, 1 October 1954, folder 25, box 511, Strauss Papers.

73. Manuscript file, dated July 1954, box 196, Strauss Papers.

74. Pearl Carroll, Time Inc., to Strauss, 10 July 1954, box 196, Strauss Papers.

75. Pfau, *No Sacrifice Too Great*, 188–89, 215–17.

76. The story of the confirmation hearings, in which Strauss barely scraped the majority vote of the committee only to be rejected on the Senate floor by three votes, is told in his *Men and Decisions*, chap. 18; and in Pfau, *No Sacrifice Too Great*, chap. 13.

77. "Senator Charges 'H-Bomb Lies.'"

78. The Dixon-Yates affair involved a proposal to generate electricity for the Tennessee region. Initiated by the Tennessee Valley Authority, the project emerged as a complex plan for the AEC to purchase power from a private source to relieve the demand on the TVA's Shawnee plant. Strauss handled the negotiations secretly, incurring the wrath of some fellow commissioners and the bitter opposition of congressional Democrats. The AEC historians Hewlett and Holl untangled what they describe as a "bizarre" plan. Hewlett and Holl, *Atoms for Peace and War*, 127–40. See also Pfau, *No Sacrifice Too Great*, 183–92.

79. Anderson to Truman, 13 March 1959, with Anderson's marginal annotation "This I question" next to that paragraph of the *Newsweek* article, Post-Presidential Papers, HST. The article is Lindley, "Case for the Defense."

80. Truman to Anderson, 16 March 1959, Post-Presidential Papers.

81. Drew Pearson broadcast on WTOP (Washington, DC), 21 March 1959. The Drew Pearson Washington Merry-Go-Round Radio Broadcast Collection is available at the University Library Archives at American University, Washington, DC.

82. Strauss to Johnson, 6 April 1959, box 472, Strauss Papers.

83. *Nomination of Lewis L. Strauss to be Secretary of Commerce: Hearings before the Comm. on Interstate and Foreign Commerce*, US Senate, 86th Cong., 1st Sess., 6 (1959) (statement of Lewis L. Strauss).

84. Anderson to Truman, 21 April 1959, Post-Presidential Papers.

85. Souers to Strauss, 3 April 1959, box 178, Strauss Papers.

86. Nevertheless, as a former president, Truman expressed anger at the harassment of scientists by Republican senators exploiting security clearance questions for political ends. Truman to Edward U. Condon, 3 December 1957, "Truman #1" folder, series 1, Edward U. Condon Papers, American Philosophical Society.

87. Souers to Strauss, 17 April 1959, box 178, Strauss Papers.

88. Strauss to Truman, 19 August 1959; "Memorandum for Files of Lewis L. Strauss," 21 September 1959; Strauss to Souers, 21 September 1959, box 396, Strauss Papers. A fuller account of these exchanges is given in Young, "Hydrogen Bomb."

89. Krock, *Memoirs*, 310–13. Krock gave thanks to Charles V. Murphy in his acknowledgments. For his part, Strauss offered gentle remonstrance that Krock had not gotten all of the details of his time on the AEC correct.

90. Wilson, interview by Gingerich.

Conclusions

1. The summary of issues that follows is an edited account drawn from Schilling's lecture notes and supporting note cards, and Schilling to Neustadt, 8 April 1966, WRS personal papers.

2. WRS interview with Paul Nitze, 1 May 1957, 2. Lest it be thought that Schilling's analyses always met with such a reception, it should also be noted that when he advanced one of his theories to Acheson—that of the intentionally minimal scope of Truman's 31 January decision—he got a scoffing response that the concept and description were high in the realm of theory and bore little relation to how the human mind actually works. Indeed, Acheson was wary of any attempts to force events into too neat and orderly a pattern, and for that matter seemed skeptical of the work of political scientists in general. WRS interviews with Dean Acheson, 21 June 1957, 1, 2; and 24 October 1956, 1. Nitze's more positive reaction was significant, as he was himself prone to dismiss "political science" writing as "chic" interpretations that "missed the point." Young, "Revisiting NSC 68," 11, 32.

3. WRS interviews with Lewis L. Strauss, 20 May 1957, 4, and 2 May 1958, 2 (comments in his interview notes indicate that Schilling had some difficulty believing that Strauss was really that isolated); Edward Teller, 14–15 December 1956, 3, 8, 11, 13; and Kenneth Nichols, 22 April 1957, 10, 11.

4. WRS interview with Henry Smyth, 7 August 1956, 6.

5. WRS interview with Edward Teller, 14–15 December 1956, 10.

6. WRS notes from John Manley's account of his diary entries, collected 16 December 1956.

7. WRS interview with George Kennan, 28 September 1956, 4–5, based on Kennan reading from his diary entries.

8. For a further discussion of the confusions involved, see Schilling, "H-bomb Decision," 32–34.

9. WRS interview with Edward Teller, 14–15 December 1956, 12. Reportedly John von Neumann also held this view about Oppenheimer. WRS interview with Kenneth Mansfield, 18 August 1956, 3.

10. For background on the Strauss-GAC and Lawrence-Oppenheimer instances of poor relations, see Rhodes, *Dark Sun*, 310–11 and 359–60, respectively.

11. For background, see Neuse, *David E. Lilienthal*, 196, 214–20.

12. WRS interview with George Kennan, 14 September 1956, 1, 4. For background, see Paul, *Nuclear Rivals*, 115–25.

13. WRS interview with Edward Teller, 14–15 December 1956, 1–2.

14. "M'Mahon Says 24 Know Atom Score."
15. WRS interviews with Dean Acheson, 24 October 1956, 1–2, and 21 June 1957, 4; Gordon Arneson, 27 March 1957, 2, 8.
16. Rosenberg, "U.S. Nuclear Stockpile," 28. In his interview with Schilling, Kenneth Mansfield told a similar tale that involved McMahon, Forrestal (now secretary of defense), and the chief of naval operations in early 1949, but he may have been conflating the early incident with a speech McMahon gave in January 1949 about making the stockpile size public.
17. WRS interview with Kenneth Mansfield, 18 August 1956, 5.
18. WRS personal discussions with Kenneth Mansfield. Schilling used Mansfield's statement in his course lectures for many years.
19. WRS interview with David E. Lilienthal, 18 June 1957, 1, 2–3. See also Bundy, *Danger and Survival*, 200–201, which has passages on this subject that, upon reading them, Schilling noted as telling.
20. WRS interview with Cyril Smith, 17 December 1956, 10.
21. WRS interview with David E. Lilienthal, 23 August 1957, 4, reveals some agreement from Lilienthal on this point.
22. WRS interviews with Dean Acheson, 24 October 1956, 7; Paul Nitze, 27 February 1957, 4–5, 8; and Gordon Arneson, 27 March 1957, 8. Arneson relates a similar story in his 1969 account of the decision, but about Oppenheimer, not Lilienthal. Whether it was the same story but his memory had shifted, or whether he saw both people get this reaction from Acheson, is unclear. Arneson, "H-bomb Decision," 29.
23. WRS interview with J. Robert Oppenheimer, 11 June 1957, 14.
24. WRS interviews with George Kennan, 14 September 1956, 1–2, 4, and 28 September 1956, 4.
25. WRS interview with Dean Acheson, 24 October 1956, 6.
26. WRS interview with Lt. Gen. Alvin R. Luedecke, 3 May 1957, 5. A similar point was made by another air force general, in WRS interview with Maj. Gen. Roscoe C. Wilson, 23–24 April 1958, 9–10.
27. For area bombing generally, see Paskins and Dockrill, *Ethics of War*, chap. 1. The deliberate targeting of civilian populations is discussed in Richelson, "Population Targeting."
28. Quoted in Bernstein, "Oppenheimer Loyalty-Security Case Reconsidered," 1415.
29. Rosenberg, "'Smoking Radiating Ruin,'" 30–31.
30. Stern, *Oppenheimer Case*, 195–96.
31. Twining, *Neither Liberty nor Safety*, chaps. 3–5, esp. 105–6, 125–26.
32. Gavin, *Nuclear Statecraft*, 23.
33. Jervis, "Perceiving and Coping with Threat," 13–14.
34. Gavin, *Nuclear Statecraft*, 23.
35. This perspective on public affairs was introduced by Donald A. Schön and Martin Rein in their *Frame Reflection*. A recent reworking is van Hulst and Yanow, "From Policy 'Frames' to 'Framing.'" The most pertinent, well illustrated with examples, is Entman, *Projections of Power*. Eden, *Whole World on Fire*, applies this analysis to the underestimation of the fire effects of a nuclear attack.
36. Recollecting "where you stand . . . ," in an article in *Public Administration Review*, Miles noted ruefully that "better known people" generally got the credit for the expression. Miles, "Origin and Meaning."
37. Allison and Halperin, "Bureaucratic Politics," 49.
38. Beard, *Developing the ICBM*, 11.
39. Allison and Halperin, "Bureaucratic Politics," 42.
40. Smyth to Steven L. Newman, 18 October 1968, Newman correspondence folder, series 1, Henry DeWolf Smyth Papers, American Philosophical Society. Also cited in Newman, "Oppenheimer Case," 165. Smyth thought Finletter's office, especially William Burden and Garrison Norton, might have been misled by the "fanatical" David Griggs.
41. *Oakeshott, Rationalism in Politics*, 54.
42. Rowen, "Evolution of Strategic Nuclear Doctrine," 140n. Emphasis in the last two sentences added.

43. Sabatier and Jenkins-Smith, *Policy Change and Learning*; Jenkins-Smith and Sabatier, "Advocacy Coalition Framework."

44. Deaile, *Always at War*, 122.

45. Bernstein, "H-bomb Decisions," 327–28, 346, 350.

46. Offner, *Another Such Victory*, xii, chap. 16.

47. Siracusa and Warren, *Weapons of Mass Destruction*, 32.

48. Costs are estimated at $409 billion for the seventy-thousand-weapon stockpile, versus more than $3.2 trillion for delivery systems. O'Neill, "Building the Bomb," 102–4. The costs quoted are in constant 1996 dollars.

49. Weida, "Economic Implications," 540.

50. Kenneth Waltz, quoted in Trachtenberg, *Cold War and After*, 39. Also see esp. chap. 1 in *Cold War and After*.

51. Alvarez, *Alvarez*, 152.

52. Gavin, *Nuclear Statecraft*, 21–22.

53. Schilling, "H-bomb Decision," 46.

Bibliography

Primary Sources

Archival Sources

American Heritage Center, University of Wyoming, Laramie, WY

Clay Blair Papers

American Philosophical Society, Philadelphia

Henry DeWolf Smyth Papers
Edward U. Condon Papers

Dwight D. Eisenhower Presidential Library (DDE), Abilene, KS

Lauris Norstad Papers

Harry S. Truman Presidential Library (HST), Independence, MO

President's Secretary's Files
Post-Presidential Papers
Dean Acheson Papers
Eben A. Ayers Papers

Herbert Hoover Presidential Library, West Branch, IA

Lewis L. Strauss Papers
Bourke B. Hickenlooper Papers

Hoover Institution, Stanford University, Stanford, CA

Robert LeBaron Papers

Liddell Hart Centre for Military Archives, King's College, London

Minutes of the meetings of the Joint Chiefs of Staff, Records of the Joint Chiefs of Staff, Pt. 2: 1946–53 (microfilm set from University Publications of America)

National Archives and Records Administration (NARA), College Park, MD

Record Groups RG 128, RG 218, RG 236, RG 326, RG 330

State Historical Society of Missouri, Columbia, MO

Papers of W. Stuart Symington

Trinity College Cambridge Library, Cambridge

Sir George Thomson Papers

US Department of Energy, Washington, DC

US Atomic Energy Commission General Advisory Committee records

US Library of Congress, Washington, DC

Hoyt S. Vandenberg Papers
Nathan F. Twining Papers
Louis N. Ridenour Papers
Paul Nitze Papers
Curtis LeMay Papers

Interviews

By Warner R. Schilling

This is an alphabetical list of all of the participants WRS interviewed in person for this project and the date of each interview, as well as the dates of any subsequent interviews and substantive communications he had with them. For a list of the interview subjects organized by their institutional affiliations and showing their positions or ranks during 1949–50, see table 2 in the introduction.

Individual	Date of interview	Date(s) of subsequent communication
Acheson, Dean	24 October 1956	21 June 1957
Alexander, Archibald	19 August 1957	
Alvarez, Luis	15 December 1956	
Arneson, R. Gordon	27 March 1957	tel. 3 May 1957

Individual	Date of interview	Date(s) of subsequent communication	
Bacher, Robert	11 December 1956		
Bethe, Hans	17 May 1957		
Borden, William L.	10 October 1956	tel. 25 Oct 1956	also letter 26 Mar 1957
Bradbury, Norris	10 December 1956		
Buckley, Oliver	13 September 1956		
Burns, James	22 April 1957		
Bush, Vannevar	19 February 1958		also letter 4 Mar 1958
Coiner, Richard	3 May 1957		
Cole, W. Sterling	20 February 1957		
Collins, J. Lawton	8 October 1957		
Conant, James	13 September 1957		
Conway, John T.			letter only 27 Nov1957
Davis, Arthur C.	21 June 1957		
Dean, Gordon	9 July 1956		
DuBridge, Lee	11 December 1956		
Durham, Carl T.			letter only, 9 Apr 1957
Everest, Frank F.			letter 10 Apr 1957
Fisher, Adrian	3 December 1956		
Gavin, James	26 June 1958	tel. 16 Jul 1958	
Groves, Leslie	6 August 1956	tel. 13 Aug 1956	
Haislip, Wade H.			tel. 30 Jul 1957
Hill, T. B.	1 May 1957		
Holifield, Chester	29 March 1957		
Hull, John E.	29 March 1957		
Jackson, Henry M.	3 April 1957		
Johnson, Louis	20 June 1957		
Kennan, George	14 September 1956	28 September 1956	
Krock, Arthur	24 April 1958		
Leach, W. Barton	30 January 1956		
LeBaron, Robert	29 March 1957	1 May 1957	29 July 1957
Leva, Marx	29 March 1957		
Lilienthal, David	18 June 1957	23 August 1957	
Loper, Herbert B.	3 April 1957	20 May 1957	
Luedecke, Alvin	3 May 1957		

(Continued)

(Continued)

Individual	Date of interview	Date(s) of subsequent communication	
Manley, John	16 December 1956	tel.16 Dec 1956	also notes from diary
Mansfield, J. Kenneth	15 December 1955	18 August 1956	
McCormack, James	21 June 1956	27 June 1957	also letter; tel. 23 Jan 1958
Morse, Philip M.	6 May 1958		
Neustadt, Richard	9 January 1956	5 October 1956,	24 Jan 1957, 7 Mar 1957
Nichols, Kenneth	22 April 1957		
Nitze, Paul	27 February 1957	1 May 1957	also informal 19 Mar 1957
Ohly, John H.	20 May 1957		
Oppenheimer, J. Robert	11 June 1957		
Pike, Sumner	31 October 1956		
Pitzer, Kenneth	14 December 1956		
Price, Melvin	2 May 1957		
Rabi, Isidor Isaac	7 May 1956	29 May 1956	
Rowe, Hartley	23 November 1956		
Russell, James	27 February 1956	3 April 1957	
Schlatter, David	24 May 1957		
Seaborg, Glenn	15 December 1956		
Serber, Robert	8 January 1957		
Smith, Cyril	17 December 1956		
Smyth, Henry	7 August 1956	26 September 1956	also notes 1954 speech
Souers, Sidney	8 October 1957		
Strauss, Lewis	20 May 1957	2 May 1958	
Struble, Dewey	29 July 1957		
Symington, Stuart			letter only, 21 May 1958
Szilard, Leo	8 May 1958		
Teller, Edward	14 December 1956	15 December 1956	
Truman, David	11 March 1957		
Truman, Harry S.	14 September 1957		
Tufts, Robert	13 March 1956	11 January 1957	
Volpe, Joseph	3 December 1956	2 May 1957	
Walker, John	24 October 1956		
Warren, Shields	27 May 1957		

Individual	Date of interview	Date(s) of subsequent communication	
Webster, William	28 May 1957		
Wilson, Carroll	23 November 1956		
Wilson, R. C.	23 April 1958	24 April 1958	also letter 2 Jun 1958
Zacharias, Jerrold	21 June 1956		

By Other Interviewers

Arneson, R. Gordon. Interview by Niel M. Johnson, 21 June 1989, Washington, DC. Harry S. Truman Presidential Library.

Luedecke, Alvin R. Interview by Terry Anderson, 29 September 1981. Cushing Library, Texas A&M University, College Station, TX.

Nitze, Paul H. Interview by Paul Hammond, 27 November 1956. WRS personal papers.

Nitze, Paul H. Interview by John N. Dick and James G. Hasdorff, 19–20 May 1981, 14–16 July 1981. US Air Force Oral History Interview Program, Air Force Historical Research Agency, K239.0512–997.

Norstad, Lauris. Interview by Hugh N. Ahmann, 13–16 February and 22–25 October 1979. US Air Force Oral History Interview Program, Air Force Historical Research Agency, K239.0512–1116.

Pitzer, Kenneth Sanborn. *Chemist and Administrator at UC Berkeley, Rice University, Stanford University, and the Atomic Energy Commission, 1935–1997.* Oral history conducted in 1996–98 by Sally Smith Hughes and Germaine LaBerge. Regional Oral History Office, Bancroft Library, University of California, Berkeley, 1999.

Strauss, Lewis L. Interview by John T. Mason Jr., 23 January and 14 February 1962, and 26 February 1963. Oral History Archives, Columbia University.

Wilson, Roscoe C. Interview by Lt. Col. Dennis A. Smith, 1–2 December 1983. US Air Force Oral History Interview Program, Air Force Historical Research Agency, K239.0512–1554.

Manhattan Project

DuBridge, Lee. Interview by Martin J. Sherwin, 30 March 1983. Voices of the Manhattan Project. https://manhattanprojectvoices.org/oral-histories/lee-dubridges-interview-part-2.

Hammel, Ed. Interview by Martin J. Sherwin, 9 January 1985. Voices of the Manhattan Project. https://manhattanprojectvoices.org/oral-histories/ed-hammels-interview.

Wilson, Robert R. Interview by Owen Gingerich, 23 April 1982. Voices of the Manhattan Project. https://manhattanprojectvoices.org/oral-histories/robert-r-wilsons-interview.

Secondary Sources

Acheson, Dean. *Present at the Creation: My Years in the State Department.* New York: W. W. Norton, 1969.

Allison, Graham T., and Morton H. Halperin. "Bureaucratic Politics: A Paradigm and Some Policy Implications." In "Theory and Policy in International Relations," edited by Raymond Tanter and Richard H. Ullman. Supplement, *World Politics* 24 (Spring 1972): 40–79.

Allison, S. K., K. T. Bainbridge, H. S. Bethe, R. B. Brode, C. C. Lauritsen, F. W. Loomis, G. B. Pegram, et al. "Let Us Pledge Not to Use H-bomb First!" *Bulletin of the Atomic Scientists* 6, no. 3 (March 1950): 75.

Alperovitz, Gar. *The Decision to Use the Atomic Bomb, and the Architecture of an American Myth.* New York: Alfred A. Knopf, 1995.

Alsop, Joseph, and Stewart Alsop. *We Accuse! The Story of the Miscarriage of American Justice in the Case of J. Robert Oppenheimer.* New York: Simon and Schuster, 1954.

Alvarez, Luis W. *Alvarez: Adventures of a Physicist.* New York: Basic Books, 1987.

Ambrose, Stephen E. *Eisenhower.* Vol. 1, *Soldier, General of the Army, President-Elect, 1890–1952.* New York: Simon and Schuster, 1983.

Anders, Roger M., ed. *Forging the Atomic Shield: Excerpts from the Office Diary of Gordon E. Dean.* Chapel Hill: University of North Carolina Press, 1987.

Arneson, R. Gordon. "The H-bomb Decision." *Foreign Service Journal* 46, no. 6 (May 1969): 27–29.

Bacher, Robert F. "The Hydrogen Bomb: III." *Scientific American* 182, no. 5 (May 1950): 11–15.

Barlow, Jeffrey G. *Revolt of the Admirals: The Fight for Naval Aviation, 1945–1950.* Washington, DC: Naval Historical Center, 1994.

Batchelder, Robert C. *The Irreversible Decision, 1939–1950.* Boston: Houghton Mifflin, 1962.

Beard, Edmund. *Developing the ICBM: A Study in Bureaucratic Politics.* New York: Columbia University Press, 1976.

Beisner, Robert L. *Dean Acheson: A Life in the Cold War.* New York: Oxford University Press, 2006.

Bernstein, Barton J. "American Conservatives Are the Forgotten Critics of the Atomic Bombing of Japan." *San Jose Mercury News,* 2 August 2014.

Bernstein, Barton J. "Crossing the Rubicon: A Missed Opportunity to Stop the H-bomb?" *International Security* 14, no. 2 (Fall 1989): 132–60.

Bernstein, Barton J. "Eclipsed by Hiroshima and Nagasaki: Early Thinking about Tactical Nuclear Weapons." *International Security* 15, no. 4 (Spring 1991): 149–73.

Bernstein, Barton J. "Four Physicists and the Bomb: The Early Years, 1945–1950." *Historical Studies in the Physical and Biological Sciences* 18, no. 2 (1988): 231–63.

Bernstein, Barton J. "The H-bomb Decisions: Were They Inevitable?" In *National Security and International Stability,* edited by Bernard Brodie, Michael D. Intriligator, and Roman Kolkowicz, 327–56. Cambridge, MA: Oelgeschlager, Gunn and Hain, 1983.

Bernstein, Barton J. "The Oppenheimer Loyalty-Security Case Reconsidered." *Stanford Law Review* 42, no. 6 (July 1990): 1383–1484.

Bernstein, Barton J. "Truman and the H-bomb." *Bulletin of the Atomic Scientists* 40, no. 3 (March 1984): 12–18.

Bethe, Hans A. "Comments on the History of the H-bomb." *Los Alamos Science,* no. 6 (Fall 1982): 42–53.

Bethe, Hans A. "The Hydrogen Bomb: II." *Scientific American* 182, no. 4 (April 1950): 18–23.

Biddle, Tami Davis. *Rhetoric and Reality in Air Warfare: The Evolution of British and American Ideas about Strategic Bombing, 1914–1945*. Princeton, NJ: Princeton University Press, 2002.

Bird, Kai, and Martin J. Sherwin. *American Prometheus: The Triumph and Tragedy of J. Robert Oppenheimer*. New York: Vintage Books, 2006.

Blackett, P. M. S. *Fear, War and the Bomb: Military and Political Consequences of Atomic Energy*. New York: Whittlesey House, 1949. First published as *Military and Political Consequences of Atomic Energy*. London: Turnstile, 1948.

Blades, David M., and Joseph M. Siracusa. *A History of U.S. Nuclear Testing and Its Influence on Nuclear Thought, 1945–1963*. Lanham, MD: Rowman and Littlefield, 2014.

Borowski, Harry R. *A Hollow Threat: Strategic Air Power and Containment before Korea*. Westport, CT: Greenwood, 1982.

Botti, Timothy. *Ace in the Hole: Why the United States Did Not Use Nuclear Weapons in the Cold War, 1945 to 1965*. Westport, CT: Greenwood, 1996.

Bradbury, Norris E. "The Los Alamos Laboratory." *Bulletin of the Atomic Scientists* 10, no. 9 (November 1954): 358–59.

"Bradbury's Colleagues Remember His Era." *Los Alamos Science*, no. 7 (Winter/ Spring 1983): 29–52.

Bradley, Omar N., and Clay Blair. *A General's Life: An Autobiography*. New York: Simon and Schuster, 1983.

Broscious, S. David. "Longing for International Control, Banking on American Superiority: Harry S. Truman's Approach to Nuclear Weapons." In *Cold War Statesmen Confront the Bomb: Nuclear Diplomacy since 1945*, edited by John Lewis Gaddis, Philip H. Gordon, Ernest R. May, and Jonathan Rosenberg, 15–38. Oxford: Oxford University Press, 1999.

Buck, Alice L. *A History of the Atomic Energy Commission*. Washington, DC: US Department of Energy, Office of the Executive Secretariat, History Division, 1983.

Bundy, McGeorge. *Danger and Survival: Choices about the Bomb in the First Fifty Years*. New York: Vintage Books, 1990.

Burr, William, Thomas S. Blanton, and Stephen I. Schwartz. "The Costs and Consequences of Nuclear Secrecy." In Schwartz, *Atomic Audit*, 433–84.

Campbell, Richard H. *The Silverplate Bombers: A History and Registry of the Enola Gay and Other B-29s Configured to Carry Atomic Bombs*. Jefferson, NC: McFarland, 2005.

Cantelon, Philip L., Richard G. Hewlett, and Robert C. Williams, eds. *The American Atom: A Documentary History of Nuclear Policies from the Discovery of Fission to the Present*. 2nd ed. Philadelphia: University of Pennsylvania Press, 1991.

Cochran, Thomas B., William A. Arkin, Robert S. Norris, and Milton M. Hoenig. *Nuclear Weapons Databook*. Vol. 2, *U.S. Nuclear Weapons Warhead Production*. Washington, DC: Ballinger, 1987.

Condit, Doris M. *History of the Office of the Secretary of Defense*. Vol. 2, *The Test of War, 1950–1953*. Washington, DC: Historical Office, Office of the Secretary of Defense, 1988.

Condit, Kenneth W. *History of the Joint Chiefs of Staff*. Vol. 2, *The Joint Chiefs of Staff and National Policy, 1947–1949*. Washington, DC: Historical Office, Office of the Secretary of Defense, 1996.

Converse, Elliott V., III. *Rearming for the Cold War: History of Acquisition in the Department of Defense.* Vol. 1, *1945–1960.* Washington, DC: Historical Office, Office of the Secretary of Defense, 2012.

Coox, Alvin D. "Strategic Bombing in the Pacific, 1942–1945." In Hall, *Case Studies in Strategic Bombardment,* 253–382.

Davis, Christopher M. *9/11 Commission Recommendations: Joint Committee on Atomic Energy—A Model for Congressional Oversight?* CRS Report for Congress. Washington, DC: Congressional Research Service, 2004.

Deaile, Melvin G. *Always at War: Organizational Culture in Strategic Air Command, 1946–62.* Annapolis, MD: Naval Institute Press, 2018.

Dean, Gordon. "The Hydrogren Bomb." *Bulletin of the Atomic Scientists* 10, no. 9 (November 1954): 357, 362.

Defense Threat Reduction Agency. *Defense's Nuclear Agency, 1947–1997.* Washington, DC: DTRA History Series, 2002.

Dingman, Roger. "Atomic Diplomacy during the Korean War." *International Security* 13, no. 3 (Winter 1988–89): 50–91.

Donovan, Robert J. *Tumultuous Years: The Presidency of Harry S. Truman, 1949–1953.* New York: W. W. Norton, 1982.

Doyle, Thomas E. "Reviving Nuclear Ethics: A Renewed Research Agenda for the Twenty-First Century." *Ethics and International Affairs* 24, no. 3 (Fall 2010): 287–308.

Eden, Lynn. *Whole World on Fire: Organizations, Knowledge, and Nuclear Weapons Devastation.* Ithaca, NY: Cornell University Press, 2004.

Elliot, David C. "Project Vista and Nuclear Weapons in Europe." *International Security* 11, no. 1 (Summer 1986): 163–83.

Entman, Robert M. *Projections of Power: Framing News, Public Opinion, and U.S. Foreign Policy.* Chicago: University of Chicago Press, 2004.

Etzold, Thomas H., and John Lewis Gaddis. *Containment: Documents on American Policy and Strategy, 1945–1950.* New York: Columbia University Press, 1978.

Evans, Medford. "An Open Letter to Dr. Oppenheimer." *National Review,* 9 March 1957.

Feaver, Peter Douglas. *Guarding the Guardians: Civilian Control of Nuclear Weapons in the United States.* Ithaca, NY: Cornell University Press, 1992.

Fermi, Laura. *Atoms in the Family: My Life with Enrico Fermi.* Chicago: University of Chicago Press, 1954.

Ferrell, Robert H., ed. *Harry S. Truman and the Bomb: A Documentary History.* Worland, WY: High Plains, 1996.

Ferrell, Robert H. *Harry S. Truman and the Cold War Revisionists.* Columbia: University of Missouri Press, 2006.

Fitzpatrick, Anne. "Igniting the Light Elements: The Los Alamos Thermonuclear Weapon Project, 1942–1952." PhD diss., Virginia Polytechnic Institute and State University, 1999.

Ford, Kenneth W. *Building the H Bomb: A Personal History.* Singapore: World Scientific, 2015.

Fox, Annette Baker. *The Institute of War and Peace Studies: The First Thirty-Five Years.* New York: Columbia University, 2001.

Friedberg, Aaron L. "A History of the U.S. Strategic 'Doctrine'—1945 to 1980." *Journal of Strategic Studies* 3, no. 3 (December 1980): 37–71.

Friedman, Norman. "The Soviet Bomber Force: Two 'Revolutions in Military Affairs.'" In *The Soviet Air Forces*, edited by Paul J. Murphy, 157–76. Jefferson, NC: McFarland, 1984.

Futrell, Robert Frank. *Ideas, Concepts, Doctrine: Basic Thinking in the United States Air Force.* Vol. 1, *1907–1960.* Maxwell Air Force Base, AL: Air University Press, 1989.

Gaddis, John Lewis. *George Kennan: An American Life.* New York: Penguin, 2011.

Galison, Peter, and Barton J. Bernstein. "In Any Light: Scientists and the Decision to Build the Superbomb, 1952–1954." *Historical Studies in the Physical and Biological Sciences* 19, no. 2 (1989): 267–347.

Gavin, Edward P. "LTG James M. Gavin: Theory and Influence." Student monograph, School of Advanced Military Studies, US Army Command and General Staff College, 2012.

Gavin, Francis J. *Nuclear Statecraft: History and Strategy in America's Atomic Age.* Ithaca, NY: Cornell University Press, 2012.

Gavin, James M. "The Tactical Use of the Atomic Bomb." *Combat Forces Journal* 1, no. 4 (November 1950): 9–11.

Gavin, James M. *War and Peace in the Space Age.* New York: Harper and Bros., 1958.

Gavin, James M. "We Can Solve Our Technical Difficulties." *Army Combat Forces Journal* 6, no. 4 (November 1955): 64–65.

Getting, Ivan A. *All in a Lifetime: Science in the Defense of Democracy.* New York: Vantage, 1989.

Getting, Ivan A., and John M. Christie. "David Tressel Griggs: October 6, 1911–December 31, 1974." In *Biographical Memoirs*, vol. 64, 112–33. Washington, DC: National Academy Press, 1994.

Gibson, James N. *Nuclear Weapons of the United States: An Illustrated History.* Atglen, PA: Schiffer, 1996.

Gilpin, Robert. *American Scientists and Nuclear Weapons Policy.* Princeton, NJ: Princeton University Press, 1962.

Goncharov, G. A. "American and Soviet H-bomb Development Programmes: Historical Background." *Physics-Uspekhi* 39, no. 10 (1996): 1033–44.

Gordin, Michael D. *Red Cloud at Dawn: Truman, Stalin, and the End of the Atomic Monopoly.* New York: Farrar, Straus and Giroux, 2009.

Grayling, A. C. *Among the Dead Cities: Was the Allied Bombing of Civilians in WWII a Necessity or a Crime?* London: Bloomsbury, 2006.

Greer, Thomas H. *The Development of Air Doctrine in the Army Air Arm, 1917–1941.* Washington, DC: Office of Air Force History, 1955.

Griffith, Charles. *The Quest: Haywood Hansell and American Strategic Bombing in World War II.* Honolulu: University Press of the Pacific, 2005.

Guilhot, Nicholas, ed. The Invention of International Relations Theory: Realism, the Rockefeller Foundation, and the 1954 Conference on Theory. New York: Columbia University Press, 2011.

Gunston, Bill. *Bombers of the West.* London: Ian Allan, 1973.

Hall, R. Cargill, ed. *Case Studies in Strategic Bombardment.* Washington, DC: Air Force History and Museums Program, 1998.

Hammond, Paul Y. *NSC-68: Prologue to Rearmament.* In *Strategy, Politics, and Defense Budgets*, by Warner R. Schilling, Paul Y. Hammond, and Glenn H. Snyder, 267–378. New York: Columbia University Press, 1962.

Hansell, Haywood S., Jr. *The Air Plan That Defeated Hitler*. Atlanta: Higgins-McArthur/Longino and Porter, 1972.

Hansell, Haywood S., Jr. *The Strategic Air War against Germany and Japan: A Memoir*. Washington, DC: Office of Air Force History, 1986.

Hansen, Chuck. *The Swords of Armageddon*. Version 2. 7 vols. Sunnyvale, CA: Chukelea, 2007. http://www.uscoldwar.com/index.htm.

Harlow, Francis H., and N. Metropolis. "Computing and Computers: Weapons Simulation Leads to the Computer Era." *Los Alamos Science*, no. 7 (Winter/Spring 1983): 132–41.

Harry S. Truman: Containing the Public Messages, Speeches, and Statements of the President; 1949. Public Papers of the Presidents of the United States. Washington, DC: US Government Printing Office, 1964.

Harry S. Truman: Containing the Public Messages, Speeches, and Statements of the President; 1952–53. Public Papers of the Presidents of the United States. Washington, DC: US Government Printing Office, 1966.

Hawkins, David. *Project Y: The Los Alamos Story*. Part 1, *Toward Trinity*. Los Angeles: Tomash, 1983.

Haynes, Richard F. *The Awesome Power: Harry S. Truman as Commander in Chief*. Baton Rouge: Louisiana State University Press, 1973.

Herken, Gregg. *Cardinal Choices: Presidential Science Advising from the Atomic Bomb to SDI*. New York: Oxford University Press, 1992.

Heuser, Beatrice. *The Bomb: Nuclear Weapons in Their Historical, Strategic and Ethical Context*. London: Longman, 2000.

Heuser, Beatrice. *Nuclear Mentalities? Strategies and Beliefs in Britain, France, and the FRG*. Basingstoke: Palgrave Macmillan, 1998.

Hewlett, Richard G., and Oscar E. Anderson Jr. *The New World, 1939–1946: A History of the United States Atomic Energy Commission, Volume 1*. University Park: Pennsylvania State University Press, 1962.

Hewlett, Richard G., and Francis Duncan. *Atomic Shield, 1947–1952: A History of the United States Atomic Energy Commission, Volume 2*. University Park, PA: Pennsylvania State University Press, 1969.

Hewlett, Richard G., and Jack M. Holl. *Atoms for Peace and War, 1953–1961: Eisenhower and the Atomic Energy Commission*. Berkeley: University of California Press, 1989. Prepared by the US Atomic Energy Commission.

Hilsman, Roger. "The Foreign-Policy Consensus: An Interim Research Report." *Journal of Conflict Resolution* 3, no. 4 (December 1959): 361–82.

Hirsch, Daniel, and William G. Mathews. "The H-bomb: Who Really Gave Away the Secret?" *Bulletin of the Atomic Scientists* 46, no. 1 (January/February 1990): 22–30.

Holloway, David. *Stalin and the Bomb: The Soviet Union and Atomic Energy, 1939–1956*. New Haven, CT: Yale University Press, 1994.

Hone, Thomas C. "Strategic Bombardment Constrained: Korea and Vietnam." In Hall, *Case Studies in Strategic Bombardment*, 469–526.

Investigation into the United States Atomic Energy Commission. Report of the Joint Committee on Atomic Energy. Washington, DC: US Government Printing Office, 1949.

Jenkins-Smith, Hank C., and Paul A. Sabatier. "The Advocacy Coalition Framework: An Assessment." In *Theories of the Policy Process*, edited by Paul A. Sabatier, 117–66. Boulder, CO: Westview, 1999.

Jervis, Robert. "Perceiving and Coping with Threat." In *Psychology and Deterrence*, by Robert Jervis, Richard Ned Lebow, and Janice Gross Stein, 13–33. Baltimore: Johns Hopkins University Press, 1985.

Jervis, Robert, Richard Ned Lebow, and Janice Gross Stein. *Psychology and Deterrence*. Baltimore: Johns Hopkins University Press, 1985.

Kaplan, Edward. *To Kill Nations: American Strategy in the Air-Atomic Age and the Rise of Mutually Assured Destruction*. Ithaca, NY: Cornell University Press, 2015.

Kennan, George. *Memoirs, 1925–1950*. London: Hutchinson, 1968.

Knaack, Marcelle Size. *Encyclopedia of U.S. Air Force Aircraft and Missile Systems*. Vol. 2, *Post-World War II Bombers, 1945–1973*. Washington, DC: Office of Air Force History, 1988.

Kohn, Richard H. *Reflections on Research and Development in the United States Air Force*. Edited by Jacob Neufeld. Washington, DC: Center for Air Force History, US Air Force, 1993.

Kristof, Nicholas D. "The Problem of Memory." *Foreign Affairs* 77, no. 6 (November/December 1998): 37–49.

Krock, Arthur. *Memoirs: Sixty Years on the Firing Line*. New York: Funk and Wagnalls, 1968.

LaFeber, Walter. *America, Russia, and the Cold War, 1945–1984*. 5th ed. New York: Alfred A. Knopf, 1985.

Leffler, Melvyn P. *A Preponderance of Power: National Security, the Truman Administration, and the Cold War*. Stanford, CA: Stanford University Press, 1992.

Leighton, Richard M. *History of the Office of the Secretary of Defense*. Vol. 3, *Strategy, Money, and the New Look, 1953–1956*. Washington, DC: Historical Office, Office of the Secretary of Defense, 2001.

Lemmer, George F. *The Air Force and Strategic Deterrence, 1951–1960*. n.p.: US Air Force Historical Division Liaison Office, 1967. https://nsarchive2.gwu.edu/nukevault/ebb249/doc09.pdf.

Lifton, Robert Jay, and Greg Mitchell. *Hiroshima in America: Fifty Years of Denial*. New York: G. P. Putnam's Sons, 1995.

Lilienthal, David E. *Change, Hope and the Bomb*. Princeton, NJ: Princeton University Press, 1963.

Lilienthal, David E. *The Journals of David E. Lilienthal*. Vol. 2, *The Atomic Energy Years, 1945–1950*. New York: Harper and Row, 1964.

Lilienthal, David E. *The Journals of David E. Lilienthal*. Vol. 3, *The Venturesome Years, 1950–1955*. New York: Harper and Row, 1966.

Marks, Anne Wilson. "Washington Notes." *Bulletin of the Atomic Scientists* 5, no. 12 (December 1949): 327–28.

McCray, W. Patrick. "Project Vista, Caltech, and the Dilemmas of Lee DuBridge." *Historical Studies in the Physical and Biological Sciences* 34, no. 2 (2004): 339–70.

McCullough, David. *Truman*. New York: Simon and Schuster, 1992.

McFarland, Stephen L. "The Air Force in the Cold War, 1945–60: Birth of a New Defense Paradigm." *Airpower Journal*, Fall 1996.

McFarland, Stephen L. *America's Pursuit of Precision Bombing, 1910–1945*. Washington, DC: Smithsonian Institute Press, 1995.

McGhee, George C. *On the Frontline in the Cold War: An Ambassador Reports*. Westport, CT: Praeger, 1997.

McMillan, Priscilla J. *The Ruin of J. Robert Oppenheimer and the Birth of the Modern Arms Race*. New York: Viking, 2005.

McMullen, Richard F. *History of Air Defense Weapons, 1946–1962*. ADC Historical Study 14. n.p.: HQ Air Defense Command, n.d.

Meilinger, Phillip S. *Hoyt S. Vandenberg: The Life of a General*. Bloomington: Indiana University Press, 1989.

Merrill, Dennis K., ed. *Documentary History of the Truman Presidency*. Vol. 21, *The Development of an Atomic Weapons Program following World War II*. Bethesda, MD: University Publications of America, 1998.

Miles, Rufus E., Jr. "The Origin and Meaning of Miles' Law." *Public Administration Review* 38, no. 5 (September–October 1978): 399–403.

Millis, Walter. *Arms and Men: A Study in American Military History*. New Brunswick, NJ: Rutgers University Press, 1981.

Mitrovich, Gregory. *Undermining the Kremlin: America's Strategy to Subvert the Soviet Bloc, 1947–1956*. Ithaca, NY: Cornell University Press, 2009.

Monks, Alfred L. "The Soviet Strategic Air Force and Civil Defense." In *Soviet Aviation and Air Power: A Historical View*, edited by Robin Higham and Jacob W. Kipp, 213–38. Boulder, CO: Westview, 1977.

Moody, Walton S. *Building a Strategic Air Force*. Washington, DC: Air Force History and Museums Program, 1996.

Moody, Walton S., Jacob Neufeld, and R. Cargill Hall. "The Emergence of the Strategic Air Command." In *Winged Shield, Winged Sword: A History of the United States Air Force*, vol. 2, *1950–1997*, edited by Bernard C. Nalty, 53–96. Washington, DC: Air Force History and Museums Program, 1997.

Morgenthau, Hans J. "The H-bomb and After." *Bulletin of the Atomic Scientists* 6, no. 3 (March 1950): 76–79.

[Murphy, Charles V. J.]. "The Hidden Struggle for the H-bomb." *Fortune*, May 1953.

Neuse, Steven M. *David E. Lilienthal: The Journey of an American Liberal*. Knoxville: University of Tennessee Press, 1996.

Newman, Steven Leonard. "The Oppenheimer Case: A Reconsideration of the Role of the Defense Department and National Security." PhD diss., New York University, 1977.

Nichols, Kenneth D. *The Road to Trinity: A Personal Account of How America's Nuclear Policies Were Made*. New York: William Morrow, 1987.

Nitze, Paul H. *From Hiroshima to Glasnost: At the Center of Decision—A Memoir*. With Ann M. Smith and Steven L. Rearden. New York: Grove and Weidenfeld, 1989.

Nye, Joseph S., Jr. *Nuclear Ethics*. New York: Free Press, 1986.

Oakeshott, Michael. *Rationalism in Politics, and Other Essays*. Expanded ed. Indianapolis: Liberty Fund, 1991.

Office of the Assistant to the Secretary of Defense (Atomic Energy). *History of the Custody and Deployment of Nuclear Weapons (U) July 1945 through September 1977*. Washington, DC: US Department of Defense, February 1978. http://nautilus.org/wp-content/uploads/2015/04/306.pdf.

Offner, Arnold A. *Another Such Victory: President Truman and the Cold War, 1945–1953*. Stanford, CA: Stanford University Press, 2002.

O'Neill, Kevin. "Building the Bomb." In Schwartz, *Atomic Audit*, 33–104.

Oppenheimer, J. Robert "Atomic Weapons and American Policy," *Foreign Affairs* 31, no. 4 (July 1953): 525–35.

Overy, Richard. *The Bombers and the Bombed: Allied Air War over Europe, 1940–1945*. New York: Viking Penguin, 2014.

Pais, Abraham. *J. Robert Oppenheimer: A Life*. With supplemental material by Robert P. Crease. New York: Oxford University Press, 2006.

Parrish, Noel Francis. "Behind the Sheltering Bomb: Military Indecision from Alamogordo to Korea." PhD diss., Rice University, 1968.

Paskins, Barrie, and Michael Dockrill. *The Ethics of War*. Minneapolis: University of Minnesota Press, 1979.

Paul, Septimus H. *Nuclear Rivals: Anglo-American Atomic Relations, 1941–1952*. Columbus: The Ohio State University Press, 2000.

Pfau, Richard. *No Sacrifice Too Great: The Life of Lewis L. Strauss*. Charlottesville: University Press of Virginia, 1984.

Pike, John E., Bruce G. Blair, and Stephen I. Schwartz. "Defending against the Bomb." In Schwartz, *Atomic Audit*, 269–326.

Polmar, Norman, and Robert S. Norris. *The U.S. Nuclear Arsenal: A History of Weapons and Delivery Systems since 1945*. Annapolis, MD: Naval Institute Press, 2009.

Ponturo, John. *Analytical Support for the Joint Chiefs of Staff: The WSEG Experience, 1948–1976*. Arlington, VA: Institute of Defense Analyses, 1979.

"President Orders Exploration of the Super Bomb." *Bulletin of the Atomic Scientists* 6, no. 3 (March 1950): 66.

Quinlan, Michael. *Thinking about Nuclear Weapons: Principles, Problems, Prospects*. Oxford: Oxford University Press, 2009.

Rearden, Steven L. *History of the Office of the Secretary of Defense*. Vol. 1, *The Formative Years, 1947–1950*. Washington, DC: Office of the Secretary of Defense, 1984.

Rearden, Steven L. "U.S. Strategic Bombardment Doctrine since 1945." In Hall, *Case Studies in Strategic Bombardment*, 383–467.

Rhodes, Richard. *Dark Sun: The Making of the Hydrogen Bomb*. New York: Simon and Schuster, 1995.

Richelson, Jeffrey. "Population Targeting and US Strategic Doctrine." *Journal of Strategic Studies* 8, no. 1 (1985): 5–21.

Ridenour, Louis N. "The Bomb and Blackett." *World Politics* 1, no. 3 (April 1949): 395–403.

Ridenour, Louis N. "The Hydrogen Bomb." *Scientific American* 182, no. 3 (March 1950): 11–15.

Rosenberg, David Alan. "American Atomic Strategy and the Hydrogen Bomb Decision." *Journal of American History* 66, no. 1 (June 1979): 62–87.

Rosenberg, David Alan. "The Origins of Overkill: Nuclear Weapons and American Strategy, 1945–1960." *International Security* 7, no. 4 (Spring 1983): 3–71.

Rosenberg, David Alan. "'A Smoking Radiating Ruin at the End of Two Hours': Documents on American Plans for Nuclear War with the Soviet Union, 1954–55." *International Security* 6, no. 3 (Winter 1981–82): 3–38.

Rosenberg, David Alan. "U.S. Nuclear Stockpile, 1945 to 1950." *Bulletin of the Atomic Scientists* 38, no. 5 (May 1982): 25–30.

Ross, Steven T. *American War Plans, 1945–1950*. Portland, OR: Frank Cass, 1996.

Ross, Steven T., and David Alan Rosenberg, eds. *America's Plans for War against the Soviet Union, 1945–1950*. Vol. 11, *The Limits of Nuclear Strategy*. New York: Garland, 1989.

Rowen, Henry S. "The Evolution of Strategic Nuclear Doctrine." In *Strategic Thought in the Nuclear Age*, edited by Laurence Martin, 131–56. London: Heinemann, 1979.

Sabatier, Paul A., and Hank C. Jenkins-Smith. *Policy Change and Learning: An Advocacy Coalition Approach*. Boulder, CO: Westview, 1993.

Sagan, Scott D., and Benjamin A. Valentino. "Revisiting Hiroshima in Iran: What Americans Really Think about Using Nuclear Weapons and Killing Noncombatants." *International Security* 42, no. 1 (Summer 2017): 41–79.

Sakharov, Andrei. *Memoirs*. Translated by Richard Lourie. New York: Alfred A. Knopf, 1990.

Schaffel, Kenneth. *The Emerging Shield: The Air Force and the Evolution of Continental Air Defense, 1945–1960*. Washington, DC: Office of Air Force History, 1991.

Schilling, Warner R. "The H-bomb Decision: How to Decide without Actually Choosing." *Political Science Quarterly* 76, no. 1 (March 1961): 24–46.

Schilling, Warner R. *The Politics of National Defense: Fiscal 1950*. In *Strategy, Politics, and Defense Budgets*, by Warner R. Schilling, Paul Y. Hammond, and Glenn H. Snyder, 1–266. New York: Columbia University Press, 1962.

Schilling, Warner R. "Scientists, Foreign Policy, and Politics." *American Political Science Review* 56, no. 2 (June 1962): 287–300. Expanded version published in *Scientists and National Policy Making*, edited by Robert Gilpin and Christopher Wright, 144–73. New York: Columbia University Press, 1964.

Schnabel, James F. *History of the Joint Chiefs of Staff*. Vol. 1, *The Joint Chiefs of Staff and National Policy, 1945–1947*. Washington, DC: Office of Joint History, Office of the Chairman of the Joint Chiefs of Staff, 1996.

Schön, Donald A., and Martin Rein. *Frame Reflection: Toward the Resolution of Intractable Policy Controversies*. New York: Basic Books, 1994.

Schwartz, Stephen I., ed. *Atomic Audit: The Costs and Consequences of U.S. Nuclear Weapons since 1940*. Washington, DC: Brookings Institution Press, 1998.

Seitz, Frederick. "Physicists and the Cold War." *Bulletin of the Atomic Scientists* 6, no. 3 (March 1950): 83–89.

Shepley, James R., and Clay Blair Jr. *The Hydrogen Bomb: The Men, the Menace, the Mechanism*. New York: David McKay, 1954.

Sherry, Michael S. *Preparing for the Next War: American Plans for Postwar Defense, 1941–45*. New Haven, CT: Yale University Press, 1977.

Siracusa, Joseph M. "NSC 68: A Reappraisal." *Naval War College Review* 33, no. 6 (November–December 1980): 4–14.

Siracusa, Joseph M., and Aiden Warren. *Weapons of Mass Destruction: The Search for Global Security*. Lanham, MD: Rowman and Littlefield, 2017.

Steiner, Barry H. *Bernard Brodie and the Foundations of American Nuclear Strategy*. Lawrence: University Press of Kansas, 1991.

Stern, Philip M. *The Oppenheimer Case: Security on Trial*. With Harold P. Green. London: Rupert Hart-Davis, 1971.

Steury, Donald P. "How the CIA Missed Stalin's Bomb." *Studies in Intelligence* 49, no. 1 (2005): 19–26.

Strachey, John. *Scrap All the H-bombs*. London: Labour Party, 1958.

Strauss, Lewis L. *Men and Decisions*. Garden City, NY: Doubleday, 1962.

Talbott, Strobe. *The Master of the Game: Paul Nitze and the Nuclear Peace.* New York: Alfred A. Knopf, 1988.

Tannenwald, Nina. *The Nuclear Taboo: The United States and the Non-use of Nuclear Weapons since 1945.* Cambridge: Cambridge University Press, 2007.

Tarr, David W. "Military Technology and the Policy Process." *Western Political Quarterly* 18, no. 1 (March 1965): 135–48.

Teller, Edward. *Better a Shield Than a Sword: Perspectives on Defense and Technology.* New York: Free Press, 1987.

Thompson, Nicholas. *The Hawk and the Dove: Paul Nitze, George Kennan, and the History of the Cold War.* New York: Henry Holt, 2009.

Thomson, George. "Hydrogen Bombs: The Need for a Policy." *International Affairs* 26, no. 4 (October 1950): 463–69.

Thorpe, Charles. "Disciplining Experts: Scientific Authority and Liberal Democracy in the Oppenheimer Case." *Social Studies of Science* 32, no. 4 (August 2002): 525–62.

Trachtenberg, Marc. *The Cold War and After: History, Theory, and the Logic of International Politics.* Princeton, NJ: Princeton University Press, 2012.

Truman, Harry S. *Memoirs.* Vol. 2, *Years of Trial and Hope.* Garden City, NY: Doubleday, 1956.

Truslow, Edith C., and Ralph Carlisle Smith. *Project Y: The Los Alamos Story, Part 2; Beyond Trinity.* Los Angeles: Tomash, 1983.

Tubbs, Arthur D. *Establishing Air Research and Development Command: Two Civilian Scientists Played Key Roles.* Maxwell Air Force Base, AL: Air Command and Staff College, April 1986.

Twining, Nathan F. *Neither Liberty nor Safety: A Hard Look at U.S. Military Policy and Strategy.* New York: Holt, Rinehart and Winston, 1966.

Urey, Harold C. "Should America Build the H-bomb?" *Bulletin of the Atomic Scientists* 6, no. 3 (March 1950): 72–73.

US Atomic Energy Commission. *In the Matter of J. Robert Oppenheimer: Transcript of Hearing before Personnel Security Board.* Washington, DC: US Government Printing Office, 1954.

US Atomic Energy Commission. *In the Matter of J. Robert Oppenheimer: Transcript of Hearing before Personnel Security Board, Record of Classified Deletions.* Washington, DC: US Department of Energy, 2014. https://www.osti.gov/includes/opennet/includes/Oppenheimer%20hearings/Record%20of%20Classified%20Deletions.pdf.

US Department of State. *Foreign Relations of the United States.* 1949. Vol. 1, *National Security Affairs, Foreign Economic Policy.* Washington, DC: US Government Printing Office, 1976.

US Department of State. *Foreign Relations of the United States.* 1950. Vol. 1, *National Security Affairs; Foreign Economic Policy.* Washington, DC: US Government Printing Office, 1977.

US Department of State. *Foreign Relations of the United States.* 1952–54. Vol. 2, *National Security Affairs.* 2 parts. Washington, DC: US Government Printing Office, 1984.

US Strategic Bombing Survey. *Summary Report (Pacific War).* Washington, DC, 1 July 1946.

van Hulst, Merlijn, and Dvora Yanow. "From Policy 'Frames' to 'Framing': Theorizing a More Dynamic, Political Approach." *American Review of Public Administration* 46, no. 1 (January 2016): 92–112.

Watson, George M., Jr. *The Office of the Secretary of the Air Force, 1947–1965.* Washington, DC: Center for Air Force History, 1993.

Weida, William J. "The Economic Implications of Nuclear Weapons and Nuclear Deterrence." In Schwartz, *Atomic Audit,* 519–43.

Werrell, Kenneth P. *Blankets of Fire: U.S. Bombers over Japan during World War II.* Washington, DC: Smithsonian Institution, 1996.

Wolk, Herman S. *Planning and Organizing the Postwar Air Force, 1943–1947.* Washington, DC: Office of Air Force History, 1984.

Yoder, Edwin M. *Joe Alsop's Cold War: A Study of Journalistic Influence and Intrigue.* Chapel Hill: University of North Carolina Press, 1995.

York, Herbert F. *The Advisors: Oppenheimer, Teller, and the Superbomb.* Stanford, CA: Stanford University Press, 1989.

York, Herbert F. *Arms and the Physicist.* Woodbury, NY: American Institute of Physics, 1995.

York, Herbert F. *Race to Oblivion: A Participant's View of the Arms Race.* New York: Simon and Schuster, 1970.

Young, Ken. *The American Bomb in Britain: US Air Forces' Strategic Presence, 1946–64.* Manchester: Manchester University Press, 2016.

Young, Ken. "Cold War Insecurities and the Curious Case of John Strachey." *Intelligence and National Security* 29, no. 6 (2014): 901–25.

Young, Ken. "The Hydrogen Bomb, Lewis L. Strauss and the Writing of Nuclear History." *Journal of Strategic Studies* 36, no. 6 (Spring 2013): 815–40.

Young, Ken. "Revisiting NSC 68." *Journal of Cold War Studies* 15, no. 1 (Winter 2013): 3–33.

Zachary, G. Pascal. *Endless Frontier: Vannevar Bush, Engineer of the American Century.* New York: Free Press, 1997.

Zaloga, Steven J. *The Kremlin's Nuclear Sword: The Rise and Fall of Russia's Strategic Nuclear Forces, 1945–2000.* Washington, DC: Smithsonian Books, 2002.

Ziegler, Charles. "Waiting for Joe-1: Decisions Leading to the Detection of Russia's First Atomic Bomb Test." *Social Studies of Science* 18, no. 2 (1988): 197–229.

Zubok, Vladislav. *A Failed Empire: The Soviet Union in the Cold War from Stalin to Gorbachev.* Chapel Hill: University of North Carolina Press, 2007.

Press Coverage

Alsop, Joseph, and Stewart Alsop. "Air Defense Ignored in Political Shuffle." Matter of Fact. *Washington Post,* 9 May 1952.

Alsop, Joseph, and Stewart Alsop. "The Indecisive Decision." Matter of Fact. *Washington Post,* 27 January 1950.

Alsop, Joseph, and Stewart Alsop. "It's Not So Funny, Really." Matter of Fact. *New York Herald Tribune,* 2 December 1949.

Alsop, Joseph, and Stewart Alsop. "Pandora's Box I." Matter of Fact. *Washington Post,* 2 January 1950.

Alsop, Joseph, and Stewart Alsop. "Pandora's Box II." Matter of Fact. *Washington Post*, 4 January 1950.

Associated Press. "Hydrogen-Helium Use in Atomic Bomb Seen." *New York Times*, 3 January 1947.

Baldwin, Hanson W. "Experts Urge Tactical Air Might; Score Stress on Big Atom Bomber." *New York Times*, 5 June 1952.

Bradley, Omar, as told to Beverly Smith. "This Way Lies Peace." *Saturday Evening Post*, 15 October 1949.

"Charge of 'Reluctance' on H-bomb Is Denied." *U.S. News and World Report*, 8 October 1954.

"Citation from the White House." *U.S. News and World Report*, 8 October 1954.

"Columbia Founds War-Peace Study." *New York Times*, 10 December 1951.

Cooke, Alistair. "Support for Senator McMahon." *Manchester Guardian*, 4 February 1950.

Coughlan, Robert. "Dr. Edward Teller's Magnificent Obsession." *Life*, 6 September 1954.

"D.C. Nominees Sought to Take Atom Courses." *Evening Star* (Washington, DC). 14 February 1950.

Dugan, George. "Stassen Proposes Church Bomb Talk." *New York Times*, 15 February 1950.

Farber, M. A. "Conant Discusses Student Activism." *New York Times*, 8 March 1970.

Flynn, Elizabeth Gurley. "Mark Women's Day—Protest H-bomb." *Daily Worker*, 8 March 1950.

Friendly, Alfred. "New A-bomb Has 6 Times Power of 1st." *Washington Post*, 18 November 1949.

Gwertzman, Bernard. "U.S. Papers Tell of '53 Policy to Use the A-bomb in Korea." *New York Times*, 8 June 1984.

Haverstick, John. "Thermonuclear Cabal." *Saturday Review*, 30 October 1954.

International News Service. "'H-bomb Not Too Valuable.'" *Omaha World-Herald*, 16 May 1950.

Laurence, William L. "Atomic Bombing of Nagasaki Told by Flight Member." *New York Times*, 9 September 1945.

Lefever, Ernest W. "Why Agonize over Hiroshima, Not Dresden?" *Los Angeles Times*, 30 August 2000.

Lerner, Max. "'The Naked Question.'" *New York Post*, 1 February 1950.

Lindley, Ernest K. "Case for the Defense." Washington Tides. *Newsweek*, 9 March 1959.

"M'Mahon Says 24 Know Atom Score." *New York Times*, 13 May 1949.

Moley, Raymond. "On Tap, Not on Top." *Newsweek*, 11 October 1954.

Pearson, Drew. "Crusade against H-bomb Planned." Merry-Go-Round. *Washington Post*, 23 January 1950.

Pettus, Terry. "Seattle Pastors Favor Effort to Ban H-bomb." *Daily Worker*, 8 March 1950.

Reston, James. "The H-bomb Decision." *New York Times*, 8 April 1954.

"Senator Charges 'H-Bomb Lies.'" *Salt Lake Tribune*, 11 May 1959.

Shepley, James R., and Clay Blair Jr. "The Hydrogen Bomb: How the U.S. Almost Lost It." *U.S. News and World Report*, 24 September 1954.

Winslow, Richard K. "12 Scientists Bid U.S. Declare It Won't Use Super-Bomb First." *New York Herald Tribune*, 5 February 1950.

Index

Page numbers in *italics* refer to tables.

AJ-1 aircraft, 102, 105
AJ-2 aircraft, 105
"Alarm Clock" model, 91–92
alignments, organizational, 155–56, 162
allies, 152–53
Allison, Graham, 162
Alsop, Joseph and Stewart: critique of
    Shepley and Blair, 144, 188n59; press
    coverage of Super debate, 37, 55–56, 60,
    106, 125, 127, 130
Alvarez, Luis: advocacy for Super,
    37–38, 45, 164; on arms race, 165; GAC
    report and, 48, 51; Los Alamos and, 19,
    89–90; Oppenheimer hearing and, 144;
    Schilling's interview with, xi, 48, 174n41
American Expeditionary Forces, 108
American Physical Society, 75, 84
Anderson, Clinton, 147–49
Anderson, Oscar, 44
Anderson, Sam, 31, 105, 112, 117
area bombing, 15, 71, 77–80, 109–10, 160
Armed Forces Special Weapons Project,
    38, 128
arms control. See international control
arms race, thermonuclear: psychological
    aspects, 98–99; Super development and,
    71, 80–83, 165; test bans and, 92–93;
    thermonuclear, 6, 16
Army Air Corps Tactical School, 109
Arneson, Gordon, 24, 56, 60, 63, 157–58,
    191n22
Arnold, Henry "Hap," 78, 114
Arnold A. Saltzman Institute of War and
    Peace Studies. See Institute of War and
    Peace Studies (IWPS)
Atlantic Pact, 25
atmospheric monitoring, 19–22. See also
    detection systems
atomic bombs: custody of, 44, 53;
    development of, 7 (see also Manhattan
    Project); size and weight of, 100–106, 124;
    stockpile, 34, 46, 156–57, 184n21, 190n16,
    191n48; strategic bombing and, 113–14;
    tactical deployment, 70; use of, 7, 18, 22,
    28. See also boosted fission bombs; fission
    bomb production; Hiroshima bombing;
    Nagasaki bombing; Super (hydrogen
    bomb) development
Atomic Energy Act (1946), 3, 21, 41, 53
Atomic Energy Commission (AEC):
    atomic weapons expansion and, 33,
    115–16; classified information and, 145;
    Defense Department and, 53–54, 161;
    feasibility and, 36–37, 88; financial costs
    and, 93–94; GAC report and, 45–47, 57;

JCAE oversight of, 4; laboratories, 68, 90,
    129 (see also Livermore Laboratory; Los
    Alamos Laboratory); military information
    and, 43–44; MLC and, 53–54; overview
    of, 3, 40–41; politics of advice and,
    151, 153, 156, 157–58, 162; production
    facilities, 69, 95; report to Truman, 57–60;
    Soviet nuclear weapons and, 25; stockpile
    and, 157; Strauss and, 147–49; Super
    decision and, 1, 16, 38, 40–47, 55–65,
    133, 134 (see also advocates for Super
    bomb; opponents of Super bomb); TVA
    and, 189n78; on unilateral renunciation,
    6. See also Personnel Security Board,
    Oppenheimer hearing
Atomic Pioneer Awards, 51
Atomic Warfare and the Christian Faith, 71
Ayers, Eben, 64

B-17 aircraft, 20
B-29 aircraft, 20, 26, 28, 29, 77, 89, 101
B-36 aircraft, 28, 102–4, 106, 111
B-47 aircraft, 104–6
B-50 aircraft, 101, 113
B-52 aircraft, 105
Bacher, Robert F., 37, 40, 83, 91, 96–98,
    119, 120
Baker, Richard D., 137
balance of power, 25–26
ballistic missiles. See missiles
bans. See international control
Beard, Edmund, 162
Beisner, Robert L., 179n33
Berkeley Laboratory, 74, 177n82
Bernstein, Barton, 2, 4, 7, 73, 74, 93, 165,
    174n38
Bethe, Hans: on GAC, 49; moral arguments
    and, 75; Schilling's interview with, xi,
    188n40; Soviet nuclear capabilities and,
    83; Super development and, 35, 136, 141,
    187n12, 188n40
bipartisanship, 69
Bison (aircraft), 29
Blackett, P. M. S., 75
Blair, Clay, Jr., 17, 139–47, 188n59, 188n61
Blue Book (air defense plan), 31
bombs. See atomic bombs; strategic
    bombardment doctrine; Super (hydrogen
    bomb) development; targets
boosted fission bombs, 34, 77, 90, 95, 145, 157
Borden, William, 24, 91, 127; Schilling's
    interview with, xi
Borowski, Harry, 184n21
Bradbury, Norris, 34, 68, 90, 96, 137, 140–42,
    145, 189n72; Schilling's interview with, 142

United States: atomic monopoly, 18–19,
22, 25, 28, 158; federal organizational
structure, 3; foreign policy, 69 (*see
also* international relations); nuclear
superiority, 2, 26, 38, 80–82; public
morale, 25; public opinion, 75–76, 79;
vulnerability, 16, 25, 71. *See also* national
security policy; *individual departments and
organizations*
University of California, Berkeley, 37, 48.
See also Berkeley Laboratory
unmanned drone aircraft, 105–6
Urey, Harold C., 81–82
US Air Force: advocacy for Super, 164;
atmospheric monitoring and, 20;
civilian control and, 44; criticism of, 131;
establishment of, 20, 29; Los Alamos
scientists and, 135; Oppenheimer hearing
and, 127–32; politics of advice and, 15,
108, 151, 162, 163; Scientific Advisory
Board, 30, 114, 119; on Soviet threat, 26;
Super bomb development and, 1–2, 17.
See also Strategic Air Command (SAC);
US Army Air Forces (AAF)
US Air Force Europe, 112, 124
US Army, 16; air defense and, 31 (*see also*
air defense); tactical warfare and, 116,
119–20
US Army Air Forces (AAF), 20, 29, 77–78,
160, 163, 170n46
use of Super bomb: debates over, 8, 15, 16,
68, 107–8; military value and, 98–100;
tactical warfare, 115–25, 151
US Navy: air defense and, 27, 31 (*see also*
air defense); on Soviet threat, 25–26;
tactical warfare and, 116, 120; targeting
doctrine, 79
U.S. News and World Report, 96, 140

Valley, George, 125
Vandenberg, Hoyt S.: advocacy for
Super, 38, 42; air defense and, 28, 30,
125; detection systems and, 20–21;
Oppenheimer hearing and, 128–29;

strategic bombing and, 111–12, 114, 119,
121, 161
van Hulst, Merlijn, 191n35
Vista report, 118–25, 129–31, 138, 160,
161, 163
Volpe, Joseph, 60, 65; Schilling's interview
with, xi
von Kármán, Theodore, 114
von Neumann, John, 10, 83

Walker, John, 88
Walkowicz, Teddy, 129
Waltz, Kenneth, 165
war plans, 22, 24–25; AEC and, 43–44; air
power and, 28, 31. *See also* capabilities;
Emergency War Plans; intent, defensive
planning and; strategic bombardment
doctrine
Waymack, William W., 40
Weapon Systems Evaluation Group, 3, 59,
66, 67, 99, 158; strategic bombing reports,
112–13, 120; on tactical warfare, 116
Webster, William, 32, 41
Western Europe, 25–26, 81–82, 115, 120, 123.
See also Europe
Wilson, Carroll, 45, 47, 95
Wilson, Robert R., 150
Wilson, Roscoe C., 42, 52, 105, 128–31,
186n121; Schilling's interview with, 131
Wolfe, Kenneth B., 106
Wolfers, Arnold, ix
World War I, 108–9
World War II, 36, 50, 109, 163. *See also*
Germany; Hiroshima bombing; Japan;
Nagasaki bombing

Yanow, Dvora, 191n35
Yoder, Edwin, 130
York, Herbert, 3, 68, 84

Zacharias, Jerrold, 126, 138–39
Zhukov, Georgy, 139
ZORC, 138–40
Zuckert, Eugene M., 134